BEYOND THE PODIUM

About ASTD

Founded in 1944, ASTD is the world's premier professional association in the field of workplace learning and performance. ASTD's membership includes more than 70,000 professionals in organizations from every level of the field of workplace learning and performance in more than one hundred countries. Its leaders and members work in more than 15,000 multinational corporations, small and medium-sized businesses, government agencies, colleges, and universities. For more information, visit www.astd.org.

BEYOND THE PODIUM

Delivering Training and Performance to a Digital World

Allison Rossett
Kendra Sheldon

Foreword by Marguerite J. Foxon

Linking People,
Learning & Performance

JOSSEY-BASS/PFEIFFER
A Wiley Company
San Francisco

Published by

JOSSEY-BASS/PFEIFFER
A Wiley Company
350 Sansome St.
San Francisco, CA 94104-1342
415.433.1740; Fax 415.433.0499
800.274.4434; Fax 800.569.0443

www.pfeiffer.com

ASTD
Linking People,
Learning & Performance

1640 King Street   Box 1443
Alexandria, VA 22313-2043 USA
Tel 800.628.2783   703.683.8100
Fax 703.683.8103
www.astd.org

ISBN: 0-7879-5526-4

Library of Congress Cataloging-in-Publication Data

Rossett, Allison.
   Beyond the podium : delivering training and performance to a
digital world / Allison Rossett and Kendra Sheldon.
           p. cm.
Includes Index.
   ISBN 0-7879-5526-4 (alk. paper)
   1. Employees, Training of.   2. Employees, Training
of—Computer-assisted instruction.   I. Sheldon, Kendra, date   II.
Title.
   HF5549.5.T7 R644 2001
   658.3'124-dc21

                                                                00-013121

Printed in the United States of America

Acquiring Editor: Matthew Holt
Director of Development: Kathleen Dolan Davies
Editor: Rebecca Taff

Senior Production Editor: Dawn Kilgore
Manufacturing Supervisor: Becky Carreño
Cover Design: Blue Design

Printing   10   9   8   7   6   5   4   3   2   1

We at Jossey-Bass strive to use the most environmentally sensitive paper stocks available to us. Our publications are printed on acid-free recycled stock whenever possible, and our paper always meets or exceeds
minimum GPO and EPA requirements.

To our mothers, Tybee and Elizabeth,
and our late fathers, Buster and Jack.

CONTENTS

FOREWORD

Read another book on training and development (T&D)? *Been there, done that!* But *Beyond the Podium* isn't just another book on the subject. Rather, it's an example-packed journey into the brave new digital world of training and performance. Allison Rossett and Kendra Sheldon unveil a future already on the horizon, where development cycle time is radically reduced, efforts repurposed and broadly accessible, learners globally networked, learner preferences acknowledged, and information imparted in minutes or hours, not days. And they provide a roadmap to help us on the journey.

For years we called "it" training and "us" trainers, but those terms became a bit passé in the Seventies and Eighties. Our profession and our titles have become more sophisticated, although admittedly less meaningful to some clients. We are known now as human performance technologists, learning solutions managers, performance improvement consultants, educational support managers, instructional designers, HRD managers, e-learning specialists, and more. But whatever name we go by, at the end of the day we're all involved in the same game — trying to help people do their jobs better by providing the knowledge and skill they require.

Back in the dark ages we had training departments and trainers. Terms like "instructional design," "performance analysis," and "Web-based learning" were not then in our vocabulary. Too often perceived as an organizational backwater, training and development existed far from the strategic purpose of the organization. In one company where I worked, the strategic plan was kept in a locked cabinet in the office of a senior vice president, and only the upper echelon of management was allowed to see it. Despite the fact that I had national responsibility for the training function, I was nevertheless considered too low on the corporate ladder to see the strategic plan.

The life of a trainer was pretty straightforward back then. Not surprisingly, we generally operated in a reactive mode, responding to management's request to fix the latest problem with the training solution they had already identified. We developed the course materials (on typewriters, can you believe!), and trainers presented it in classrooms. Needs analysis was often discounted as an unnecessary exercise and sure to prolong the development of the training material. Evaluation didn't fare any better—it cost too much and, in management's mind, didn't tell them anything they didn't already know. Butts on seats—that was the metric that counted. And when the budget needed to be cut, management started with the T&D department.

Fortunately, things have changed. As we look back over the journey from the dark ages to the enlightenment of today, we can discern several trends that have enhanced our field and the credibility of T&D. The principles of instructional design enhanced our practice. Constructivists offered an alternative perspective on learning and instructing. The notion that training should make a measurable difference in terms of outcomes such as costs, productivity, and quality took hold. Needs analysis ceased to be an optional extra. Indeed, Rossett's 1987 book, *Training Needs Assessment,* was a significant influence in that regard. The focus shifted from training to performance. We've even coined the ungainly term "human performance technology" to describe this new focus.

Recently I was leafing through HRD books written twenty years ago. One author posed a simple question: What if a paradigm shift—a fundamental change in the nature of the game—were to occur in T&D? Well, we've seen that transformation, that fundamental change, and it continues to evolve. We're now living in an e-world, a digital age. In a newspaper interview in October, John Chambers, CEO of Cisco, was asked about "killer business applications." His response underscores the profound changes occurring in relation to training—how it is perceived, what is expected of it, and how it will impact organizations. He remarked that "Another killer application is e-learning. E-learning is where e-commerce was three years ago. You remember when ordering things was terribly slow and difficult? That's where e-learning is today. It's going to get faster and easier to use. We accurately predicted that e-commerce would be business-to-business first, then business-to-consumer. We think e-learning will follow the same trend. But it will radically change traditional education as well."

So why are Allison Rossett and Kendra Sheldon writing a book about training? First, they want to challenge us to stop, catch our breath, and take another look at our profession.

Rossett and Sheldon refresh our understanding of the fundamental elements as well as the new directions in T&D. They look at the differences between training, development, education, learning, information, and performance. The core instructional design components are there in chapters on analysis and figuring out what to do with problems and requests, designing great training, and evaluating the impact and success of an intervention.

Second, Rossett and Sheldon unpack some of the exciting learning technologies, the trends, and the new digital age stuff infiltrating the training profession faster than most of us can stay abreast of it. They examine the role of knowledge management, informal learning, independent learning, globalization, certification, e-learning, networking, career self-reliance, object-oriented design, and more.

Finally, Rossett and Sheldon seek to redefine the nature and role of training and trainers. They provide us with a bigger picture of T&D than most of us are currently dreaming. They want us to reflect on the changes around us and expand our view of our professional world and to educate our sponsors, customers, and colleagues about the possibilities. In their view of the future, "It won't be about on-line or instructor-led classes as much as it will be about relationships with customers, knowledge distribution, tailoring solutions from all these options, and integration of learning throughout the organization. It will be about speed too."

Management is now pressuring T&D to provide faster, cheaper, and better training. Increasingly, learners are asking for the same. The challenge is to find ways to meet and shape these requests, addressing performance and learning needs in new formats, using more effective delivery media, and developing a more integrated function within the organization. Rossett and Sheldon open our eyes to the possibilities that already exist or are emerging as organizations move more deeply into the digital age. They present us with compelling evidence that training (or whatever we want to call it) is alive and well and is undergoing another "fundamental change in the nature of the game."

Beyond the Podium is not a book only for newcomers to the T&D field. It is for T&D leaders, designers and developers, learners, techies, and non-techies. It's for all of us who are committed to improving the performance of our customers and who want to add significant value to our organizations through T&D. Twenty years ago none of us dreamed of the future we are in today—pervasive computer and Internet technology, Web-based learning, global needs, reusable learning objects, and more. Rossett and Sheldon take us into the heart of the shift—with a sense of humor if not a little irreverence—and challenge us to expand our vision of training.

Nor is *Beyond the Podium* a book that envisions the future but leaves you wondering how you can get there. The authors have drawn on their years of combined experience in consulting, academia, and practice to provide rich illustrations and insights. They have liberally sprinkled nifty job aids, tables, tips, and examples of good practice throughout the book. At the end of each chapter they add additional resources. For example, there are substantive interviews with outstanding training practitioners and leaders who share insights, hints, and tools. They also provide valuable takeaways in the form of PowerPoint® slides summarizing the chapters' main points and responses to potential objections. I especially like their suggested resources to bring us up to snuff if we have a spare hour, a day, or a week.

Whether you started out in the T&D field in the dark ages or are joining up in the digital age, this book will challenge you, teach you, excite and inspire you. And you'll have fun reading it too!

April 2001   Marguerite J. Foxon
                                                                                    Motorola

PREFACE

Friends were surprised that I would write a book about training. One said, "Hasn't it all been said and said again?" I don't think so. Not even close.

I wrote the book because I think the profession deserves a fresh look from those close to it, those new to it, and from our sponsors, customers, and colleagues. *Beyond the Podium* is devoted to encouraging and shaping that look.

But why? The first reason is that too many people appear frozen in their view of the possibilities. Many training professionals are locked into what they do every day, with little time to consider more strategic options.

The people around us are, not surprisingly, even less familiar with the field today. On an airplane I asked an investment banker about training, "What picture do you get in your mind when you hear the word 'training'?" He said something like this, "Training—haven't thought about it much. We have a big training group, I know. I guess I see a room with some people in it, maybe twenty people, and an instructor who is good at holding their attention."

At long last we bask in the attention of many of those in charge.

I tried the same question with others on planes and on terra firma. They responded similarly, with one adding that her organization had begun to do something with computers, but she wasn't sure what.

Not much interest in training. Not much knowledge either.

Why write the book now? At long last we bask in the attention of many of those in charge. Executives are ratcheting up expectations for training and development. Perhaps they do it because of the magnitude of the challenges they confront as they roll out enterprise systems and new products, create surprising alliances, seek new customers, and move their operations and aspirations all over the world. Success depends on their people.

Unfortunately, significant challenges loom. U.S. Federal Reserve Chairman Alan Greenspan said, "Human skills are subject to obsolescence at a rate unparalleled in American history." *Business Week* (November 13, 2000, p. 42) described American workers as "grumpier," according to a Conference Board study. Satisfaction at work has dropped significantly over the past five years, with training as one of the culprits on the list of causes. The same *Business Week* article bemoaned a deficit of engineering and scientific skills.

Other executives are turning to us not because of worries, but because of opportunities. In their view, training professionals can bring new ideas and approaches to the table. Leaders are compelled by the economic benefits presented by Web training, lured to the plentiful resources that learning portals promise, and eager to capture and nurture organizational smarts through knowledge repositories and on-line conversations. As it dawns on them that training and development can mean much more than twenty people in a room with a dynamic instructor, interest quickens.

As it dawns on them that training and development can mean much more than twenty people in a room with a dynamic instructor, interest quickens.

A final reason for writing this book is the litany you've probably heard: *training is dead.* Kendra Sheldon, my co-author, and I don't think so. Far from it.

There is no way you can read this book, engage with its questions and answers, examine the examples, hear stories from spotlight interviews, and come to conclusions that include words like "death" or "dying." A big tent view of the field presents tasty opportunities and alternatives: solution systems; change management; e-learning; learning management systems; goal-based evaluation; constructivist strategies; click and brick; informal learning; problem-based learning; electronic performance support; knowledge management; object-oriented design; certification; and wireless technologies. Training is not dead at all; it's reborn.

You'll find those topics, and more, in the book, along with

- *Many views on many topics.* Take "training is dead." Our two spotlight interviews in Chapter Three take opposite positions on this statement. Others throughout the book weigh in as well, with strong words on this topic and others.

- *Many featured interviews.* Marc Rosenberg, Roger Chevalier, Margo Murray, Roslyn Price, Thiagi, James Li, Jack Phillips, and Ruth Clark. Those are just a few of the two dozen spotlight interviews that pepper the book.
- *A focus on the questions you and others have.* The book is for you if you've been wondering: What kinds of skills, knowledge, perspectives, and alliances will be required? What should I be thinking about and planning for? Toward what should I be leading my unit and organization? What new approaches are on the horizon? What about the tried and true? How can I explain all this to my customers? How can I position and educate them?

  And it's for you if your customers and colleagues are asking: Why don't we just change your title from trainer to performance consultant? Why don't we just change your title from trainer to Web trainer? I went to a conference and really liked what they said about knowledge management. How can we use that in what we do? What can you people do for us?
- *A tour of the possibilities.* If you want to know where to start on a performance analysis or evaluation, suggestions and tools are here. If you want a primer on many technologies for learning, that's available too. And if it's Web training or informal learning or knowledge management that intrigue you, you'll find all that here too, in substantial detail. We use real projects and people to talk about what's happening now and to push our thinking forward, into the future. We've tried to create a book that is chock-full of engaging possibilities and practical stuff. There are many dialogues, examples, charts, job aids, anecdotes, and quotes. Want questions to use to screen your ideas about Web strategy? It's here. Want suggestions for how to handle resistance to performance analysis? It's here. Concerned about screening your organization's readiness for knowledge management? That's here too.
- *A guide to professional development.* The purpose of the book was not to provide a how-to. It is meant to generate ideas and to open up doors and windows to an expanded view of the profession. Because we're introducing new topics, however, we took responsibility for what happens to you next. Every chapter presents four kinds of professional development resources. First, we present a table keyed to how much time you're able to invest in learning more about the subject. Got an hour or a day? We suggest options to match available time. Second, a substantive resource list is associated with each chapter. Third, each chapter is speckled with recommended on-line resources. And fourth, we ask each of the people we interviewed for their ideas for suggested resources. Most share favorite books, articles, and electronic resources.
- *Something old, something new.* Some familiar training topics are here, such as analysis and evaluation, both linked to performance improvement. So too is

an extensive treatment of what makes great training great. And we revisit audio and video as training technologies. At the same time, we press into emergent topics associated with training and development, examining knowledge management, wireless options, object-oriented design, international training, e-business, and the Web.

- *A focus on the essentials.* Long reviews of the literature aren't here, but key citations and studies are. I apologize to the wise people whose thinking has influenced this book (such as Joe Harless, Harold Stolovitch, Robert Mager, Peter Pipe, Sue Markle, Dave Jonassen, Rob Foshay, John Keller, Walt Dick, Pat Smith, Tim Ragan, Gloria Gery, Tom Gilbert, Roger Addison, Geary Rummler, Joe Durzo, Marc Rosenberg, Dave Merrill, Ruth Clark, Judy Hale, Elwood Holton III, Diane Gayeski, Mary Broad, Ron Zemke, and many others) for not making frequent allusions to their contributions. My purpose here is to make it easier for human resource professionals to get their jobs done, to get to the heart of the matter, as Robert Mager might have put it.

- *American admittedly, but with some international flavor.* Two Americans wrote this book, with experiences that are primarily American. We do, however, work hard to include international perspectives and examples and to pose issues that professionals are dealing with as their organizations take on global partners and goals. The topics and trends covered here, from informal learning to the cognitive influence on instructional design to evaluation to knowledge management, are as important to an Indonesian or Israeli training professional as to a North American.

- *Irreverent and varied examples.* We've worked hard to make the examples vivid. We visit computer companies, museums, investment houses, and government agencies. We talk about sales, sexual harassment, data warehousing, ethics, food, teams, safety, retirement accounts, software, and management development. Examples and dialogues come from real projects in real organizations and, where possible, we identify the company or agency. Sometimes, experiences are exaggerated to illustrate points. The gist will ring true. Given the choice of several examples or quotes, in this book as in others, you'll find the more irreverent. We want your reading experience to be a good one.

Co-author Kendra Sheldon and I are upbeat about the field. Just look at the smorgasbord we put on the table for readers. We are not, however, Pollyannas. While we cover emergent perspectives, approaches, and technologies, we also note that profusion rhymes with confusion. The expanding training terrain raises serious questions about quality, brand, responsibility, and meaning. What roles will we play in making certain that e-learning and knowledge management, for example, make meaningful contributions—that they do not turn into turn-of-the-century fads?

The book is meant to entice and encourage. If it prompts you to read a book, visit a Website, raise questions with a customer or colleague, interrogate a vendor, or propose new strategic possibilities for your career or unit, then Kendra and I have succeeded. Know that we tried.

San Diego, California Allison Rossett
March 2001 arossett@mail.sdsu.edu
http://edweb.sdsu.edu/people/ARossett/ARossett.html

ACKNOWLEDGMENTS

When we set out to write this book, we promised it would reflect many viewpoints. We think we've delivered there. Many are here in *Beyond the Podium,* some in obvious and others in more subtle ways. Thanks to Roz Price, Carla Fantozzi, Jack Phillips, Cathy Bolger, Terry Bickham, Frank Rogalewicz, Lynn Richards, Roger Chevalier, Margo Murray, Marci Bober, Marguerite Foxon, Marc Rosenberg, Barry Shelton, Jim McGee, James Li, Sivasailam Thiagarajan, Cathy Tobias, Marty Murillo, Ruth Clark, Janice Sibley, Jill Funderburg Donello, Mark and Jessica Fulop, Laura Schmidt, Leigh Kelleher, Rebecca Vaughan, Laura Schmitt, Sharon Young, Fernanda Groenendijk, Bernie Dodge, Cheryl Leedom, Leigh Kelleher, Jim Marshall, Joe Katzman, and Suzanne Valery. Their brilliant and funky selves add incalculably to the book.

We also have friends and family who are a joy to acknowledge. Kendra thanks her family, Steve, Leslie, Greg, and Kara Sheldon, for their sacrifices, support, and love; Chris Haddock for his friendship and inspiration; Stuart Grossman, Marcia Olson, and Bob Hoffman for their help, patience, and generosity; and dear friends Mona Meyer, Brett Clapham, Caleb Clark, Russ Davidson, and Chris Volkl for contributions to *Beyond the Podium.* She also appreciates the support that came from her on-line community, Soend, and Allison Rossett, for support, motivation, and the opportunity of a lifetime.

Allison, in turn, could write a book of acknowledgments. First, to the SDSU educational technology community. Their influence is here, in some of the names mentioned above and in some not mentioned, such as colleagues Pat Harrison, Brock Allen, and Donn Ritchie and students and alumni too numerous to name. The adventurous spirit in our community, the surprising urgency and enthusiasm in an academic program, incubates new ideas and approaches.

Allison also wants to acknowledge Sue Reynolds for all she did, from the sublime to the ridiculous. Thanks to Sue for helping to clarify ideas, for demanding yet another example, and for cooking more than her fair share.

PART ONE

THE BASICS

CHAPTER ONE

WELCOME TO TRAINING!

Ann: I thought I was joining the training group, but they had another name when I got there. Now we're called "Performance Development."

Al: I saw the new name on the Web page.

Ann: From what I can tell after only two weeks, it's still mostly training going on. You know, this name thing is interesting. Two of my classmates from grad school were hired into training and development groups. I'm in performance development now. Another has the title of "curriculum architect," would you believe? Still another is an instructor. And yet another is a consultant, plain and simple—a road warrior for one of the big accounting firms.

Al: One of the guys in our group is now the "Web training manager."

Ann: It looks to me as if people in our business can be defined by *what* they do mostly or by the *people* they serve or even the *services* they want to move toward offering.

Al: I see what you mean. I could use a better fix on the field. I'm interested in what training is today and in the future, especially with the performance movement and new technologies. Getting clear about all that would enable me to explain it better to my customers—and even my family. You know, my parents have never really understood what I do for a living.

Welcome

The purpose of this book is to respond to questions just like the ones Ann and Al are raising. Ann, Al, their customers and sponsors, and even their families, seek a contemporary view of training and development. They want a picture of the field that incorporates the opportunities and concerns generated by new organizational goals, new customers, international vistas, new technologies, and the performance improvement movement.

That's what we will do here. We'll answer the questions that we believe are on your mind. Not yet of concern to you? We'll attempt to put them on your plate for consideration.

Here we're attempting to welcome you again to the charms of the training profession and to provide you with facts, figures, examples, and reasons that will help you rekindle the interest of others too.

This book is not a how-to-do training technologies or a how-to-do performance consulting. It isn't even a how-to-do training, although you'll find descriptive and detailed chapters on topics such as analysis, evaluation, and informal learning. Instead of how-to, we've focused attention on why-to, on touring the terrain and possibilities, on providing assistance in thinking about learning and performance, and in positioning the profession in a world with high expectations for results, speed, and performance.

Technologies and performance goals supply the backdrop for the book.

Technologies and performance goals supply the backdrop for the book. In it we look at services, products, practices, and standards associated with training and development in a world where performance improvement and learning technologies are everywhere.

Is This Book for You?

This book is for you if you've found yourself wondering

- Who am I? Who am I going to be? What about my career? What kinds of skills, knowledge, perspectives, and alliances will be required? What should I be thinking about and planning for? Toward what should I be leading my unit and organization?
- What new approaches are on the horizon? What about the tried and true?

- Is greatness different today than it was before? What is great training? Isn't great training what it has always been?
- Is the classroom dead?
- Must I become a Web developer? Must we *all* become Web developers?
- What difference will all this technology make? How can I play a role in turning hype into reality?
- What does all the talk about performance mean for me and my colleagues?
- How can I explain these topics to my customers? How can I position and educate my customers about learning, performance, and technology?
- How do I plan more effectively for my unit, organization, and self?
- How do I prove the contributions we're making? How do I improve the contributions we're making?
- What are the emergent possibilities for our business? For me?

This book is for you if the people around you are saying

- What difference does training make?
- Why don't we just change your title from trainer to performance technologist?
- Pick a learning portal and get back to me with your recommendations.
- I'll work with the executive committee to pick the learning portal and let you know.
- Pick a learning management system and get back to me with your recommendations.
- I'll work with the executive committee to pick the learning management system and let you know.
- Why are you talking to me about this other stuff? Just train them. That's what we've always done. That's what they expect and like. You guys are good at that.
- Should training and human resource people be doing things differently, given our global initiatives? Shouldn't you be doing more than just classes? What else could you be doing?
- How can we capture more of the smarts of our people? I'm concerned because we're losing so many to retirement and to other companies.
- What is it you folks have been doing?
- How do we enhance informal learning here?
- I went to a conference and really liked what they said about knowledge management. How can we use that in what we do?
- Can we move 75 percent of the training to the Web by the third quarter?
- In a nutshell, what's happening in training and development that can help us here?

How the Book Works

Beyond the Podium is divided into two parts, with four chapters in the first and six in the second.

Part One offers the basics. In it we define and position training, focusing on eternal verities, such as the elements of great training no matter the delivery mode, and instructional design, analysis, and evaluation.

Chapter One: Welcome to Training! In this chapter we describe the reasons for the book, how it works, how we're defining training, and why we think the topic deserves your attention and enthusiasm.

Chapter Two: How Can We Figure Out What to Do? This chapter is about performance analysis. It serves as the underpinning for the shift from training to performance, where analysis helps professionals figure out what to do and then sell solution systems within the organization.

Chapter Three: What Is Great Training? Some things don't change all that much, and here we visit the enduring aspects of the work. The examples are modern, including e-learning sites, but the emphases on meaning, purpose, activity, and humanity remain.

Chapter Four: Proving Our Contributions. We provide a lively tour of the options that range from goal-based to goal-free evaluations, from Kirkpatrick to Phillips, and from interviews to focus groups to on-line data gathering.

Part Two looks at learning and performance technologies, informal learning, knowledge management, and the future.

Chapter Five: What Does Performance Have to Do with It? In this chapter we discuss the halting shift from training to performance. Why? How? Who? Where? Why should a trainer or HR professional attend to this issue? How can we retain a commitment to learning and also enhance performance?

Chapter Six: What Are Our Technology Options? Here we survey the possibilities, applauding the options and admitting to the constraints. We'll look at the upsides and downsides of familiar media, such as audio and video, and introduce videoconferencing, DVD, and wireless technologies.

Chapter Seven: What About the Web? Chapter Seven is nothing but net. Here we look at the implications of the Internet for the things training and development professionals have always wanted to do. Our enthusiasm, however, is tempered by caution. We also review what's necessary to begin to take advantage of e-learning and on-line performance support.

Chapter Eight: What About Informal Learning? What is informal learning and how can professionals nurture rather than snuff it? We look at the many ways informal learning is currently happening in organizations and how to play positive roles in the movement.

Chapter Nine: How Can We Use Knowledge Management? Here we define knowledge management and encourage a big tent view of training that includes many approaches and tools associated with knowledge management (KM).

Chapter Ten: Where to from Here? We have opportunities and concerns that can and will keep us up at night. This chapter presents eight thorny and intriguing topics looming on the horizon:

- E-business and training and development
- Object technology
- New roles and permeable boundaries
- Taming choices
- International vistas
- The knowledge cocoon
- Career self-reliance
- Sorting a pile of this from a pile of that

Chapter Features

The chapters follow a pattern. You'll find:

Opening Dialogue. Meet Ann, Al, Carlos, Omar, Herta, Minjuan, Brock, and many more people just like us. They're talking about training and development and framing the issues that are discussed in each chapter.

Friendly Definitions and Discussions. We'll attempt to crystallize the subject and then to explore many ways of thinking about it. Our main focus is on why it matters.

Why should a training and development person pay attention to evaluation, knowledge management, object technology, or informal learning, for example? In Chapter Four, we examine many ways of defining and doing evaluations. In Chapter Seven, we do the same with e-learning, and in Chapter Eight, we tour informal learning opportunities, from breakfasts that boost repair skills to on-line communities of practice.

Questions and Answers. The chapters are arranged around the questions that we think are on your mind. At the same time, we've established a table in each chapter that presents questions you, customers, and colleagues would be likely to pose and answers for them. Is training dead? I love my job the way it is; do I have to change? Why are you writing about training when performance is what's important? Why are you writing about performance when my job is training? What might a training professional bring to the knowledge management effort? These are just a few examples of questions (and answers) that are peppered throughout the chapters, focusing on concerns we know you and your sponsors have.

Time-Sensitive Resources. Got an hour? A day? A week? Every chapter includes suggestions about how to spend limited moments boning up on the topic at hand.

Spotlight Features. Thiagi. Marc Rosenberg. Margo Murray. Jack Phillips. Zhongmin Li. Ruth Clark. And many, many more. Each chapter features an interview with experts and practitioners, people with something to say about the chapter subject. In vivid ways, and with peeks at their personalities, we provide multiple perspectives about each chapter topic.

Slide Briefings. Every chapter, except Chapters Six and Ten, includes a slide briefing that summarizes key points. These presentations were constructed with the sponsor in mind. What do they want to know about the topic? What concerns them? What's important here? Our purpose is to help readers to carry out customer and sponsor education.

Extended Resources. Although we attempted to avoid writing an academic text thick with citations, we also tried to give credit where credit is due. This wasn't easy. Each chapter includes many resources honored for their contributions to our thinking, with hope that readers will pursue them further.

Technology Everywhere. Two chapters (Six and Seven) concentrate on technology, but every chapter reflects the way it permeates the work that we do.

Performance Everywhere. Two chapters (Two and Five) concentrate on performance consulting and solution systems, but every chapter reflects the ways performance concepts permeate the work that we do.

Defining Training

Let's start at the beginning.

What, then, is training? Let's agree to a generous and big tent definition. We recognize that reasonable people could and will quibble here.

Training, then, is what the organization provides to help its people to become more effective and satisfied individuals and employees.

Training experiences can be long and elaborate, such as the curriculum involved in the development of a surgeon, or short and sweet, such as a half-hour class introducing salespeople to a new parts database. Some training is formal, such as a class or video product rollout, or informal, which might happen when a colleague helps out with new software. And training can focus on getting the job done; this happened when a razor blade company taught its operators to use a new piece of equipment. Or it can be broader in purpose, more educational in nature, such as when a computer company offered workshops to its manufacturing employees about learning to learn and English as a second language.

Expanding Purposes

In the old days, when you said "training," it evoked a vivid picture of a group of participants gathered together in a classroom for the purpose of learning to do their jobs. An instructor stood at the front of the room, perhaps at a lectern, on the podium. Now, in most organizations, while that picture still resonates, much more is expected of the training enterprise and of training professionals. Table 1.1 presents widening purposes for training.

The learning enterprise is not at all what it used to be. It just plain looks different.

New purposes for training are dwarfed by the even more dramatic and changing face of training. The learning enterprise is not at all what it used to be. It just plain looks different.

TABLE 1.1. EXPANDING PURPOSES FOR TRAINING.

Training, Typically	*Training, into the Future*
Individual growth and development	Individual *and* organizational growth and development
Skills	Skills, knowledge, *and* perspectives
Know-how	Know-how *and* know how to learn
Learning	Learning, performance, *and* strategic results
The right way to do it	The right *ways* to do it, including understanding about several possible acceptable ways of approaching the work
Training has immediate impact	Impact is immediate *and* continues on into the future
Trainees are prepared for the next task *and* the current job	Immediate implications *and* as preparation for the unforeseen
Participants learn by heart (memorize)	Knowledge bases are key reference
The mind is an impenetrable black box	We educate the mind to learn, learn faster, *and* learn better
Skills for the work	Work related skills *and* those with implications for a lifelong career trajectory

Expanding Approaches and Roles

Training magazine's annual training census (Industry report, 2000) reported that in 1997, 81 percent of training in organizations with more than one hundred employees occurred in classrooms. By 1998, classroom training had slipped to 70 percent of the offerings. In the not-at-all-distant past, the world of training was podium oriented, focused on four walls, presentation skills, and group dynamics.

Certainly, those words and domains retain resonance today, but they are now joined by new emphases: the Web, systems, partnerships, performance, and knowledge bases. Obviously, by most measures and to some extent, now and in the near future, we confront fresh possibilities, responsibilities, and relationships. Tables 1.2 and 1.3 call out these advancing approaches and roles. Chapter Ten discusses them in more detail.

Individuals and organizations, of course, vary in how far along they are on this continuum of change. Some are already engaged in the shift from the "sage on the stage" to the "guide on the side." Perhaps they are at the table when criti-

TABLE 1.2. EXPANDING APPROACHES TO TRAINING.

Training, Typically	Training, into the Future
Training events, materials, and products	Systems, where events and materials are only one aspect
Classroom-based	Convergence of learning and work
Instructor-led	Learner-centered
Simplification and reduction in errors	Authenticity and the desire for engagement with real situations
Instructor responsibility	Expanding learner responsibility
Instructors test students on their new skills and knowledge	Classroom and technology-based self-assessments are included
Instructor-led OR self-instructional	Instructor-led *and* self-instruction in the same system
Professionals make, revise, or purchase training or training services	The organizational role expands, including brokering with vendors and "siblings" in the organization
Enhanced by technology such as video, audio, and self-instructional print	Technology is key player, delivering significant aspects of the training and work support
Instructors teach what students need to know by heart; some key materials are provided as documentation and job aids	Professionals gather best practices and perspectives into on-line knowledge bases and learning communities which engage employees over time
Training experience is a moment in time	Development extends over time and into work, and might commence with a conversation with a supervisor, move the worker to the Web for a self-assessment, include a class offering, and follow up with on-line chats for participants and their supervisors

cal decisions about the business are made. Others, perhaps most, admit that they and their organizations are inclined in those directions, pressured by more competitors and more reasons to involve vendors in the work of the organization. The *Training* census found that 40 percent of training is now coming from outside sources.

What is certain is that no matter where you work in training and development, the people next to you and around you must begin to think hard about new ways of being. The opportunities are just too tasty to ignore. The expectations are pointed. Cost pressures and far-flung employees and customers demand

TABLE 1.3. EXPANDING ROLES OF TRAINING PROFESSIONALS.

Conventionally	*Now, Increasingly, into the Future*
Developer of individual brainpower	Manager of organizational brainpower
Designer and developer	Developer *and* purchaser from outsources
Deliverer or coordinator of classes	Less delivery, more focus on organizational readiness and management of knowledge resources
Develops and produces events and products	Creates and nurtures placebound and on-line environments that continuously support and develop
Coordinator of short-term events and interactions	Broker of systems that start before classes and continue afterward
Concern about high-quality experiences for participants	Focus on the systems that encourage and support performance, learning, and strategic results
Meeting needs by delivering from inventory	Performance analysis to customize and tailor
Developer of content knowledge	Developer of individual learning power, of the ability to establish associations, find relevant materials, and make meaning
Sharing skills and knowledge	Managing knowledge resources
Demonstrating skills in training analysis, design, development, and delivery	Doing what is needed, working in teams, configuring groups that transcend conventional boundaries, ensuring quality
Focusing on students	Developing programs for supervisors as well as students
Measured by butts in seats and hits on Websites	Measured by contributions to strategic goals and results
Solves problems when they emerge	Anticipates and mitigates

immediate responses. And customers grow increasingly impatient for tangible contributions to the goals that matter to them.

Why Is Training Important?

For all the changes that are happening, one aspect remains stable. Training is popular. It is perceived as critical to individual and organizational success. *Training* magazine's annual census reported that 56.6 million Americans received some formal training in 1997 and 54.5 million in 1998.

Money and hope are now more firmly associated with the training enterprise. In fact, education and training, once the place where employees went to wind down their careers, has become a pretty good place to linger and grow. This halo extends to Wall Street, whose quickening interest in the field was heralded by a cover in *Barron's*. Both *Training & Development* and *Training* magazine have also acknowledged the emerging excitement about the business case for training and development. Merrill Lynch estimates that thirty-nine IPOS and $3.4 billion in equity were invested in new education and training businesses in the last five years of the century. Boston-based Edventures.com estimates that $2.5 billion in venture capital was invested in education companies in 2000, up from $500 million in 1997. W.R. Hambrecht & Co. (www.wrhambrecht .com/research/newsletters/wrh/issue002023/index.html#elearning) now covers e-learning enterprises in ways that are parallel to their investment coverage for wireless technologies, electronics, finance, and health industries. IDC (www .idc.com) is predicting that e-learning will be a $14 billion dollar business by 2004, a stunning number when compared to the $54 billion total reported by *Training* magazine in its year 2000 census.

What, beyond habit, is generating all the interest in education and training? Perhaps it is the flood of change with which employees must contend. There is a plethora of new products, technologies, and customers. Leaders recognize that a shift from analog to digital, for example, or the introduction of Kosovan or Somalian refugees into an HMO, creates pressing development needs in employees.

Globalization too is creating demand for training, because an employee charged with negotiating contracts in Uzbekistan is sorely challenged. So too is the accountant from Lisbon who will be making his first trip to Detroit or the new McDonald's franchisee from Moscow. Their cravings for training and support are enormous.

Many thus turn to training because they want to help employees ready themselves for their work, in particular, for the unforeseen, such as circumstances they might confront in negotiating in Uzbekistan or when a customer or computer does the unexpected.

Another force for change is government mandates that require employees to be trained about topics such as safety. Close kin to government mandates for new and refresher training is risk avoidance. Outcomes from lawsuits can be more positive for organizations when they demonstrate and document serious efforts to address concerns before they endanger people, relationships, reputations, or productivity. Training represents one key approach to mitigation, for example, for sexual harassment. *Training's* census 2000 includes a stunning factoid: sexual harassment training is the fourth most prevalent type of training, with 90 percent of all organizations doing something in that area. This is even more startling when compared to the topic that is slightly more popular, performance appraisals, and the one slightly less so, leadership.

Cost can't be ignored as a motivation for the renewed interest in training and development, especially for technology delivery. Rich options are now available with appeal to even the stingiest organization. For example, a graduate student at San Diego State University was delighted with a snappy on-line e-commerce "course" that cost $7.95 and was offered by Element K (www.elementk.com).

Interest in the brain is another factor. Intructors and teachers are talking about it, as are parents and executives. How do people learn? How can they learn different types of material? How can we ensure that they are supple and flexible in their ability to learn, necessary because our challenges and environments continuously change? A Website that translates neuroscience for the rest of us is www.brainconnections.com.

Executives display tenacious preference for training, continuing to believe in quick fixes delivered by the training unit or external training and development vendors. A sad-but-true example was provided by one leader's solution for a work team that just couldn't get along. The executive pointed to a binder that housed a video-based, team-training module with certainty that it was the answer to the team's problems. When pressed on the issue, she was willing to consider bringing in a dynamic "trainer" to offer a class on team dynamics.

New technology lures as well. Even Jack Welch, famed leader of GE, caught the e-learning bug. He has mandated that 50 percent of GE's training be delivered on-line. Qwest Communications is now pushing for 100 percent of its training on-line. While the promises are tantalizing, too often the execution is idiosyncratic. The benefits remain to be seen, establishing a pivotal role for training and human resource professionals.

Beyond impulse and entrenched habits is reality. Does training and development also attract its landmark business because of concrete contributions? Peter Drucker's views appear to be somewhat optimistic. In his classic 1992 article in the *Harvard Business Review,* Drucker noted that "Knowledge is the primary resource for individuals and for the society overall. Land, labor, and capital—the economist's traditional factors of production—do not disappear, but they become secondary" (p.95). Thomas Stewart (1997) also recognized the centrality of intellectual capital, although he certainly does not assume that knowledge is owned and nurtured only by the training department.

Beyond impulse and entrenched habits is reality.

Stewart cited a 1995 study by The National Center on the Educational Quality of the Workforce: "In a report issued in 1995, which controlled for factors like age of equipment, industry, and establishment size, EQW showed that, on average, a 10 percent increase in workforce education level led to an 8.6 percent gain in total factor productivity. By comparison, a 10 percent rise in capital stock—that is, the value of equipment—increased productivity just 3.4 percent. Put another way, the marginal value of investing in human capital is about three times greater than the value of investing in machinery" (p.85).

A California State University Northridge study for the California Employment Training Panel (ETP) found the impact of training on employees to be almost too good to be true. Dr. Richard Moore identified $400 million in benefits for a $73 million dollar state investment in training. New employees, veterans, and entire organizations profited, as Moore found increased worker earnings and organizational growth, and reduced unemployment. The ETP press release (June 28, 2000) noted that forty-five states have ETP-like entities, providing publicly funded worker training to selected organizations and groups across the United States.

ASTD's Bassie and McMurrer (1998) presented preliminary evidence showing that companies that invest more heavily in training are more profitable. These findings are based on a sample of forty publicly traded firms across many industries. Although these results do not meet standards of statistical significance, they are tentatively encouraging. After comparing two groups of companies—those whose average 1996 expenditures per employee placed them in the top half of training expenditures versus those in the bottom half—they reported that companies in the top half had higher net sales and higher annualized gross profit per employee. While caution about claiming causation is appropriate, the relationship intrigues.

Bassie and Van Buren (1998, 1999) have worked to tease out the impact of training on business results. They used a statistical technique to categorize participants in ASTD's benchmarking study as "leading edge," seeking to discern organizations judged to exemplify the best practices of the training industry. They then demonstrated how these leading-edge training investments resulted in higher performance compared to the larger benchmarking sample. They found that leading-edge firms, with increasing resources devoted to training, technology, and outsourcing, correlated with better sales performance, profitability, and quality of products and services. Effects were greater with such commitments invested over time, according to Bassie and Van Buren (1999). Companies that increased their training expenditures per employee and as a percentage of payroll, and the percentage of employees they trained from 1996 to 1997, improved their performance over that same period.

TABLE 1.4. QUESTIONS AND ANSWERS.

Questions	Suggested Answers
Why are you writing about training when performance is most important?	We are writing about training because training is still at the heart of our business in the view of customers. We still do it. What must change is how we support it, the systems we wrap around it, the partnerships we establish in the organization, and the care we use to rivet training to important opportunities and problems. Indeed, the purpose is performance; training is one portion of the performance effort.
Aren't education and training distinct? Haven't you been combining them?	Yes, many do consider them distinct, and we have been talking about them as if they are synonymous. It is important to recognize that training has been historically linked to immediate job performance, while education has been associated with longer-term experiences that build individual capacity. A training organization that only develops skills for today will need to train and train and train repeatedly. On the other hand, an organization inclined only toward education will swiftly lose support from line supervisors. Both are called out and respected in Table 1.1.
What is knowledge management? Is a training professional the same thing as a knowledge manager?	The transition of the workforce from brawnpower to brainpower rivets attention on what the people in an organization know and how to collect, stir, store, and refresh it. That is the charge of the knowledge manager. This is a growing area of opportunity for training professionals with skills at capturing best practices, representing many perspectives on success, and nurturing dialogue in an organization.
There's a lot of talk about training technologies. Is it happening? Is it making a difference?	Technology is definitely finding its way into training and development. Lakewood and ASTD studies agree on that, pointing to a steady rise in technology-based training. The impact is murkier. While many with expertise and stakes in technology and training point to increased learning and reduced costs, independent studies are still needed. One thing is certain: training tomorrow will involve more and better technology than today. Our challenge is to take advantage of the benefits of technologies, while addressing valid concerns about superficiality and failure to persist.

TABLE 1.4. (*CONTINUED*)

Questions	*Suggested Answers*
If what we care about is performance, why even talk about training?	We may "care" about performance, according to ASTD's Bassi, Cheney, and Van Buren (1997), but we don't necessarily focus professional energy on it. Rossett and Tobias (1999) found that fewer than two-thirds of professionals conduct analysis prior to selecting a solution and only 18 percent describe their organizations as boundaryless. Try effecting strategic performance without collaboration across organizational boundaries. It can't be done. Training remains at the core of our business, for good and some not-so-good reasons. We must take advantage of our current vantage point in order to contribute to performance.

Questions and Answers

Table 1.4 presents typical questions and suggestions for responding to them (Q&As). Use this table to craft responses that are tailored to your own context. This particular Q&A is directed at the reader; Q&As in subsequent chapters are meant to help training professionals respond to likely sponsor and customer queries.

Getting Smarter About Training and Development

How can professionals update their knowledge about the field? One answer, of course, is this book. We hope it is a trampoline for new vistas and continuing professional development. Time is always a factor. Table 1.5 attempts to match developmental needs with the time you're able to invest.

TABLE 1.5. RESOURCES.

Time	Resources
"I have an hour"	Tour the ASTD Website at www.astd.org
	Tour the Training and Development Community Center at http://www.tcm.com/trdev
	Tour the ISPI site at www.ispi.org
	Tour the Training Supersite at http://www.trainingsupersite.com
	Tour the Masie Center, The Technology and Learning Thinktank at http://www.masie.com/train96.html
	Read Rossett and Barnett's article in *Training* magazine, "Designing Under the Influence."
	Gayeski, D. (1998). "Out-of-the-box instructional design." Retrieved May 26, 1999, from the World Wide Web: http://www.astd .org/CMS/templates/template_1.html?articleid=11475
"I have a day"	Tour the Education, Training, and Development Resource Center for Business and Industry at http://www.tasl.com/
	Tour the Training Net site at http://www.trainingnet.com
	Read the rest of this book
	Subscribe to the Masie technology and training newsletter at www.masie.com
	Read Billcom Publishing's *Training* magazine annual census issue, published each year in October and November
	Visit www.ibstpi.org, an organization that has generated instructor, instructional designer, and manager competences
	Read Robert Mager's "What Every Manager Should Know about Training" and "Goal Analysis"
	Tour Instructional Technology research on-line at http://intro.base.org
"I've got a week"	Join the American Society for Training and Development, attend a conference, subscribe to *Training & Development*
	Join International Society for Performance Improvement, attend a conference, subscribe to *Performance Improvement*
	Consider attending an Influent Technologies (www.influent.com) conference or the annual training conference and training and technology conferences at www.lakewoodpub.com
	Check out Pac Bell's searchable index of educational Websites at http://www.kn.pacbell.com/wired/bluewebn/
	Read the *Journal of Interactive Learning Research* at http://www.aace.org/pubs/jilr/
	Read Smith, P. L., and Ragan, T. J. (1999). *Instructional design.* 2nd edition. Upper Saddle River, NJ: Prentice-Hall.

Spotlight on People

Cathy Bolger

Dr. Cathy Bolger is a San Diego–based training professional in the best of the familiar mold, garnering kudos for her ability to stand up and train. She is very, very good at teaching and delighting the people who take her classes. Bolger offers presentation skills, meeting/facilitation skills, conflict resolution, and stress management classes to corporate and government clients. She also facilitates outdoor team-building experiences. In addition, Bolger enjoys a long-term relationship with the Center for Creative Leadership; through it, she coaches managers using data from 360-degree feedback instruments and assessments.

The Hard Parts Bolger's clients are, like most, eager to buy a class, schedule the room, and fill it with participants. Bolger acknowledges that even her much appreciated events are only a portion of the solution critical to achieving strategic goals. She believes that the shift to performance improvement perspectives is indeed real, for those who "get it." She continued, "For instance, trainers are starting to see themselves as 'brokers' of services as part of a solution system. However, many are still doing what they have always done, which is to use a training class as a solution."

As someone who has offered many classes repeatedly, she admitted a personal challenge familiar to training professionals: "Staying fresh can be a challenge. I try to treat every coaching session or training as if it is an athletic event. I come well rested and well prepared. I take a break (could be a day a week, a month or a year) if I find myself getting a bit stale. For instance, I cut back on my outdoor team-building facilitation for a few years, and just recently have been scheduling more work as I again find it very enjoyable."

People Are the Pleasure While technology is a growing influence on our field and Bolger uses it as a productivity and communications tool, it's the people she coaches and teaches who make her eyes light up. She put it this way: "I enjoy helping people move in a positive direction toward their goals, whether it is giving a better presentation, leading a better meeting, or balancing task and people skills." She also is actively involved in the local ASTD chapter and noted that networks of colleagues have added to the joy she derives from her work.

In the Future When asked to give advice for people new to the field, Bolger highlighted quality and customer focus. She said, "Become known as someone who has good service skills such as quick follow up, openness to feedback, and good interpersonal skills." Bolger also remarked on the importance of professional associations and technology.

Lynn Richards

From a position as a learning center manager with Hewlett-Packard, Lynn Richards moved to Peregrine Systems, an infrastructure software company. At up-and-coming Peregrine, she leads a group responsible for, among other things, providing software training and certification for external customers and channel partners. Richards now heads up a cadre of twenty-eight instructional designers and developers, instructors, and technical experts. Richards noted that she is responsible for "making sure that people are ready for what needs to be done today and tomorrow."

From Training to Training and Performance In over twenty years of experience at companies as diverse as Kimberly Clark and M&M Mars, Richards has seen it all. Her career mirrors trends and transitions typical of the larger field of training and development. She has moved from delivering training to analyzing, designing, and developing learning products to her leadership role. Now she sees herself as making certain that learning and education are aligned with business goals. She is responsible for standards and processes that will result in integrated solution systems. Richards put it this way, "I've evolved as the profession evolved and continue to grow and learn."

For Richards, the shift from training to performance was natural. She was there early, and now she's delighted to be joined by so many others, including the major professional associations. She remarked, "I believe the excitement of others is still in its infancy. The process of moving through awareness, to understanding, and to application is slow. I see it requiring someone in a group, not necessarily the manager, to champion and model the shift to performance." Richards' natural sense of systems is at work here. She recognizes that the commitment to analysis and integrated solutions has to be in the minds and hearts of leaders across the organization, not just in human resources and training.

Richards recognized that some colleagues in our business resist. She said, "Some education and training colleagues are fearful that their classroom 'business' will be threatened and reduced. I wish that they could see the shift to performance as merely that, a shift, rather than a possible 'take away.' By partnering, we can show how combined solutions will not only provide better solutions but also generate greater satisfaction from our customers."

The Hard Parts Richards admitted that it isn't always easy to facilitate group processes that will result in shared standards and efficient procedures. Her job is to serve a far-flung customer base, to implement these high standards and processes, and to acknowledge and appreciate individual differences. She explained, "To reach an overall balance between often competing needs and priorities, the scale will tip from one side to the other over the short term. One group of people will be temporarily better off or happier. I just have to ride this out like they do, keeping the longer term vision and goal in mind, in view of the staff, and encouraging them throughout."

The Joy Richards remarked on the pleasure she derives from perceiving growth in the staff. One instance she remarked on is how she experiences their successes, the gratification she feels when their high-quality deliverables lead to profitable business results and increased customer satisfaction. She is motivated by how much she learns from staff members and by how her development process is also continuous. Richards cited examples, such as seeing the design and development of a Website emerge and benefiting from significant improvements in instructional design/development processes via recommendations from staff members.

Commitment to Technology Richards acknowledged that she chose a prior position because it enabled her to explore electronic learning. She commented, "I'm especially excited about the possibilities offered by intranet solutions, including just-in-time access to learning and information, independent self-paced and scheduled options, and how such options fit with existing instructor-led resources. Managers in the business units are more easily attracted to cost-effective learning solutions offered at the desktop. They see these solutions as more efficient than classes. Of course, the obvious travel cost savings are real, but also the accessibility and customization possibilities attract favor."

In her new role at Peregrine, she sees increasing opportunities for technology, with an emphasis on integrating classroom and electronic options. Richards highlighted the importance of customer readiness for emergent technologies and integrated systems. She pointed to a problem that is omnipresent in the training business: "There seems to be a wider excitement about Web technology than there is a focus on when it is appropriate to use it or what must be done in the organization to support successful implementation."

In the Future Richards was a perfect person to ask for advice about the future. She said

- Create a professional vision and think about what you want to *do* with these skills so that there will be a context and purpose for your learning
- Work to become clear about your personal values, principles, standards, boundaries, and ethics so that if (when) confronted with unusual or uncomfortable situations, you will be somewhat prepared to deal with that situation, for example, time pressure inevitably challenges quality, so be prepared to deal with the conflict
- Continuously self-assess so that you are aware of what satisfies you and in what areas you are strong and in need of development
- Cultivate relationships with successful practitioners so you can learn from them

- Be prepared to be flexible about inevitable constraints
- Take as wide a view as possible and continue learning so that you have more options for employment
- Keep your defenses low so that you are ready and able to learn new things and respond to advances in the field
- Learn to ask for help
- Collaborate generously

Terry Bickham

A long-time U.S. Coast Guard officer and manager of a large training center, Terry Bickham now manages a training unit at Peregrine Systems. When we interviewed Bickham, he'd just retired from a long, successful career in the Coast Guard.

Bickham described his work with the Coast Guard this way, "As producing skilled Coast Guard men and women who save people from the sea and protect the sea from people."

Technical Training with a Focus on Performance The Coast Guard has received kudos for its commitment to performance improvement. Bickham's efforts at the Petaluma training center provide a model for large organizations attempting to infuse performance perspectives into their organizations. He described the leadership he provides this way: "Each of the schools has a very capable school chief, so I leave the day-to-day training management up to them. I focus on three equally important functions: providing the schools with the support and resources they need; coaching my staff of performance consultants who work with the schools; and working with our clients to provide them with the results they really want, on topics as varied as telecommunications, network maintenance, law enforcement, and emergency medical services."

Even in the Coast Guard, with established commitments to performance improvement, line leaders aren't always on board. Bickham put it this way: "We spend quite a bit of time with clients talking with them about performance improvement and the need to make sure training is what they really need. We have been pretty successful at convincing them to pay for analysis, but we've not been so successful at getting them to follow through on the non-training pieces of the puzzle. Frankly, they know we'll give them a first class training product and the other stuff is just too hard. Because my training center doesn't have the influence to make the systemic changes needed, we now require the clients to designate one of their folks as the project manager. That shifts responsibility for the success of the endeavor from the training provider (us) to the clients themselves. They find it harder to blame the training system if it doesn't work out and are more open to including reps from human resources, operations, et cetera, in the effort."

Here Bickham demonstrates one of the strategic shifts occurring in our business. While continuing to produce knock-your-socks-off training and support materials, he and his team worked as change agents and at redefining and sharing responsibility for performance improvement with the line.

Great Training with a Systems View Bickham's statement about where he derives pleasure in his work is interesting. Note how his focus is on the implications of the effort—in this case, for the ways a job aid helps to get the work done. He said, "We've adopted what we call our 'core purpose.' It's a simple statement that our mission is to 'improve performance in the field for technical specialties we serve.' What it doesn't say is that we will put on great training or that we will graduate five thousand students each year. My greatest joy is that every one of my staff truly takes that statement to heart and uses our core purpose as the litmus test for all that we do. They eagerly search for ways to build skill and knowledge that really have an impact beyond the classroom. For example, they'll build an on-line job aid for calibrating a piece of equipment that is perfect for use in the field. They'll then design a training module for their school based on using that job aid instead of the traditional lecture and lab. I guess I get a real charge out of seeing my instructors view themselves as more strategic in the organization and then contribute."

Technology Contributes and Complicates When queried about technology and training, Bickham said, "I'd say there is intense excitement about technology in two-thirds of our staff and intense fear in the other third." He noted that there are some wonderful benefits, for example, "We've recently saved more than two thousand student days a year in just a few courses by using 3-D modeling and animation to get complex electronic concepts across. That's very real, and the peer pressure is on in all my schools for similar results." At the same time, Bickham is concerned about the tendency to use technology as an information dump, continuing habits associated with one expert presenting to many, and the familiar "sage on the stage." He said, "The trouble is that some of the schools are focusing on converting classroom lectures to basic PowerPoint. We're addressing this by attempting to develop our folks to think about the strategies, not just the technologies, to make these folks more comfortable with new software and teaching and interaction strategies, but it will take a while."

In the Future Bickham acknowledged his roots in training. Here is the caveat he offered as he encourages training people to retain specializations: "As performance has become in vogue, I've seen some people give an almost Judas-like denial of their former lives as training professionals. I think that's silly. While it's fine to consider yourself a performance consultant, I believe it is important to specialize in a particular intervention or two. Training management with a true performance foundation can have a huge impact on the organization. If you keep that larger perspective and purpose alive in your team, the opportunities are endless and exciting."

At the Heart of the Matter

The following slides are designed to help professionals explain and win support for their training, development, and performance improvement efforts. The focus here is on encapsulating the business so that others can support and participate.

Slide 1.1

What Is Training?

Training is what the organization provides to its people to help them become more effective humans and employees.

Presenter's Notes

Ask your audience to think about training that has made a difference for them. List a few ways that it contributed to your growth. What made it successful? How could it have been even better?

Slide 1.2

What Training Looks Like Today

- ■ **A class at the training center**
- ■ **When the supervisor coaches**
- ■ **Use of a Web-based checklist to prepare for a performance review**
- ■ **Review of callbacks with a manager**

Presenter's Notes

Note that we're keeping it simple. Use real examples. Where we've spoken about the generic class or Web checklist, fill in real examples from your setting. The important thing here is to give a sense of the richness of things that are going on as part of the training enterprise and, of course, to link those efforts to strategic goals.

Slide 1.3

Why Train?

- ■ **New products, customers, technologies, and locations**
- ■ **Prepare people to learn independently**
- ■ **Prepare for the unforeseen**
- ■ **It matters, resulting in better performance, retention, sales**

Presenter's Notes

Once again, focus on your own setting. What new technology is being rolled out? Who are the new customers and why do sales and service people need information about them? What data do you have about the impact of training on results? Share it here.

Slide 1.4

Is Training Sufficient? NO!

- Role of the supervisor
- Importance of clear expectations
- Match with metrics and recognition
- Strong sponsorship
- Matching technology and processes

Presenter's Notes

This is a classic challenge. How do you convince the larger organization to play a part in the performance improvement effort? First, be clear about their role. Keep it simple. Focus on managers and supervisors and how critical they are to the success of any initiative. Then move on to talk about each of the factors listed above, all of which are best explained by grounding them in a real effort, one that is familiar to executives. Resistance is typical. Meet it with examples of past training efforts (quality, customer service, sexual harassment) unsupported and thus unsuccessful.

Slide 1.5

Helping Trainers Develop People

■ Are "sibling" relationships encouraged?
■ Are they at the table before the emergency?
■ Are you an active sponsor?
■ Are you judging goodness by butts in seats?

Presenter's Notes

Many professionals have not told their leadership how to help them do their jobs in a more strategic way. Do that. It is also important to talk about the shoemaker's children, as there are many training and development units that lag behind in their own development.

Resources

American Management Association. (1997). *Training results: achieving results that last.* Washington, DC: Author.

Bassie, L., Cheney, S., & Lewis, E. (1998, November). Trends in workplace learning: Supply and demand in interesting times. *Training & Development, 52*(11), 51–77.

Bassie, L. J., Cheney, S., & Van Buren, M. (1997, November). Training industry trends 1997. *Training & Development,* pp. 46–59.

Bassie, L. J., & McMurrer, D. P. (1998, May). Training investment can mean financial performance. *Training & Development,* pp. 40–42.

Bassie, L. J., & Van Buren, M. (1998, January). The 1998 ASTD state of the industry report. *Training & Development,* pp. 21–43.

Bassie, L. J., & Van Buren, M. (1999, January). Sharpening the leading edge. *Training & Development,* pp. 23–33.

Clark, D. (1999). *Learning, performance and training glossary.* Retrieved May 25, 1999, from the World Wide Web: www.nwlink.com/~donclark/hrd/glossary.

Craig, R. L. (Ed.). (1996). *The ASTD training and development handbook* (4th ed.). New York: McGraw-Hill.

Dobbs, K. (2000, October). The coming shakeout in e-learning. *Training, 37*(10) 114–120.

Drucker, P. F. (1992, September/October). *Harvard Business Review,* pp. 95–104.

Eline, L. (1999). *A trainer's guide to skill building.* Retrieved May 26, 1999, from the World Wide Web: www.astd.org/CMS/templates/template_1.html?articleid=12697

Gayeski, D. (1998, April). Out of the box instructional design. *Training & Development.* (Online) www.astd.org/virtual_community/td_magazine/td_0498_contents.

Hall, B. (1997). *Web-based training cookbook.* New York: John Wiley & Sons.

Industry report 1997. (1997, October). *Training,* pp. 33–75.

Industry report 1998. (1998, October). *Training,* pp. 43–76.

Industry report 2000. (2000, October). *Training,* pp. 45–94.

Mager, R. F. (1999). *What every manager should know about training: An insider's guide to getting your money's worth from training* (2nd ed.) Atlanta, GA: Center for Effective Performance.

Masie, E. (1998, December 20). *TechLearn trends online newsletter* (#96). Retrieved May 25, 1999, from the World Wide Web: www.techlearn.com/trends/trends96.htm

Masie, E. (1999, April 24). *TechLearn trends online newsletter* (#119). Retrieved May 25, 1999, from the World Wide Web: www.techlearn.com/trends/trend119.htm

Rossett, A., & Barnett, J. B. (1996) Designing under the influence. *Training, 33*(12), 33–43.

Rossett, A., & Tobias, C. (1999). A study of the journey from training to performance. *Performance Improvement Quarterly, 12*(3), 30–42.

Smith, P., & Ragan, T. (1999). *Instructional design.* Upper Saddle River, NJ: Prentice-Hall.

Stewart, T. (1997). *Intellectual capital.* New York: Doubleday.

CHAPTER TWO

HOW CAN WE FIGURE OUT WHAT TO DO?

Gustavo: Look at this e-mail. It's my first contact from the new vice president of sales, Gerhard von Hoff, over in Frankfurt. He wants a three-day class on sales basics for just about everybody. Remember, we did something similar to that in a two-day class last year? And then there's the fact that our sales force is all over the world. I hope he's not thinking about investing in a globetrotting road show for sales training.

Emily: And we get so much resistance from the territory sales managers whenever we pull their folks out of the field for training! Will they support a three-day class? And why three days? Will they attend themselves? Maybe they will, since Gerhard is their new VP.

Gustavo: And what do we put in the class? How do we make it relevant and meaningful? I want to please Gerhard, but I also want to make sure we don't produce a frivolous program.

Emily: Gus, maybe you need to do a quick analysis to find out what the sales force *really* needs. Of course, you'll need to convince Gerhard to hold off on the classes for a bit, but the data will be a great way for him to learn more about the global sales force.

Defining Analysis

In a nutshell, *analysis is the study we do in order to figure out what to do*. Through analysis, Gustavo, Emily, and the rest of us take a fresh and data-driven look at the work, worker, and workplace. We do that so that recommendations will be based on many opinions throughout the organization, rather than fiat, convention, or whim.

Analysis matters because it helps divine better plans. In his quest to do the right thing for Gerhard and the organization, Gustavo, for example, will turn to sales people, managers, the literature on best sales practices, sales results, customer feedback, and Gerhard's top priorities for excellence.

Thus, analysis is what professionals do to gain insight into the organization, job, workplace, and individual. For doctors, architects, and performance professionals, analysis is the process that ensures movement from ambiguity to what Robert Mager dubbed "the heart of the matter." The doctor determining why the adolescent is fatigued, the architect observing work flow in an office, and the trainer seeking what the sales force *really* needs are all using sources and data to figure out what to do.

Repeated Analyses

It makes good sense to carry out at least two waves of analysis. The first wave is performance analysis (PA). Think about it as scoping, a reconnaissance effort used to determine what is needed. Gus must turn to performance analysis to find the most promising initiative for the global sales force. He will ask questions about the strengths and weaknesses of the sales force, review data reflecting customer perceptions and sales patterns, and eventually seek the causes for gaps between the way it is and the way Gerhard wants it to be. Performance analysis is a process that identifies sweet spots and then seeks information that will help to tailor a system targeting those opportunities.

Once performance analysis ensures that skill, knowledge, and motivation are part of the mix, more explicit and focused needs assessments can be carried out. Needs assessment, or training needs assessment (TNA), is the study done in order to design and develop appropriate instructional and informational programs and materials (Rossett, 1987; Rossett, 1999) (Figure 2.1). Training needs assessment might involve in-depth subject-matter study, audience analysis, determination of prerequisite skills and attitudes, establishment of consensus approaches and standards, and determination of the details that underpin learning, information, and even knowledge management programs.

In this case, after a performance analysis that captures choice opportunities for improvement and growth, Gus would turn to model performers, experts, and the literature to hone in on the details associated with basic selling skills such as closing the deal, contact management, competitive intelligence, or product knowledge.

Table 2.1 captures the differences between performance analysis, the brisk once-over that crafts the plan, and the more extensive training needs assessment to generate the details of the solution.

There are, of course, similarities between training needs assessment and performance analysis. Both represent methods for figuring out what to do, although at different levels of detail and with varying proximity to the solution. They are efforts to understand and serve customers and to engage people throughout an organization in the effort. And they are based on asking questions of sources, as Rossett (1987, 1999), Robinson and Robinson (1995), Hale (1998), and Swanson (1994) have emphasized. The differences are also worth considering. Performance analysis is mostly about sketching out the approach. Training needs assessment, on the other hand, generates the meat in the solution, which might be a class, on-line learning, job aids, documentation, an on-line help system, or some combination.

TABLE 2.1. PERFORMANCE ANALYSIS AND TRAINING NEEDS ASSESSMENT.

Performance Analysis	*Training Needs Assessment*
Scopes to determine what to do	Is the process to gather sufficient detail to enable development of a solution
Results in a data-driven description of what is needed and why	Results in classes, job aids, on-line reference and training, documentation
Is the initial response to the request for assistance from the customer	Directs attention to those needs that are linked to gaps in skills, knowledge, and motivation
Results in a report	Results in tangible learning and support products
Defines the problem or opportunity	Provides details regarding the right way or ways to do it, to achieve the strategic goals
Defines cross-functional solution systems	Identifies the details of exemplary performance and perspectives so that they can be authenticated, communicated, and taught

FIGURE 2.1. PA TO TNA.

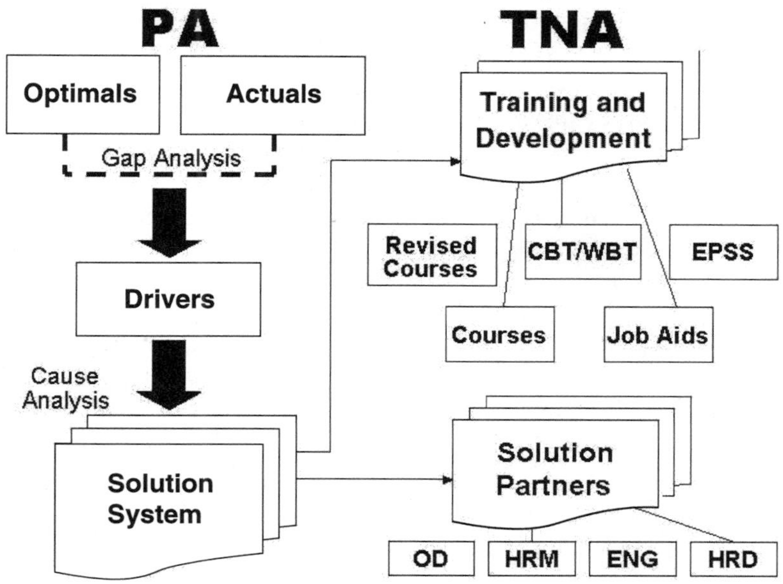

FIGURE 2.1. PA TO TNA.

Strategic and Virtual Analyses

Some years back, during introductions at the commencement of an analysis class at a global computer company, an engineer rose to tell the group what he was up to. He said something like this: "I'm tasked with doing the corporate needs assessment for our engineering population, and I've been at it now for sixteen months. I decided to take this class because I sense now that some of my executive support is eroding and I need to get this thing wrapped up swiftly."

Analysis in this case would never be complete, because the data would be out of date as soon as his "final" report had emerged from the printer. Instead, that engineer must establish a system for continuously gathering, reporting, and recommending based on numerous waves of contacts in the field.

A recent article in *Business Week*'s E.BIZ (November 1, 1999, p. EB 54) lamented cumbersome planning processes that serve to tether the organization. The concern was that planning inevitably yields products and approaches that must be marketed and sold, no matter the customer's need. We've seen this in training organizations that devote substantial resources to planning and developing and then find themselves focused on marketing their inventory, no matter the changes in the organizational strategy or marketplace. A colleague at a telecommunications company lamented how resources were often directed at trivial incentives for attendance, such as t-shirts, personal digital assistants, and lottery tickets, rather than on customized solutions.

The alternative is continuous and virtual engagement with customers, so that products, services, and systems are tailored to match emergent needs and priorities. That's a far cry from selling from inventory, where unloading that inventory becomes the top priority.

The challenge for professionals, then, is to be both responsive and anticipatory, immediate and perpetual. . . .

The challenge for professionals, then, is to be both responsive and anticipatory, immediate and perpetual—to help Gerhard with developing his global sales staff and to recognize that it is critical to already have some handle on the global sales staff's strengths and weaknesses, *even before asking.* Emily and Gustavo should possess prior knowledge about the sales force and be continuously updating their intelligence about new products, sales directions and priorities, and customer perceptions. Wouldn't that be better than waiting for a request and then being abruptly catapulted into action? Problem number one under those circumstances is tempering the sponsor's enthusiasm and buying time to conduct an analysis.

Why Is Analysis Important?

Bracketing the profession in the new century are enthusiasm about workplace training *and* cynicism about the ability of training in and of itself to influence what really matters—performance improvement linked to strategic results.

Analysis contributes here, as we use systematic study to figure out how to contribute in meaningful ways to everything from better sales to parenting skills to reduced service callbacks to improved project management.

Analysis makes two overarching and critical contributions. First, it defines what the professional should do to provide valuable services to the sponsor and organization. For example, what sales training would contribute to the performance of Gerhard's global sales force? What else besides sales training will they need? What roles should the line organization play?

The second contribution is political. Analysis allows people up and down the organization, and even outside it, such as suppliers and customers, to put their fingerprints on the effort. That yields a better and more palatable result, one they are more likely to support. Gerhard and Gus's initiative will be defined by opinions beyond their own.

Here is an example of both contributions provided by Lieutenant Commander Laura Schmitt. Laura tells this story about a problem the U.S. Coast Guard was having with transmitters:

> Reports of equipment trouble kept coming in. The problem wasn't that this particular type of transmitter seemed to break any more often than was expected, but when the transmitters did break it took forever to fix them. A little digging by managers also showed that the electronic technicians charged with fixing them were both available at the transmitter sites and had been to a one-week training course. What conclusion did the managers come to? They decided that the course was at fault and should be revised.
>
> Thus, a request came in to our performance consultant team at the training facility. Could we please look into the situation? A performance consultant partnered with an instructor from the course to conduct a performance analysis. We made sure we had both funding and buy-in from the managers at every step of the way. We found a few small ways that the course could be improved, and we initiated those changes. We shared equipment information with the people who order spare parts. We shared our performance analysis results on the electronic school's Web page so that technicians and managers could learn from the effort as we proceeded, too.
>
> And, we found the real reason for the long downtimes associated with this broken equipment. It was a confidence problem on the part of the electronics technicians when it came to working with high voltage. For the technicians, the bottom line was that they preferred to call in a "more experienced" technician rather than face fixing what they perceived as dangerous equipment on their own.
>
> The solution? To training we added more practice time and a few knowledge-based objectives so that students had a clearer picture of what was happening with the voltage, so that they could understand what was dangerous and what was not. We used the analysis to educate managers so that the "more experienced" technicians could establish supportive relationships during scheduled visits that would translate to telephone support during equipment failures. Most importantly, we ensured that every unit had job aids and technical manuals available to the technicians at the job site in a format they could use while fixing the equipment. Those documents were the same documents used to practice in the classroom. Our contribution was to speed up the maintenance of the transmitters at low cost, always good news for Coast Guard people and the public.

Doing Analysis

The purpose of analysis is to cast a wide net for needs and solutions. How are we going to do that? What follows is a simplified approach to analysis. It is not meant to replace any of the sources detailed in Table 2.2. Rather it is designed to show that analysis can be done swiftly in a way that will involve many in planning.

The purpose of analysis is to cast a wide net for needs and solutions.

Six ideas are central to analysis:

1. Analysis has two purposes: (1) defining the effort and response and (2) reaching out to an array of sources in order to define the effort *and* create support for it.
2. Requests for analysis come in many flavors, such as, "I want our sales force to have a really good three-day class on sales basics"; "We're rolling out new

TABLE 2.2. RESOURCES.

Time	Resources
"I have an hour"	Tour the First Things Fast Website at www.josseybass.com/rossett.html
	Read "Analysis" in Stolovitch and Keeps's *Handbook of Human Performance Technology,* pp. 139–162.
	Read Rossett (January, 1999), "Understanding the people in the organization who aren't us: Communication strategies for analysis." *Performance Improvement,* 38 (1), 16–19.
"I have a day"	Read Rossett's *First Things Fast: A Handbook for Performance Analysis,* published by Jossey Bass/Pfeiffer.
	Read Robert Mager and Peter Pipe's *Analyzing Performance Problems.*
	Read Judith Hale's *Performance Consultant's Fieldbook*
	Read Rossett (1997, July). "That was a great class, but . . . " *Training & Development,* 51(7), 18–24. http://www.astd.org/CMS/templates/index.html?template_id=1&articleid=10988
"I've got a week"	Read Ron Zemke and Tom Kramlinger's *Figuring Things Out*
	Read Dana and Jim Robinson's books about performance consulting
	Consider taking a class about analysis offered by Influent, for example, at http://www.influent.com/seminars/needs.htm
	Some relevant software tools are at http://www.perseusdevelopment.com http://www.surveymaster.com http://www.bnhexpertsoft.com

project management software across the globe—maybe we need an on-line class or something"; "What are we going to do about the performance appraisals? I was thinking we might want to rework the forms and then train everybody"; or "What can we do to make certain that our hospital administrators are ready for all the changes that are coming down the pike?" Then there are the situations in which there will be no requests at all. Does that limit our responsibility? The silent colleague might be the one on auto-pilot or the one with the greatest need to look at opportunities to improve performance of people and the organization.

Figure 2.2 presents a page from the *First Things Fast* Website, where approaches to analysis are linked to the kinds of requests training people are asked to handle.

FIGURE 2.2. STRATEGY TABLE.

Strategy Table

Here's an abbreviated example. Let's presume that you were asked to help determine what the engineer of the future might need to know and do. Don't forget to alter this template to match your unique circumstances.

Stages	Sources	Possible Questions
One	Customer, client or sponsor	Why are you focusing on the development of engineers NOW? What do you hope to accomplish by developing engineers? Are all engineers of equal interest or is one group the focus? What do you see as key skills for the future? What are the emergent challenges? Have you established an on line community that captures the ideas of thought leaders or enables collaboration between engineers, no matter their location?
Two	The Literature and Professional Associations	What trends have they identified? Emergent skills? Perspectives? Emergent challenges? New technologies? Additional sources? Implications of worldwide outreach?
Three	Internal and external experts	What trends do they see as most critical? Emergent skills? Perspectives? Emergent challenges? New technologies? From all these, what are the priorities that they associate with this organization and vertical market?

what you're looking for fast on this web site and in *First Things Fast.*

‹GO›

About the Author Get to know the author of *First Things Fast.*
‹GO›

Site Index Lost? Find exactly what you're looking for on the site.
‹GO›

Buy the Book Order your copy of *First Things Fast* from the Jossey-Bass On-line Bookstore.
‹GO›

Source: Rossett, A. *First Things Fast* Website. Copyright © 1999, Jossey-Bass/Pfeiffer. Reprinted by permission of John Wiley & Sons, Inc.

3. Both formal and informal methods of analysis are worthy, including data gathered during walks from the parking lot to the building or while standing in line for a cup of coffee, as well as through surveys, focus groups, and review of exit interviews or accident reports.

4. Many sources of information are better than one or two. Possible sources include experts, incumbents, model performers, supervisors, work products, and customers.

5. It is important to select directions by defining a gap between the desired and current situation, thus directing resources to where they are most needed.

6. Root causes or drivers are sought and then used to define systemic solutions, recognizing, for example, that a question about why they don't or won't is just as critical as what they do and do not know.

It is possible to simplify analysis into four broad stages.

Stage One: Target Directions

During Stage One, the professional is seeking a picture of the directions the effort will take. What aspects of sales are most critical, to continue our focus on Gus's challenge?

This picture of directions can be generated in two ways. First, it might come from nailing down details about a desired future state (such as great team sales or more effective selling of a particular product or being able to speak the language of physicians). The second option is to concentrate on defining current problems and then jumping from them to target directions.

Defining That Desirable Future State

The desired future state can be captured in the following ways: by interviewing the client or sponsor; by reviewing the literature; by examining specifications and policies; by talking to experts; and by watching successful performers.

Gustavo might launch his analysis by asking Gerhard about his priority directions for sales excellence. Where are his emphases? What does he think makes a difference in sales for the company? What does he believe is most essential to effective sales performance? Does it vary by territory or by product line? Here are nine sample questions that might help Gus elicit critical information from Gerhard. Adapt these questions to unique situations and sources:

- What are your top priorities for the sales force now?
- When you think about our global sales force, what pleases you? What concerns you?
- As you look at other organizations, what are they doing that you most admire, that you'd most like to bring to our sales force?
- What do you perceive as the drivers of sales excellence?
- What skills, abilities, and competencies for the sales force will grow in importance in the near future?
- What have you read or heard that might have the potential to improve sales performance in the organization?
- How does our global reach affect your priorities for sales excellence? For sales teaming across geographic boundaries?

Focusing on Problem Areas

While springboarding from a desired state can be useful, sometimes it makes sense to start by focusing on the present, especially on current problems. Safety training provides a vivid example. Would you want to focus on generic safety or target the places where injuries have occurred? The latter, typically.

Consider Gus' situation. Should he begin with Gerhard's sales priorities and views for optimal performance? Or should he start by targeting sales dips or customer complaints or the concerns voiced by regional sales managers about weaknesses in teams or follow-up? In this case, you could argue in any direction.

In other situations, such as problems with performance reviews or sexual harassment training or safety, it makes sense to ground the effort in both the current situation and past problems and successes. *Cynicism is bred by chronically dipping employees in new directions without regard to the realities of past performance and context.*

Professionals would increase the authenticity of the effort by asking sponsors the following questions. Again, alter them to match individual circumstances. Note that slight editing readies these questions for supervisors and the sales force as well.

- What measures do you use to think about the performance of the sales force?
- How is the global force doing in light of the measures? Where are they strong? Where could they be stronger?
- Consider what you've seen since you've taken over the sales function. Where could sales performance improve?
- Why are our salespeople running into problems? What will they tell us when we ask what they need to improve their results?
- What keeps you up at night as you think about our salespeople?

- Consider the sales figures. What problems pop out at you? Which issues demand your attention?
- What do customers tell you? What compliments do you receive? What concerns are they raising?
- Consider the geography. How do sales skills and results vary across the globe?
- To what do you attribute the differences? What causes some territories to sell effectively and others to be less effective?
- Look across product lines. Why are we strong in some lines and not in others? What causes these differences?

Stage Two: Describe Drivers

During Stage Two, the professional seeks to find what it will take to move toward the desired state as identified in Stage One. If we are looking at a problem in an ongoing situation, such as performance reviews or sales, the question is *why*. Why are reviews flawed? Why are they tardy? Why are salespeople not selling a particular product or closing sales in a particular way? If, however, the mission relates to rolling out a new approach to the work or a new piece of software, then the focus in Stage Two is more prospective. What will it take to move this idea into practice? What might get in the way? How can we support the introduction of this software? How can we contribute to what might be a substantive change effort?

Table 2.3 summarizes possible drivers for performance—also known as root causes, barriers, and constraints. This model owes a debt to prior work by Robert Mager, Peter Pipe, Joe Harless, and Tom Gilbert.

How would we figure out which drivers are present in this situation? The answer, of course, is to query key sources, such as incumbents, their supervisors, and the published literature. All are likely to have views on the forces that encourage and discourage movement in the desired directions. Direct the following questions to the sponsor, altering them to match individual circumstances. Note that slight editing readies these questions for supervisors and incumbents. These questions are predicated on a rollout situation, where the organization is changing something, perhaps introducing a new product or shifting to team selling. Because the challenge is to introduce something new into an organization, Dormant's (1999) work on key factors in change management are relevant here:

- Do you think employees share your enthusiasm for this initiative?
- Do you think employees are already aware of this change? What do they know? What more do they need to know?

TABLE 2.3. EXAMPLES OF DRIVERS FOR PERFORMANCE.

Drivers	Examples
Focus on Individuals Skills, Knowledge, Expectations, Information	Teachers leave their computers in the closet because they don't know how to use them.
	Contracts administrators resist making decisions because they don't know they are expected to.
	Analysts resist using the software to generate reports from the database because they can't find the documentation and the online HELP is clunky and unfriendly.
Motivation	Clerks don't see the value in the new software. The old works just fine.
	Many salespeople resist using computers, noting that they're "people-people," not techies.
Focus on Culture Environment	The documentation and directories are housed way across the office and frequently misplaced.
	Personnel re-enter a nine-digit code three different times during an order-fulfillment process.
	Zookeepers prefer to keep their knowledge about the animals to themselves, since it's always been that way.
Incentives	Supervisors who rate employees as other than stellar are expected to fill out forms and attend meetings to justify these ratings.
	Job security and recognition go to the individuals who know the most, not share the most.

- What will managers and supervisors say? Are they enthusiastic, in your view?
- Will local units and managers be able to tailor the effort to their situations?
- Are the people who will be expected to carry this forward currently sufficiently knowledgeable to do it? What must they learn to do it with fluency?
- Are they confident about their skills in this area?
- Do you think they know why you and the leadership have elected to move in this direction? Do they see the relative advantages of a shift in this direction?
- Are the necessary software and hardware and other tools readily available to them?
- Do they "get it"? Is the shift clear and understandable?
- What questions will they have about this new direction? How do you plan to answer these questions?

Stage Three: Match Solutions to Drivers

What will the professional do about the situation now? Stage Two delivers some clarity about direction and the forces or drivers associated with those directions, but where to go from there? In Stage Three we help the organization move in the defined directions.

. . . [T]his effort is predicated on assumptions about the power of systems and alignment to improve performance. Training and the resulting learning are aspects of that system.

As you can see from Table 2.4, the solutions that emerge go much beyond training and development. That's because this effort is predicated on assumptions about the power of systems and alignment to improve performance. Training and the resulting learning are aspects of that system.

TABLE 2.4. DRIVERS AND SOLUTIONS.

Driver	Description	Solutions
Lack of skill, clarity about expectations, knowledge or information	People don't because they don't know how, or they've forgotten, or there's just too much to know.	Education/training Information support (job aids) Documentation Coaching and mentoring Clarity re: standards Communications initiatives
Weak or absent motivation	People don't because they don't care, don't see the benefits, or don't believe they can.	Education/training Information support (job aids) Documentation Coaching, mentoring Participatory goal setting Communications initiatives
Ineffective environment, tools, processes	People don't because processes or jobs are poorly designed, or necessary tools are unavailable.	Reengineered work processes New or improved tools or technologies or work spaces Job design or redesign Job enrichment Participatory decision-making
Ineffective or absent incentives	People don't because doing it isn't recognized, doing it is a hassle, or not doing it is ignored.	Improved appraisal/ recognition programs Management development New policies

Table 2.4 is based on the assumption that training is good but not sufficient. In Stage Three, we take the drivers and causes identified in Stage Two and match them to an array of interventions, as detailed in Table 2.4.

Stage Four: Build and Collaborate

Table 2.4 yields interventions that touch people and resources throughout the organization. A job might need clarification or redefinition. Computer systems might require additional memory or speedier connections. A recognition program might be called for. And managers and incumbents might need a whole lot of convincing, if Stage Two uncovered that they harbored doubts about why the organization has elected to go in this direction.

Could training be an appropriate part of the mix? Indeed. In fact, it's likely. In this era of new systems, technologies, products, and customers, there is much to learn and understand. Place-bound or on-line training could be a key component. But it is only one aspect of what it takes to contribute to meaningful and consistent choices and performance.

As Figure 2.1 shows, no trainer is an island. Analyses point to an array of aligned efforts. Admittedly, these collaborations can not be taken for granted. On too many occasions, trainers have heard, "Why are you asking *me* to help with *your* project? I work in the quality unit" or "Why is somebody from training and development talking about job redesign and process reengineering?" Here are some strategies to encourage enhanced collaborations:

1. Don't wait for the analysis to be complete to involve sibling units such as organization effectiveness, compensation, or quality in the effort. Share the sponsor's enthusiasm or concern and the request for assistance right from the start. Solicit broad involvement.
2. Share findings with resonance for colleagues across the organization when those finding emerge, rather than waiting to deliver the final report. For example, if global participants are complaining about their undependable technology platforms, let management information systems (MIS) know about the rumblings. If a clunky process appears to be a factor, share that news with those tasked with reengineering.
3. Don't assume that you are the only one who is concerned about the issue. If sales are at issue or customers are complaining or enrollments have plummeted, consider it likely that many in the organization are worrying about the situation. Bring people together to facilitate a systemic approach.

4. Who is the sponsor? Gerhard, our example here, should be in a position to attract attention across the global organization. Solicit his assistance to make certain that the people who need to participate are ready, willing, and able.

5. Nurture collegial relationships. It's much more likely that people across the organization will generously collaborate if you respect the quality of the contributions offered in the past. Can you point to ways that your organization has contributed to their prior efforts? Have you established a history of shared services to support key customers? Do you know and like one another?

Resistance to Study Prior to Action

At the beginning of this chapter, Emily expressed certainty about the benefits of study prior to action. She and Gus decided to save Gerhard from himself, from his inclination to turn to the proverbial training "silver bullet." Gerhard, in his eagerness for that three-day class, joined many other executives in grabbing for a seminar, workshop, or on-line module. Many prefer quick, visible, and habitual fixes.

Emily and Gus recognized that Gerhard's request is fraught with risk. Will the line support it? Will they take their people out of the field for training? Afterward, will they coach it, contributing to transfer? Given the far-flung nature of the sales force, how will distant and global implementation challenges be handled? And about what aspects of sales should the class be directed? What's in? What's out?

Those are not trivial questions. Unfortunately, it is by no means certain that Gus will receive a welcoming response to the idea of study prior to the requested action. In 1996, Carl Czech and Allison Rossett asked training and performance professionals about the reception their performance improvement ideas were receiving in the organization. The results were not encouraging. The Rossett and Czech study identified gaps between what professionals viewed as critical (such as analysis and solution systems) and the ways that their managers and customers perceived those ideas. Two other recent studies for financial and tax services companies also pointed fingers at customers. In the view of those inclined to analysis, customers do not "get it." Training and development professionals often lamented that sponsors resist the idea of analysis prior to action.

Why?

The root reason for resistance to analysis is that sponsors don't understand *why*. What benefits derive from analysis? They prefer action to delay and study.

Try four approaches to counter this resistance. First, identify prior initiatives that were launched precipitously, without prior study, and that lacked support throughout the organization. Point to major investments in training that produced more cynicism than results because they were singular and unsupported. The quality movement and telephone skills might be fertile places to look for examples. Remind the sponsor about those frittered resources.

A second approach is to ask questions that the sponsor will recognize as reasonable and to which he or she lacks an answer. A question about the eagerness of the people in the job to move to the new system is a good example. Another is a question about the knowledge and skills of the supervisors and their willingness to coach. Good questions with obvious ramifications for program development and transfer will open the door for subsequent and speedy analyses. Many sponsors will admit that they aren't sure, for example, about where the supervisors are on the subject and note that maybe they ought to find out up-front.

A third suggestion is to stop using phrases such as performance analysis and training needs assessment. They don't mean much to customers and executives, and if they do, they often stand for lengthy studies that have not historically made much of a difference. Instead, substitute words such as customize and tailor. These concepts have more immediate appeal. Here's a possible interaction:

Gerhard: I was hoping we could get that class going by the end of the quarter. Momentum is important.

Gustavo: Yes, I see what you mean. I want to focus the sales training in the right directions. It's critical to tailor it to *our* sales force so that the effort reflects *our* priorities and *the recent feedback* we've been hearing from customers. I don't want to take a vanilla sales training package off the shelf. Let's customize this for our people and this moment in time.

Gerhard: I agree that we need a customized program. That would be better; but can we do it swiftly?

Gerhard brings us to a fourth reason for resistance to analysis. Time. Most analyses take too long. How can we shave time off the effort?

The best strategy for reducing time is to be continuously engaged in analytical effort, continually trolling for information about where the organization

TABLE 2.5. SPEEDY STRATEGIES AND STORIES.

Strategy	Stories
Perennial Analysis: Do it all the time, not just when somebody requests a class or an on-line HELP system.	Chanda arranges to have several questions included on the annual corporate climate survey. Victor, tasked with developing and retaining the engineering staff, visits lunch tables and queries regarding needs, satisfaction, and emergent trends. Jorge reads everything there is to read about higher education, because he needs to know in advance what is likely to be important on campus.
Virtual Analysis: Use technology to capture information everywhere, all the time.	In addition to reading about new directions in higher education, Jorge needs to know what faculty and administrators are thinking and doing on his campus. He establishes a technology listserv and monitors conversation, including salting it with key ideas from the literature. He uses on-line forms to collect information about advising, course delivery, assessment, and back-office issues. He establishes an on-line help desk and monitors questions and concerns.
Use Straw Not Tabula Rasa: Few respondents are eloquent. Provide models, examples, and scenarios that will stimulate worthy contributions.	When Vic is tasked with developing a global teaming class, he starts with the literature and benchmarking. From that he derives several alternative possibilities for how it might work. Then he briefs the leadership, seeking to educate them, fill in details, and identify the approach they are most likely to support.
Randomize: The beauty of randomization is that it allows generalization from a few to many.	Gerhard wants to solicit the regional sales manager's views on the needs of the global sales force. He randomly interviews fifteen of them, using a variety of e-mail and phone interviews. He assumes that the trends that emerge from that strategy can be generalized across the organization.

Source: Rossett, A. (1999). *First Things Fast: A Handbook for Performance Analysis.* San Francisco: Jossey-Bass/Pfeiffer.

and its people are going, where it is, and associated drivers. When a request arrives, much is already known. Table 2.5 summarizes strategies for speeding up analysis.

Questions and Answers

Table 2.6 shows typical questions that might be raised by sponsors and executives and suggestions for responding to them. Use this table to craft responses that are tailored to your context.

TABLE 2.6. QUESTIONS AND ANSWERS.

Questions	Answers
Is analysis really important?	It is really important. Sure, you can skip it, and you might turn out a fine program, but certainly not dependably. Analysis enables you to figure out what to do in a robust way and to involve many sources in the discovery process that yield better, aligned programs AND more support during rollout and implementation.
What if my sponsor won't let me do analysis?	That happens. Handle it by not being completely dependent on swinging into action after the request emerges. Instead, continuously gather needs-related information. Don't be surprised by a request—anticipate.
When I said I wanted to do a needs assessment, the client said, "No way." What do I do?	Customize and tailor the effort by examining work products and interviewing key players. Don't worry about perfection or permission to "do a needs assessment." Instead focus on getting close to a meaningful picture of what's going on, from several perspectives. Lose the words, especially if they enrage the sponsor. Frame the data in a way that resonates. And avoid waiting until the end of the analysis to report. Provide continuous status reports in informal ways, by dropping by and sending e-mails.
What if the data suggests that the sponsor's original view of the situation is off base?	This happens. For example, Gerhard wants a three-day sales training course. That might not be what's needed. Gus can use one of two approaches. The first is the masterly approach. Here you would make a compelling and data driven case about how the sales force needs X and Y, not Z. This case would be rich with quotes and numbers and clearly point to what needs to be done and how. The alternative is more discovery oriented. Here you would share data, findings, quotes, trends, but NOT exactly how to address them. The challenge would be to engage Gerhard in the meaning of the data and to work with him to generate an appropriate approach for the sales force, in light of the data.
The sponsor wants an external person to conduct the analysis. I'm internal—what do I do?	Work together. No external has your understanding of sources and possibilities. And that external certainly will not be able to implement an aligned system. Learn from each other.

Spotlight on People

Fernanda Groenendijk

Born in Argentina, educated there and in the United States, and now living in the Netherlands, Fernanda Groenendijk works as a performance consultant for Origin Corporation. She is responsible for the analysis, design, implementation, and evaluation of training, communication, and performance support solution for global clients. She has worked as a consultant in the United States, Latin America, and Europe and specializes in multinational and multicultural projects.

Opportunities for Analysis In the European market, in Groenendijk's view, analysis and performance technology happen for the most part as a consequence of information technology (IT) projects that are not working well. She noted that most projects commence with a welcome but without a clear picture from the client about what they hope will be accomplished. Origin Corporation's first step is to define what success will look like or where the most critical pain is. Groenendijk reported that she then interviews the client contact. She said, "This person, often a project manager, is typically a stressed out man with an IT background who claims that the business units do not understand what the project is about. In his view, the IT project is about implementing a system on time and on budget. For the business units, it is about improved performance through many changes supported by a new system."

In this first contact, Groenendijk and her colleagues attempt to find out the IT manager's expectations, no matter how far from reality they may sound. She said, "We let him see that we understand how he feels and how he thinks. And then, in his language, we explain that to be able to write an implementation plan to solve his problem, we need to see a bit more of what is going on." She noted that often she must emphasize that the planning aspects of the effort will be speedy.

That enables Groenendijk to expand her inquiry to business unit managers, consultants, and key users. She also talks to internal training professionals about what works and what does not and returns to the project manager to share findings and capture his view of the situation.

This rich data enables Groenendijk and her colleagues to determine how to proceed: "What should be recommended? Where is the support? Is there resistance? How are people feeling about this? Are the organization and key people ready to hear what will be said?" Groenendijk believes that direct and rational arguments work better in North America. Inside Europe, she noted, messages must be carefully tailored to the people and situation.

Difficulties with Analysis Groenendijk admitted that the analysis process demands much of people in the organization. She said, "You make noise in the organization and you have very little for them to see until your analysis is ready. In most cases, when you come in, people are very busy; they have problems, frustrations, and other things on their minds. They are not always cooperative, and some do not believe that you can be a part of a solution to their problems. Some people use you as a dumping place for all their frustrations, problems, incredible ideas, and sorrows. You have to keep a cool head, but let them feel empathy, try to manage their expectations, and win their trust."

Revelations That Have Emerged Groenendijk put it this way: "All problems have more than one face and therefore more than one possible solution. The art is to find the best solution for the organization. What has come to my attention in Europe is that they tend to overkill with training, and in most cases we found that

- So much training is not needed. A combination of communication (clear expectations), training, and performance support are a stronger solution.
- Too much information (training or presentations) gives top management a sense of security, middle management a headache—or more—and end users a sense of chaos.
- The Web and Web-based solutions are not yet very popular in Europe. People look for social contact and interaction during training and information sessions. They have a more conversational style than in the United States."

Differences Between Europe and Latin America Groenendijk noted some differences between Europe and Latin America: "There are many differences. In Latin America there is no money and no time for analysis. Clients hire experts, and they want a solution—no questions asked. They want a solution that is quick, and at low cost. This may be related to the fact that the shaky labor market in Latin America in the last years favors the company more than the employee. With the high unemployment rate, there are some clear messages inside and outside the organization, for example

- If you do not adapt here, you are out of work.
- There are no jobs for you elsewhere, but there are many people ready, willing, and able to fill your job even better than you.

"In Europe, clients want the expert to tell them a possible solution—and why. Then they want to 'buy' a solution that will fit in their organization. So we use analysis phase to build the relationship with the client, to first sell ourselves, and in the second place, to sell the solution. This is why we take the time to do the analysis— to find out what makes the clients tick and what they can handle at this point in time. Sometimes we recommend a partial solution. Some clients want training and nothing but training. Solutions such as performance support are unfamiliar to them, so we recommend the training that has a chance to contribute and come back around later to introduce other aligned interventions."

Groenendijk concluded: "Be careful and be fast!"

Frank Rogalewicz

Frank Rogalewicz is the manager of a regional group training department for Guardian Life Insurance. He is responsible for meeting the training and development needs of approximately twelve hundred employees in a fast-paced, customer-centered processing operation. Rogalewicz noted that his staff members are the true heroes, as it is they who actually perform the analyses and design and implement the solutions to meet real performance needs.

Why to Do Analysis Rogalewicz said: "We do analyses to ensure better individual and organizational performance. Although analyses obviously take some time, money, and resources to conduct, good ones—heck, even mediocre ones—tend to pay off in ways that *far* exceed the up-front investment."

He continued, "Imagine the dollars saved by not throwing expensive training solutions at problems that won't or can't be fixed by training to begin with. Imagine the time saved by not over- or under-training people. On top of the savings, imagine the potential returns in terms of worker commitment and productivity, management efficiency and credibility, et cetera, when you're able to meet people's true *needs* rather than just fulfilling arbitrary *wants.* In a past company, I watched a committee prescribe a $70,000 sales training rollout to sales reps in order to jump start sagging credit insurance sales. That $70,000 didn't even factor in the time and opportunity costs of having the salespeople attend these half-day sessions. We reluctantly did the sales training, and results barely changed. Interestingly, an early informal inquiry into the situation showed that an archaic company policy was the real culprit. The few offices with already high sales were not following the policy, while the low-performing offices were. When that policy was modified, credit insurance premiums soared by over $1 million in the first month alone. It's not that the training was bad; it was well-received actually. But it couldn't fix this problem. We could've kept another $70,000 in the bank."

When to Do Analysis Rogalewicz acknowledged that it isn't always obvious when to use analysis, as client language can conceal many opportunities. He noted that his organization has developed a healthy skepticism whenever someone approaches them to fix a problem or capitalize on an opportunity through training all by itself. He noted that training in and of itself is rarely sufficient.

Difficulties with Analysis Rogalewicz identified the following areas as most challenging:

- Knowing *when* you have enough data to make a reasonably sound call. On the other hand, too much data can lead to paralysis.
- Conducting an analysis *efficiently* (that is, which 20 percent of the questions will reveal 80 percent of the problem or situation).
- Conducting the analysis in a way that doesn't *look* like an analysis to the time-strapped, production-focused client.
- Getting clients to buy into the benefits of "analysis first."
- Understanding and working through your own biases. It's easy to fall into the trap of simply confirming your own biases rather than truly analyzing a situation objectively.

Revelations That Have Emerged Rogalewicz confided: "The biggest revelation that has emerged from conducting analyses is how many situations and problems can be fixed more easily and quickly *without* training (which can feel like a dangerous thing for a manager of a training department to say). Think of all the things you can do and perform both on and off the job for which you were never 'trained,' at least not formally. It's absolutely phenomenal.

"When a child is behaving unacceptably, do you propose that she or he needs training ('Honey, I think we should send the boys to a class on how to share their toys')? Nah. You normally look to modify something else in 'the system' first to correct the behavior (for example, consequences, feedback, expectations, removal of environmental obstacles or temptations, et cetera). Skill and knowledge are some things to look at, but it's often the presence or absence of other factors at the root of most problems.

"More than anything else, this has led us to change where we *start* our analyses. We'll look at potential skill and knowledge deficits, but not necessarily first—and never alone."

Strategies to Increase Support Here are some strategies that Rogalewicz uses to educate his organization about analysis:

- He demonstrates and describes real benefits that clients have realized from analyses (for example, reductions in training time, decreases in learning curves, improvements in individual performance as measured in post-training assessments and on-the-job production, positive performance changes without having held a class, and so forth).
- He talks to clients continuously about how analysis is *part of* the training process, not a separate, expendable component.

- He seeks client input into analyses and recommendations and acknowledges their contributions to such processes.
- He informs clients that we *will* ask questions (that is, sets the expectation) and provides them with examples of the questions. In most cases they can see why those particular queries are worthy and important.

Interestingly, Rogalewicz also described some strategies he has used to keep his own unit focused on analysis. His unit highlights analysis as the very first point in the departmental mission and practices. They integrate analysis accountabilities—small and large—into the training and development department. A small example is a departmental norm "outlawing" use of the question "So, what are your training needs?" A larger, more positive example is preparing structured proposals and contracts with clients that outline analysis findings and the resulting solution systems.

Advice for Practitioners Rogalewicz provided the following advice for practitioners:

- "There are many analysis models, and they're more alike than they are different. Pick one that's simple for you, internalize it, and use it to guide your analyses. A well-known, valid model can make your analyses much easier. Models such as those developed by Robert Mager, Allison Rossett, or others provide practical frameworks for studying the problem, issue, or situation with far greater objectivity. Use of valid models can also lend credibility to analysis in management's eyes.
- Learn to balance logic (for example, what the analysis model says) with intuition (what you feel).
- A partial analysis is better than no analysis.
- A linchpin in any performance analysis is the answer to the question, 'Is this a training problem?' If you're only able to answer that question, even without further analysis, you've done a ton of good.
- Question, question, question. Develop a short list of analysis questions that you can ask in every analysis.
- Ask the question, 'Why?' at least one more time than feels personally comfortable. You'll be amazed at what insights that question will yield.
- Guard against overconfidence in your own judgments. Regardless of whether you may be right, it can distance you from your clients."

At the Heart of the Matter

The following slides are designed to help professionals explain and win support for their efforts to conduct analysis prior to building solutions.

Slide 2.1

Figuring Out What to Do

A presentation about planning

Presenter's Notes

This is a presentation about planning, about how we figure out what to do. You're probably wondering why it's necessary and how we do it. That's the terrain we'll cover.

Slide 2.2

Analysis at the Heart of Change

Training center	➜	Distributed and desktop
Respond	➜	Anticipate and consult
Instructor dominated	➜	Learner centered
Teaching and learning	➜	Business results
Bureaucratic control	➜	On demand
Curriculum architectures	➜	Small, targeted objects

Presenter's Notes

Let me begin by describing the environment in which we plan and work. There's a great deal of change. The old assumptions no longer hold true. In order to figure out what to do and target services within an organization, we want to ask some questions before we hastily move forward. Your mechanic asks some questions and does some testing before acting. That's true too for your doctor. Look at this as a quick diagnosis. We want to plan systematically so that our programs are based on reality, not habit.

Slide 2.3

What Is Analysis?

- **It is what we do to figure out what to do, how best to serve customers and clients**
- **It is important because we want to tie our efforts to organizational initiatives, rather than to be driven by habit or whim**
- **Analysis enables us to do the right things for our organization**

Presenter's Notes

Several years ago, a training director asked a vendor to develop some training for contract administrators. The purpose was to empower them, so that they would make better decisions and be able to determine next steps without asking a supervisor or the corporate legal staff. It was also important, of course, for them to know when it was indeed appropriate to go up the chain of command and to involve the lawyers. The vendor was suspicious. Would training really make a difference? Perhaps the contracts people were afraid of making a mistake, doing the wrong thing. A short analysis was done. Trust was established with the administrators. The vendor was amazed to discover that the administrators did not understand the system or the reason for regulations or even where to look for information to help with decisions. They did indeed need training and access to better reference materials. They reported no fear at all, just confusion. That analysis conducted in a single intense day provided clarity about what to do.

Slide 2.4

Critical Success Factors for Analysis

- ■ **More sources are better than just one or two**
- ■ **Continuous quests for data, such as reviews of customer comments and exit interviews, are better than waiting to be asked**
- ■ **Formal and informal methods of analysis are worthy, including chats in the cafeteria line and on-line surveying**

Presenter's Notes

Who were the sources for the contracts administrator study? First was the sponsor, the leader of the contracts administration group. We also talked to managers in that group and then to eight randomly selected contracts administrators. We also examined the existing work-reference materials and prior training. All those sources influenced the effort.

One friend who leads training for a petrochemical company described how she eats lunch in the company cafeteria. Her goal—to share a meal with people she doesn't know and capture their views. It helps her anticipate what's likely to land on her desk in the near future. It also helps her nudge the organization in key directions, rather than waiting to be asked.

Slide 2.5

Critical Success Factors for Analysis

■ **Questions are at the heart of analysis—seeking information about direction, current situation, and drivers. Let's imagine that we're working on teaming.**

— **When you envision an effective team, how does work get done? How is the team directed? [directions]**

— **Consider the teams now operating here. What pleases you about the effort? What is working? What isn't? Where are we missing out? [current situation]**

Presenter's Notes

Let's move away from contracts administrators and think instead about an initiative that focuses on encouraging teaming in the organization. Here are some questions that might be asked. Can you generate others that would be of interest to us, that would help us plan a program to improve teaming in the organization?

Slide 2.6

Critical Success Factors for Analysis

■ **A picture about key gaps and needs emerges. Then questions about drivers and causes can be targeted.**

— **Why are the teams not producing in speedy fashion, in your view?**

— **What are the causes for the additional time that teams appear to be needing to complete their work?**

— **Do you think our people know how to be effective team members?**

— **Do they want to work on teams?**

Presenter's Notes

There are some structured ways of thinking about what drives performance in your organization. We use questions to get at those kinds of drivers. Do they know how? Do they care? Do they feel confident about their ability to do it? Do they have the necessary materials and tools? Do the supervisors coach and encourage? Does the organization recognize their efforts? Those questions are critical to putting the right programs in place.

Slide 2.7

Analysis Results in Systems, Not Just in Training

- **Clarity about expectations, perhaps new job descriptions and selection procedures**
- **Reengineered processes, such as a new and better way to track global team performance**
- **Recognition and incentive systems**
- **On-line training and coaching systems**

Presenter's Notes

The right programs are typically made up of training and other aligned efforts. While training is certainly a key strategy for improving and maintaining performance, that makes it good but not sufficient. Think how much more likely you are to move your engineers or analysts into teaming if you also alter job descriptions, performance standards, processes, and the way supervisors support the effort.

Slide 2.8

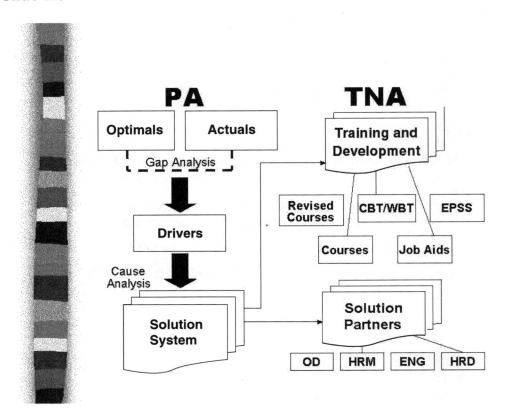

Presenter's Notes

This visual represents an iterative process, where we begin with performance analysis and our general effort to sketch the approach, and then move to training needs assessment, which will help us write or develop the programs.

Slide 2.9

Consider the graphic in Slide 2.8. How do you perceive that it will alter roles in your organization? What does it mean for the way you think about your work? For others?

Presenter's Notes

How will this affect training professionals? How will it affect colleagues in other related services, such as organizational effectiveness or information technology? How will it affect customers? Might it create new relationships with outside vendors?

Resources

Argyris, C. (1993). *Knowledge for action: A guide to overcoming barriers to organizational change.* San Francisco: Jossey-Bass.

Dormant, D. (1999). Implementing human performance in organizations. In H. D. Stolovitch and E. J. Keeps (Eds.), *Handbook of Human Performance Technology* (2nd ed.). San Francisco: Jossey-Bass.

Foxon, M. J. (1997). The influence of motivation to transfer, action planning and manager support on the transfer process. *Performance Improvement Quarterly, 10*(2), 42–63.

Fulop, M., Loop-Bartick, K., & Rossett, A. (1997, July). Using the world wide web to conduct a needs assessment. *Performance Improvement, 36*(6), 22–27.

Gilbert, T. (1978). *Human competence: Engineering worthy performance.* New York: McGraw-Hill.

Hale, J. (1998). *Performance consultant's fieldbook.* San Francisco: Jossey-Bass.

Langdon, D. G. (1997). A look into the future of human performance technology. *Performance Improvement, 36*(6), 6–9.

Mager, R. M., & Pipe, P. (1984). *Analyzing performance problems.* Belmont, CA: Pitman

Prahalad, C. K., & Hamel, G. (1990, May/June). The core competence of the corporation. *Harvard Business Review, 68,* 79–87.

Robinson, D. G., & Robinson, J. C. (1995). *Performance consulting.* San Francisco: Berrett-Koehler.

Rossett, A. (1987). *Training needs assessment.* Englewood Cliffs, NJ: Educational Technology Publications.

Rossett, A. (1996, March). Training and organizational development: Siblings separated at birth. *Training, 33*(4), 53–59.

Rossett, A. (1997, July). That was a great class, but. . . *Training & Development, 51*(7), 18–24. On-line at www.astd.org/CMS/templates/index.html?template_id=1&articleid=10988

Rossett, A. (1999). *First things fast: a handbook for performance analysis.* San Francisco: Jossey-Bass/Pfeiffer. Available at 800-956-7739. www.jbp.com/rossett.

Rossett, A. (1999, May). Knowledge management meets analysis. *Training & Development, 53*(5), 62–68.

Rossett, A., & Czech, C. (1996). They really wanna but. . .: The aftermath of professional preparation in performance technology. *Performance Improvement Quarterly, 8*(4), 114–132.

Rossett, A., & Tobias, C. (1999). An empirical study of the journey from training to performance. *Performance Improvement Quarterly, 12*(3), 31–43.

Rummler, G., & Brache, A. P. (1990). *Improving performance: How to manage the white space on the organization chart.* San Francisco: Jossey-Bass.

Stewart, T. A. (1997). *Intellectual capital: The new wealth of organizations.* New York: Doubleday.

Stolovitch, H. D. (1997). Introduction to the special issue on transfer of training-transfer of learning. *Performance Improvement Quarterly, 10*(2), 5–6.

Stolovitch, H. D., & Keeps, E. J. (1992). *Handbook of human performance technology: A comprehensive guide for analyzing and solving performance problems in organizations.* San Francisco: Jossey-Bass.

Swanson, R. A. (1994). *Analysis for improving performance: Tools for diagnosing organizations and documenting workplace expertise.* San Francisco: Berrett-Koehler.

Watkins, R., Leigh, D., Platt, W., & Kaufman, R. (1998, September). Needs assessment—A digest, review and comparison of needs assessment literature. *Performance Improvement, 37*(7), 40–53.

Zemke, R., & Kramlinger, T. (1982). *Figuring things out: A trainer's guide to needs and task analysis.* Boston: Addison Wesley.

CHAPTER THREE

WHAT IS GREAT TRAINING?

Kiyoma: Read these evaluations. He is so good. I wish all our trainers got the reactions Carlos does.

Leslie: He is famous across the company. We're fortunate that the Latin American group is willing to let us borrow him as much as we do.

Kiyoma: Ever wonder what makes that class so good? Oh, Carlos, of course. But the class gets positive reviews when others offer it too.

Leslie: I like the way we've structured the class, and the materials participants take away with them are useful. And we prep people for it with e-mails to their supervisors and to them prior to the class. All that helps.

Kiyoma: With all the initiatives on our plate now, it's good to step back and think about what makes great training great. We can lose all that too easily when looking at a sizzling presenter or a dazzling Website.

Defining Great Training

Great training makes a difference in the lives of people and the work of the organization. Outcome-oriented, it is authentic and active. Afterwards, you know you've been involved with something compelling, vivid, and memorable—something you can take back to your work and life.

What Is Great Training?

How do we know what constitutes great training? Well, we'll use the literature, of course. But above all, what we present here should ring true to you. It should parallel the moments you remember, the lessons you continue to draw on, the teachers who pop into your head, and yes, even the print materials and technology products to which you repeatedly return.

There is no simple or single answer to a question about the attributes of great training. What we'll do here is present elements associated with it. Most will be familiar. A few will be less so; they find a place in this chapter because of personal experiences with great teaching, learning, and support and the possibilities presented by emergent technologies.

The focus here will not be on centralization or decentralization, on outsourcing or insourcing, or on instructor- or technology-based training. Here we'll attempt to get to the heart of the matter about great training, to elements that endure across approaches and situations.

Great Training Has Strong Purposes

Great training is about something, not about everything. It teaches an approach to technology integration, teaming, or the tango. Typically, it has a point of view, although sometimes that point of view is a review of many points of view associated with the matter. In the end, the training should say or allow the participant to discover something clear and useful about the topic, something that participants can walk away with, ponder, and use.

Great training is about something, not about everything.

What might a training and development professional want to accomplish? The goals always are improved individual and organizational performance. But what's beyond those lofty purposes?

Perhaps you want the sales staff to understand the logic that underlies a motherboard. Perhaps you're attempting to help nurses understand Somalian culture and how it influences presentation of symptoms. Or perhaps you want to urge teens to reduce the risks they take when driving. In these three cases, there is much to be learned by heart, so-called declarative knowledge, so that the technicians, nurses, and teens have the answers in memory when needed to handle the typical as well as the unforeseen.

Table 3.1 presents some questions to use to isolate the purposes associated with your efforts. Note that your reach can extend to their ability to reference information as well as to what colleagues learn by heart.

TABLE 3.1. MEANINGFUL PURPOSES FOR TRAINING.

Emergent Purposes

Do we set purposes that influence both the individual and the organization?

Do we communicate our purposes to participants and their managers?

Do we communicate these purposes directly and repeatedly?

If we are using a more constructivist approach, one that encourages participants to find purpose and meaning individually, is there meaning for them to find?

Will our purposes have resonance for our students?

Do we use our purposes in all the ways we might: to focus participants' attention, to establish objectives, to define practices and program assessment, and to provide clarity for self assessment?

Do our purposes influence both immediate and long-term performance?

Is reference and contribution to the knowledge base an aspect of our goals?

Do our purposes touch the mind, heart, and belly?

A brief foray into the topic of behavioral objectives belongs here. Some trainers believe that a four- or three-part objective is mandatory because such objectives provide the underpinnings for learning and evaluation strategies. Good objectives will indeed accomplish that (see Mager's classic texts, *Preparing Behavioral Objectives* and *Goal Analysis*). For example, consider these two objectives:

1. Given at least ten x-rays with and without instances of osteochondral desecans (OCD), the orthopedic surgeon will be able to identify where the condition is present and where it is not and any cases necessitating further studies through x-rays or MRIs.
2. Given the x-rays that necessitate further studies to determine OCD, the orthopedic surgeon will be able to write the reports justifying those studies in such a way that insurers allow the procedures.

These objectives provide useful direction to both the person building the training and the orthopods who must learn the material. The strategies pop out. Practice and testing materials practically write themselves. Relevance to the work at hand is obvious.

Where is the quibble with objectives then? Perhaps it is that we've seen behavioral objectives serving as a slippery slope, where perfunctory objectives lead to perfunctory designs. And perhaps the problem is in the word "behavioral," an approach more associated with the last century than this new one.

Still, objectives remain a robust way to establish purposes. When written well, they result in a neat and desirable alignment between where you're attempting to go, how you get there, and how you assess that it happened.

Great Training Touches Hearts as Well as Minds

As seen in Table 3.1, there is more to it than the cognitive. The orthopedic surgeon must choose to use what she knows about OCD diagnoses. Will that teen choose to make good choices when three tipsy *What value do we add if the training is* pals are beckoning her into a car? Will that *shrugged away at the classroom door?* nurse exercise care and caring? Will the technician go the extra mile? In all these cases, the heart and belly are involved as well as the mind. What value do we add if the training is shrugged away at the classroom door?

For training to be successful, our work must extend to helping employees reach beyond *knowing how* to *knowing why*. They can't do it if they don't know how. And they won't do it unless they know why and possess confidence about it.

Table 3.2 is a recap of strategies for influencing attitudes during the training experience. The table includes strategies for use in both classroom and e-learning experiences. Later in this chapter, we'll touch on the systemic features that must wrap around training to boost the impact on performance, a topic treated in more detail in Chapter Five.

Scott Parry (2000) goes even further in his aspirations, recognizing a larger role for enthusiastic trainees in changing the organization that wraps around them: "Trainees should be viewed as catalysts and agents of change whose impact on the work environment will produce organizational growth and development in desired directions."

Great Training Is Active, Engaging

Too often, training is passive. Not long ago, one of the authors stumbled on a CD ROM with scores of PowerPoint slides dedicated to *training* managers to handle instances of sexual harassment. What's surprising is the frequency with which we run into such PowerPoint content dumps, page-turner Websites, and lecturing instructors.

Of course, we can do better. The American Museum of the Moving Image (www.ammi.org) illustrates some of the possibilities (Figure 3.1)). Animated images explain how moving pictures move, how TVs work, and how sound is recorded and they do all this in understandable and compelling ways. One of the

TABLE 3.2. TOUCHING HEARTS AS WELL AS MINDS.

Strategies to Incline Participants Toward the Purposes

Talk about the sources for the program; explain why they are credible and similar to participants.

Use two-sided arguments to make points. In most cases, they are more powerful than a litany that ignores multiple perspectives on the topic.

Innoculate learners so that they can anticipate the reactions and obstacles they will encounter. Provide ways of responding and thinking that maintain a positive view.

Use role models and role plays.

Use war stories to add authenticity and texture.

Active participation by learners is important. Practice on real problems and cases.

Structure and encourage discussion.

Structure and encourage reflection.

Provide opportunities for individuals to experience success early in their exposure.

Provide continous, repeated exposure to the messages through contacts with supervisors and reference materials, for example, not just a singular class or video or Web experience.

Use takeaway materials, ongoing involvement with on-line communities, and coaching to extend and reiterate the messages.

Use extrinsic rewards for boring and repetitive tasks.

authors found herself riveted to the beautiful FLASH images and nodding, "I didn't know it worked like that!"

Why then does so much of training and development fail to engage participants? Perhaps a review of the possibilities will help.

Let's look at the way key schools of thought incline us to engage students and participants. The behaviorists, dominant in the first half of the 20th Century, riveted attention to practice and testing. Their message urges observable activity, from circling correct answers to soldering errant wires. It's hard to argue with the value of relevant activity.

Cognitivism, as Smith and Ragan (1993) point out, places more emphasis on factors within the learner than on factors within the environment. Parallel in many ways to the popular tenets of constructivism, this school of thought emphasizes generative experiences and is more about the learner's process than the professionals' preordained intentions. Grabinger (1996) wrote about it in a way that is useful for trainers. Grabinger called it REAL, *real environments for active learning*. When REAL is in place, people learn by addressing authentic challenges

FIGURE 3.1. SAMPLE IMAGE FROM
THE AMERICAN MUSEUM OF THE MOVING IMAGE.

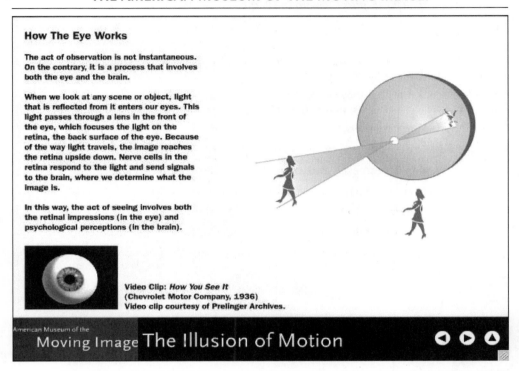

How The Eye Works

The act of observation is not instantaneous.
On the contrary, it is a process that involves
both the eye and the brain.

When we look at any scene or object, light
that is reflected from it enters our eyes. This
light passes through a lens in the front of
the eye, which focuses the light on the
retina, the back surface of the eye. Because
of the way light travels, the image reaches
the retina upside down. Nerve cells in the
retina respond to the light and send signals
to the brain, where we determine what the
image is.

In this way, the act of seeing involves both
the retinal impressions (in the eye) and
psychological perceptions (in the brain).

Video Clip: *How You See It*
(Chevrolet Motor Company, 1936)
Video clip courtesy of Prelinger Archives.

American Museum of the
Moving Image The Illusion of Motion

Source: Copyright © 2000, American Museum of the Moving Image.

anchored in what they confront at work. He reminds trainers to provide experiences that are social, collaborative, realistic, and predicated on their needs and experiences. Cases, problems, in-basket experiences, and simulations would be associated with Grabinger's REAL.

Duffy and Cunningham (1996) draw a useful distinction. In Table 7-1 (p. 175), they compare the cognitive constructivist and social constructivist viewpoints. Cognitive constructivists would encourage learners to consider a realistic situation, to find and use relevant tools and resources, to organize and reorganize information and views, to construct positions based on analysis and research, to compare perspectives, and to assess results and efforts. Social constructivists, on the other hand, would nudge affiliation, bonding, mentoring, collaboration, chatting, lunching, and sharing.

There is no need to choose here. See these points of view as support for strategies that are predicated on the world of work and encouraging of reflection, organization, teaming, and self-assessment. Consider also how the Web might contribute to delivering on the promises of both forms of constructivism.

Great Training Motivates

Great training matches the learners with experiences that they will perceive to be right for them. If too easy, too hard, or too useless, the learning experience is more likely to be abandoned by tuning out or clicking away.

Keller's ARCS. John Keller (1983) defines motivation as learner choices that move individuals toward or away from a topic or learning experience. In class, a student moves toward the topic by locking on it and thinking about its meaning applied to his or her work. On-line, the student does the very same thing. Keller offers tangible suggestions about how to motivate through his ARCS model: *attention, relevance, confidence,* and *satisfaction.*

Attention. Attention can be grabbed by offering stimulating, varied, and novel events. For example, one trainer became modestly famous for staging an altercation in class to set up the topics of conflict and resolution. Quisic, formerly IEC, kicks off many technology-based modules with pithy interactions, during which, for example, an employee and customer are at loggerheads over a broken product or missed appointment.

Relevance. Use concrete language and real-world examples that highlight familiar challenges and document real needs. One of the authors was invited into an insurance company to offer a seminar about analysis. Prior to the event, she determined through a quick analysis that there was some concern that a similar class had been offered five years earlier. To motivate them, the author launched the class by sharing data that established the persistence of the need. She said something like, "Of seven customers who were interviewed, only one strongly agreed with the statement, 'Our HR people take a fresh look at the challenges we have by gathering data from the field.'"

The best way to be perceived as relevant is to provide what is needed.

The best way to be perceived as relevant is to provide what is needed. One can envision a course on Java programming, for example, where objectives are tied to a specific work project or errors that employees know have caused re-work.

Another strategy to enhance relevance is to provide learners with choices. The Web works well here, as can be seen in the sample DigitalThink screen shown in Figure 3.2. While modules are numbered and driven by a bottom arrow, the left navigation bar adds many choices for engagement.

Confidence. Here are some strategies to boost confidence, a factor that cannot be ignored if motivation and persistence are the goal:

- Remind participants about their prior knowledge of the subject; mention related topics and achievements, linking new material to the old.
- Provide early successes with the material. For example, in a class about software, an instructor provides clear directions and encourages timid participants to use them to format text so that they immediately experience success and a boost in confidence and are ready for the bigger challenges to come.

FIGURE 3.2. SAMPLE DIGITALTHINK SCREEN FROM AN E-COMMERCE CLASS.

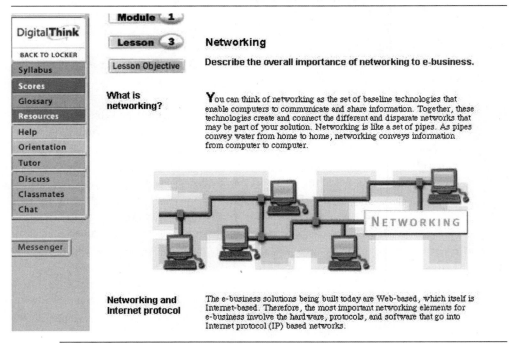

Source: Copyright © 2000, DigitalThink. Used by permission.

- Watch out for ambitious pre-tests that reveal inadequacies. In 1996, when Rossett and Barnett looked at CD-ROMS devoted to soft skills training; they found many that pre-tested in ways that assured a very poor showing for students. The impact was not good for confidence and thus not good for persistence on that technology-based program.
- Offer human communications and coaching. Researchers El-Tigi and Branch (1997) pointed to studies that demonstrated that participating in on-line discussion and chats increases confidence and motivation. Element K offers on-line classes that are fueled and supported by a tutor, infusing a human element into e-learning.

Satisfaction. Create an experience during which users have a chance to swiftly use their new knowledge on familiar problems, rather than having to wait. For example, every educational technology class at San Diego State University, even the most introductory, includes opportunities for students to work on something that the students and faculty agree is meaningful.

Andersen Consulting's "coach" is a sophisticated engine, called an "agent" by the development team. Coach monitors user progress, knows where individuals need to go based on their performance, and, based on this information, determines what feedback to display. And it praises in plain English. This praise is not a canned response, but it is tailored to student progress in the course.

Great Training Is Devoted to Inclusion and Opportunity

In a book about the wonders of new ideas, services, and technologies devoted to growth and development, it's critical to remember that two-thirds of the world's population has never heard a dial tone. Bill Gates made a similar point in a speech to a global technology audience in autumn 2000; he admitted that a personal computer could not produce food for a poor woman in a mud hut with starving children.

If conditions throughout the world overwhelm, perhaps it makes sense to focus attention where contributions can be more immediate. There are closed doors in the United States that often are described under the umbrella phrase "digital divide." Many sources tell the story, including several sites supported by the federal government:

http://racerelations.about.com/newsissues/racerelations/msubdigdivide .htm?iam=ask&terms=%22digital+divide%22

http://racerelations.about.com/newsissues/racerelations/gi/dynamic/ offsite.htm?site=http%3A%2F%2Fwww.digitaldivide.gov

http://www.pluggedin.org/

http://www.wigsat.org/

http://www.digitaldividenetwork.org/

We can start by attending to the issues. What advocacy will bring people from different backgrounds, cultures, and origins into the organization? How are they welcomed? How is excellence spelled out and supported? Are objectives associated with management development, for example, infused with concerns and outcomes about inclusion and opportunity?

Where are development resources devoted? Does career development attend to those who come to the organization with fewer advantages? Does the organization continue to focus learning opportunities, as is typical, on executives, sales, marketing, and managers, or are substantial resources devoted to upward mobility for clerks, service representatives, and operators? Are there ways for those with less education to continue their development within and without the organization?

Do learning opportunities, on-line and place bound, reflect the diversity in the organization and its customers? Do instructors come in all sizes, shapes, and hues? Do examples reflect the cultures and countries into which the organization sends its services and products? How does the organization acknowledge that not everybody is equally ready for independent learning, a mode that is very much a part of the new century? A project for a manufacturing plant in Silicon Valley provides an example. The organization purchased CD-ROM-based independent learning materials for its employees. What they soon discovered was that assemblers, many of whom were new immigrants with limited English-language skills, were uncomfortable with that isolated modality. The organization brought coaches to the situation and instituted learning programs that highlighted strategies teaching learning-to-learn.

Finally, how do your efforts recognize inclusion as a priority? Can your efforts, as manifested in programs, relationships, and products, be characterized by words such as welcoming, diverse, intense, extensive, omnipresent, inclusive, vivid, useful, and ongoing?

Great Training Has Shape

Many years ago, a friend explained that instructional systems development (ISD) was created in large part because military trainees in World War II were wasting time learning in too many and idiosyncratic ways. At each new training school, they had to figure out not only the technical skills, but also the approach to acquiring those skills. Time was wasting.

Ruth Clark (1999a, 1999b, 2000), influenced by M. David Merrill and Robert Horn, has crafted four useful learning architectures: receptive, behavioral, guided discovery, and exploratory.

Receptive Architecture. The receptive architecture is familiar to every trainer, even retired trainers. Deliver a lecture. Create video and supportive print materials. Stream audio on-line. Build an on-line help system.

The assumption is that the expert or developer can produce a source that structures materials to enable participants to learn. That's a big assumption. As we know, some are unfamiliar with the subject matter, lacking prior knowledge of the specific domain; others are distracted by different priorities; still others lack the learning-to-learn skills so essential to this architecture.

Behavioral Architecture. This architecture increases the involvement of the learner in many and significant ways. Clark emphasized these aspects of the behavioral architecture: knowledge divided into small and hierarchically arranged components, short lessons that build on each other, action and feedback to shape what the learners know and do. She notes that early computer-based training programs are based on this model, where small steps and branching reduce demands on the learner. Employees themselves don't have to know when they need another example or should re-read the materials. The program tests them and then tells them whether to watch the demonstration again, try the practice items, or move on to new material.

Guided Discovery Architecture. This strategy reflects the more cognitive era we find ourselves in. Ruth Clark notes that the role of the instructor or program is to provide resources and experiences that promote individual construction of knowledge or insights. While behavioral approaches attempt to teach a predetermined set of objectives, guided discovery creates authentic circumstances that encourage individuals to figure things out for themselves. Scenarios are created. Roles are established. Cases dominate. Teams work on real world circumstances and then compare their efforts with several examples of effective practice. This model matches a world of work that has many knowledge workers, ill-defined problems, and varied perspectives on what constitutes effective performance.

Exploratory Architecture. E-learning portals today provide rich opportunities for the exploratory architecture. Interested in more sales skills? Eager to learn about a new product in light of a competitor's offerings? Want to test the ability to determine which product is most appropriate for a client with a particular set of characteristics and which is contraindicated? As you can see here, the onus in this architecture is on the employee. The employee needs to know what she needs to know and then needs to martial the will and skill to go get it. It is up to the individual to engage with the rich resources, to make them matter.

The Internet is germane here. So too is the movement that blends training and knowledge management (see Chapter Nine), where learners move freely between experiences that drive material into memory and rich knowledge bases to which they refer at the moment of need.

All four architectures have implications for contemporary training. As employees become familiar with their varying requirements for effort, memory, structure, and persistence, they can adjust and benefit. Learning and performance professionals are also supported in their efforts, as they are able to transcend habit and choose systematic approaches.

Great Training Is Measured

Measurement, practice, testing, and feedback are very much a part of great training. For example, Ellie, a niece of one of the authors, called to announce success on her driving test. It went well, she crowed, "Once I'd gotten the parallel parking done on the first try; from there on, I was fine. I knew I could do it." Ellie was ecstatic because she did well on the road test, while there was more muted applause when she passed the written test, a piece of the challenge far more removed from the real world of stop signs and U turns. And there's been even less enthusiasm for high school, in general, where the effort and tangible outcomes are not so obviously or immediately linked.

The topic of measurement is treated in detail in Chapter Four, but deserves some attention here because we believe that measurement is at the heart of a great training experience—not so much for the administrative aspects, which tend to be favored by executives, but more for the opportunities to try out what is being learned.

Let's look at the how and who of measurement.

How. The best measurement looks like the situation for which it is preparing people. Consider Ellie's driving test. Consider the driving practices that she experienced during the weeks she prepared for her licensing. She drove and drove and drove, with escalating challenges over the weeks and months prior to the road test.

Sometimes measurement cannot mimic real-life challenges. For example, we wouldn't want to put a pilot up in a plane before he or she practiced in smaller and more controlled situations away from danger. In these cases, challenges are linked to the enabling elements or objectives associated with the authentic task. A pilot will practice at using the instruments to identify wind shear in a simulator before confronting such a crisis at twenty-four thousand feet.

Teacher training provides another example. Pre-service teachers write lesson plans and receive feedback from experienced teachers before they are tossed into a classroom with actual students. The neophyte teacher offers short lessons before taking over for a day, an experience that demands several stints and the classroom management associated with the interstices between those lessons.

Motorola's Marguerite Foxon (1997) said, "Assessment should measure the results of training over time—a week, a month, a year—it should not be a snapshot of learning taken at the end of a training class."

Portfolios are also worth considering here. What might an instructional designer's portfolio include? Perhaps it would hold a needs assessment document, a design specification, an evaluation plan and report, a Website, feedback from visitors to the Website, student test scores, and letters from customers and clients. As you can see, better even than testing itsy-bitsy aspects of performance is to give students a chance to create a compilation of their efforts, reflecting growth and commentary on the work.

Will participants be encouraged to work with access to references or to perform on their own? Are we asking them to recognize a given good or right answer or to recall one by heart? The answer is to include aids and references appropriate to the task and the circumstances. When should the surgeon turn to the *Physician's Desk Reference* and on-line references? When would that be inappropriate? During surgery, for example, there is little time to refer to resources. Prior to surgery, to prepare patients, families, and surgical colleagues, it's wise.

What about the sales professional who is tasked with tailoring solutions for customers? In front of the customer, most salespeople want to be fluent and at ease, only using reference materials to check a volatile price or assure compatibility between products. But prior to the sale or when planning for the meeting, use of databases with sample presentations, questions, and information about products and competitors is just plain smart. Practices and tests should force professionals to find and use resources and to perform by heart without them, depending on the situation, customer expectations, and professional role.

Who. There are four possible players here: the learner, the peer, the program, and the instructor/mentor. Let's put the individual learner at the center of the conversation and examine the possibilities:

The Learner and a Peer. One of the important approaches emphasized by the social constructivists is the use of peers to coach, tutor, and even measure success. With a checklist, peer sales professionals can effectively help their colleagues do many things, including make better presentations, construct better proposals, and write better letters to clients.

The Learner and the Program. E-learning supports measurement and learning management. Figure 3.3 shows one program's assessment and communication about one author's not very stellar performance on a DigitalThink test about LANs and WANs.

The Learner and the Instructor/Mentor. Ellie's driving test is a good example. In a car with an instructor, she drives and he comments on how she is doing. In a classroom, everyone watches a video about lifestyle decisions and their influence on driving; Ellie and her classmates discuss the challenges associated with peer pressure and

FIGURE 3.3. SAMPLE FEEDBACK ON PERFORMANCE.

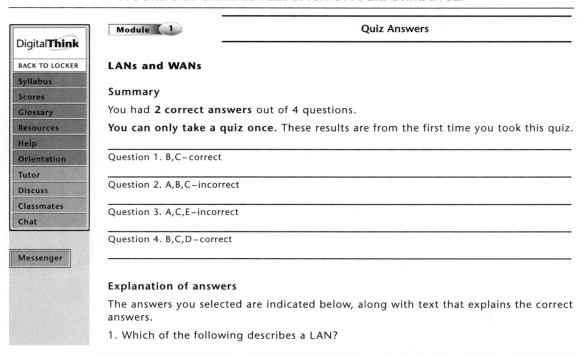

DigitalThink

BACK TO LOCKER
Syllabus
Scores
Glossary
Resources
Help
Orientation
Tutor
Discuss
Classmates
Chat

Messenger

Module 1	Quiz Answers

LANs and WANs

Summary

You had **2 correct answers** out of 4 questions.

You can only take a quiz once. These results are from the first time you took this quiz.

Question 1. B,C–correct

Question 2. A,B,C–incorrect

Question 3. A,C,E–incorrect

Question 4. B,C,D–correct

Explanation of answers

The answers you selected are indicated below, along with text that explains the correct answers.

1. Which of the following describes a LAN?

Source: Copyright © 2000, DigitalThink. Used by permission.

driving; she makes choices; the instructor comments and coaches. The instructor in this example is observing performance and following it with feedback.

Another option is to use prior measurement to coach subsequent performance. The driving instructor might have noticed that Ellie was not very good at merging into traffic on a highway. Knowing where her problems are, as they approach an opportunity to merge, he suggests that she thinks about X and do Y, thus using prior measurement to support performance just before the challenge appears.

The Learner on His or Her Own. We should take every opportunity to help colleagues to become more thoughtful and reflective about their performance. One nifty driving technology-based program goes beyond the behavioral aspects and asks new drivers to act as though driving is knowledge work, which it is, of course. This approach asks neophyte drivers to share their thinking while they are driving. On-line video streams a road situation. "What do you see going on here?" it asks. What might you anticipate could happen? What should concern you? Students then compare their individual think-aloud answers to an expert driver's perspectives in order to judge how they have done.

Ready to meet with the new client? Turning in a report that will hit the mark? Finished with the audit? Ready to take a class on-line? All are opportunities for self-assessment, for looking at the self in light of some criteria. Figure 3.4 provides a portion of an SDSU rubric that helps prospective students judge their readiness for on-line learning. Figure 3.5 enables self-assessment by providing a sample answer against which the professional may compare his or her efforts.

Great Training Is Human

People and characters are important in training. Carlos, the fabulous instructor lauded at the beginning of the chapter, is appreciated for who and how he is, as well as for what he knows and teaches. He brings himself to the classroom, enriching the group's experience with his expertise, war stories, and emotions.

Think back on great instruction. Isn't it the people we remember? Isn't it their stories that rivet us? Hearken back to the tenth-grade English teacher who forced repeated re-writes and then gave dramatic readings of the work. Picture that first sales coach who demonstrated cold calling techniques over and over and over and then shared out loud how he handles the inevitable rejections. And then there was the professor who convinced you that you should give it a try, even though you doubted you could, as he walked you around the campus to chat about an internship with the potential to stretch you. You might even remember a doctor in an on-line scenario, caught in an ethical dilemma, because her situation and approach struck a chord.

FIGURE 3.4. SDSU SITE TO MEASURE READINESS FOR ON-LINE LEARNING.

How to get the most out of online learning		
Activities	Rate Yourself	Explanation
I can troubleshoot basic software and hardware problems.	Disagree Agree 1 2 3 4 5 ○ ○ ○ ○ ○	
Activities	Rate Yourself	Explanation
I have CONVENIENT access to a multimedia capable computer, a printer and a reliable Internet connection.	Disagree Agree 1 2 3 4 5 ○ ○ ○ ○ ○	
Activities	Rate Yourself	Explanation
I am self-motivated and comfortable working alone.	Disagree Agree 1 2 3 4 5 ○ ○ ○ ○ ○	

Source: Copyright © 1999, San Diego State University. Used by permission.

One former student spoke of orientation at Andersen Consulting (now Accenture) in St. Charles, Illinois. She remembered how it influenced her. Why? She described a panel of experienced consultants kind enough to admit how hard the travel was, but full of stories about the rewards. Most of all, she pointed to the time with the other new consultants, all engaged in an experience that encouraged them to form networks and relationships. A decade later, she continued to count on the friendships begun during that orientation.

On-line and in class, it is far better to grab and retain the learner with reality and with authentic human touches.

Recently, one of the authors reviewed on-line training programs about topics such as communications, leadership, and diversity. The producers were striving to be entertaining and funny because of legitimate concerns about student

FIGURE 3.5. EXPERT ANSWERS FOR COMPARISON.

Experts
Responding to

Jossey-Bass
Pfeiffer

Home
What is PA?
About the Book
Responding to:
 Managers
 Customers
 Experts
Ask Allison
How to Handle:
 Rollouts
 Performance
 People Dev.
Resources
Seminars
Buy the Book
Site Index

Content by:
 Allison Rossett
Developed by:
 Chris Haddock
 Kendra Sheldon

"In the Asia Pacific region, we have a very particular way of handling this. I don't see any reasons to come up with a standard approach that is detailed on the web or anyplace else. I just don't agree with the way the other regions are handling this."

Your Answer

Allison's Response

"I want to hear exactly how you handle it in the Asia Pacific region and why it's so unique. What is it here that necessitates going it your own way? How have you managed to be successful with it? What can we learn from your approach so that others across the organization can benefit?

You raised issues about standardization and I want to explain why that's important to us. As the company has become more global, we're concerned about achieving a balance between those things that are common to us, at our core, part of the way we do business, and those things that are unique to countries, regions and

GUIDED TOUR

Ask Allison
a question and
enter to win an
exciting prize!

Ask Allison

Responding to
How you would
overcome
resistance from
a customer,
client or
sponsor?

⟨GO⟩

How to Handle
Performance

Source: Rossett, A. *First Things Fast* Website. Copyright © 1999, Jossey-Bass/Pfeiffer. Reprinted by permission of John Wiley & Sons, Inc.

persistence on-line. For amusement, they developed exaggerated characters, with huge flaws and mammoth strengths, with the sage communicator character wearing a Superman-like cape, for example.

But it didn't work. It was too difficult to identify with the situations; it was too easy to dismiss the lessons offered by Superman. On-line and in class, it is far better to grab and retain the learner with reality and with authentic human touches.

IBM is encouraging an intriguing initiative called the Knowledge Socialization Project, www.research.ibm.com/knowsoc. Their focus in on stories, characters, and storytelling, all of which bring people and emotion to the learning experience, on-line or off.

Great Training Is More Than a Moment in Time

How can we extend key messages and create mantras to more effectively influence learning and performance? Through print and on-line materials, such as job aids, documentation, and help systems, we are able to break the physical and temporal boundaries associated with training experiences.

Consider a craving to eat ratatouille or to change the oil in your car. Imagine the need to make a sales presentation to Eastern European university administrators. As critical as these desires are at the moment, none warrants the effort associated with memorization. Far better to develop resources to which people will turn at the moment of need than to invest in building memories that will fade from lack of use. There's no shame in not knowing by heart the details about LANs and WANs appropriate in a university setting or oil changes or exotic food; the shame would be if the reference materials were unavailable, disorganized, or out-of-date.

These external support systems come in all shapes and sizes, from a recipe for Thai peanut barbecue sauce to software documentation to an on-line Thesaurus that suggests synonyms to knowledge bases with sales presentations. What all have in common is that they support performance by providing help at the moment of need, or just before, substituting step-by-step guides, checklists, and knowledge bases for a human coach and a large investment in learning. This topic is described in more detail in Chapter Nine.

When should we use this information support? As much as possible. Every orientation and training program can extend its influence through supportive materials that reiterate key messages on the job. Do the training *and* augment with supportive reference resources.

In addition, Rossett & Gautier-Downes (1991) point out that some circumstances merit the use of information support *rather than* training. They say that these approaches should be used when a task is performed infrequently; when it involves many steps and decisions; when the consequences of making a mistake would be grave; when knowledge is changing, vast, and complex; and when resources are tight. Here are three examples. The first is all training. The second represents a blend. The third demonstrates the possibilities for information support alone:

> Ellie, the young driver, was wise to invest in conventional face-to-face training conducted in a classroom and on the road. She needs to know how to drive by heart and to acquire a suitable amount of respect for the decisions and consequences associated with driving. We don't want her turning to an onboard help system or print job aid while navigating a turn or rejecting risky teen choices.

> A pilot, on the other hand, although heavily trained, relies on a great deal of information support, from onboard computer decision support systems, to pre-flight check lists, to job aids that serve to coach during low frequency and high criticality conditions. The sales professional represents another example of an individual whose performance is enhanced by a judicious blend of training and reference materials.

> Changing the message on the answering machine and taking money out of the automatic teller provide examples of tasks supported by external references.

A critical thing to consider when scheduling training is timing. When will the participants use the new skills, knowledge, or attitudes? Training should be scheduled to be as "just in time" as possible so that, when employees complete training, they are able to swing into action or reflection in a way that uses what they learned.

The Web offers possibilities here. House modules and materials on-line. When the need emerges, employees can click to just the right source, whether for software documentation or examples of product launch strategies or a short class on presentation skills.

Great Training Transfers

Transfer to work or life is the bottom line when it comes to education and training. No matter how scintillating a class was, no matter how memorable or exciting, if the effects of training do not linger, it raises serious questions about value added to the organization that funded it. Great experiences that are untapped at work or in life eventually are perceived as wasteful.

At the beginning of this chapter, when Leslie and Kiyoma are marveling at Carlos, they acknowledge that the course itself is effective, with elements that prepare students beforehand and engage them afterward. Elwood F. Holton III (2000) offers a tool that diagnoses learning transfer. Dubbed the Learning Transfer System Inventory, it recognizes the complexity involved in ensuring that what happens in a learning situation influences what happens at work. According to Broad (Broad & Newstrom, 1992), who has written extensively on the topic, effective training is not just about what happens in the classroom, but about what happens before and after.

Before Training Focus on the supervisor here. Will he describe the purposes for the training and point to needs in his unit for these skills? Will he direct the employee's attention to critical topics that will be covered? Will he show potential uses for what is to be covered? Many supervisors will contribute, if they are expected to do so and if the nature of the class and its value are communicated and realized. Another useful strategy is to establish a performance contract, upfront, so that supervisors are certain about ways to turn the training into results.

Ask yourself, "Why is supervisory participation not what we need it to be?" Ask supervisors themselves. Then do something about it.

But still, some supervisors won't participate or know how. In those cases, go directly to participants. Send a class description to them; write it in a way that emphasizes what they'll be able to do as a result of attending and participating. Ask them questions about their situation. Focus their attention on matters that will be discussed and on why the topic has value for them, their unit, and the organization. Provide a Website with a self-assessment for potential participants to check their readiness for the particular class. Offer pre-reading, when relevant. Point to prior students and the impact that the training has had on their success.

During Training Launch training by offering reasons, data, and statistics that document the need and the value of the material. Show many ways that what is being taught matters at work, rich with examples, so that employees can envision these skills in action in their own settings. Encourage them to try out new approaches and attitudes in class. Showcase success stories, highlighting the achievements of people like themselves.

Provide practice at using relevant tools, job aids, documentation, and knowledge bases. Bring those materials right into the classroom and present cases that press them to refer to a knowledge base to write a sales proposal or to tailor an existing sales presentation for a particular given audience.

There will be obstacles. Anticipate that the world will present numerous challenges to transfer and help participants rehearse ways of handling these barriers. Reveal obstacles and detail ways to handle resistance. Admit both the downsides as well as the upsides, especially when participants already have opinions. Inoculate participants so that they know the reactions they are likely to receive when they attempt to incorporate what they have learned at work.

After Training Here managers play the critical role. According to Brinkerhoff and Montesino (1995)—and no surprise to training professionals—supervisory conversations with trainees boost transfer. Foxon (1997) found that the perception of supervisory support is most influential in transfer.

Build a role for supervisors and encourage them to carry it out. Is there a way to use technology to extend the physical reach of the instructor or sponsor? Will participants participate in a post-class listserv? Will they visit a Website to talk about their experiences? Will participants contribute to knowledge bases that capture their efforts and commentary? Will they be intrigued with a continuing dialogue with the instructor or other experts?

Questions and Answers

Table 3.3 presents typical questions that might be raised by sponsors and executives and suggested responds. Use the table to craft responses tailored to your context.

TABLE 3.3. QUESTIONS AND ANSWERS.

Questions	Suggested Answers
Why are you writing about training when performance is what is most important?	Training is still at the heart of our business *in the view of customers.* It's what they ask for, how they find us, how they title us. We want to provide great training that influences performance, of course.
Are performance and outcomes all that matter? Don't we care about the "feel" of the training experience?	Yes, we do indeed. The beauty of training is in the people and groups, in the influence of an individual instructor, in the magic that happens when fourteen auditors grapple with a problem, under the caring eye of an experienced person. "Feel" counts for e-learning too. How can we make certain that on-line materials include stories, commentaries, and characters?
Is training dead, since we're moving on-line with knowledge bases and reference materials?	No, training is not dead, but neither is it all there is. Professionals will devote themselves to judicious decisions about what to do on-line and what to do in rooms with instructors. There will most assuredly be more focus on technology support during work, with some reduction in placebound teaching.
Does the organization need fewer training professionals?	Likely, we'll need fewer individuals who tour the world teaching classes. However we will also need more people who collaborate with the line, anticipate needs, design classes and information support systems, engage sponsors and colleagues in strategic alignment, measure results, enlist line management in the effort, and collaborate to repurpose training materials into knowledge bases for ready access.
A trainer's job is to train. Right?	Wrong. Well, training is part of it, especially training that educates customers about the role of the line in supporting key messages. Our job now is to make sure that learning and knowledge are infused throughout the organization, including and going much beyond scheduled classes. Are you talking to sponsors? Are you preparing people for classes? Are you collecting best practices and making them widely available? Are you nurturing on-line communities? Are you continuously scanning for needs and resources? Are you at the table as change in the organization is contemplated?
When I think about training, I see four walls and a great teacher.	That's one way to perceive it. And it's still good, just not sufficient. The purpose of this book and chapter is to expand the possibilities.

Great Training in a Hurry

Some resources keyed to the time you are able to devote to the topic are shown in Table 3.4.

TABLE 3.4. RESOURCES.

Time	Resources
"I have an hour"	Gayeski, D. (1998). "Out of the Box Instructional Design" *Training & Development,* April. http://www.astd.org/CMS/templates/index.html?template_id=1&articleid=11475
	Read Rossett (1997, July). "That was a great class, but . . ." *Training & Development,* 51(7), 18–24. http://www.astd.org/CMS/templates/index.html?template_id=1&articleid=10988
	Visit http:www.astd.org, the American Society for Training and Development's Website
	Visit www.billcom.com, *Training* magazine's home site
"I have a day"	Rossett, A., and Barnett, J. (1996). "Designing under the influence." *Training,* December, 35–41.
	Visit http://www.learnativity.com
	Skim Mel Silberman's *101 Ways to Make Training Active,* published by Jossey-Bass/Pfeiffer
"I've got a week"	Read Pat Smith and Tim Ragan's *Instructional Design,* published by Merrill/Prentice Hall
	Take an on-line class at San Diego State, Boise State, Indiana University
	Skim Jonassen's *Handbook of Research for Educational Communications and Technology* (1996).

Spotlight on People

Ruth Clark

Ruth Clark's professional focus is human performance improvement, with an emphasis on training design, development, and evaluation. As president of Clark Training and Consulting for over twelve years, she and her staff have offered skill-building seminars on needs assessment, design of training for classroom and computer delivery, and cognitive principles of learning and instruction to a wide variety of business and government clients. Clark has authored two best-selling books: *Developing Technical Training* and *Building Expertise.*

Training Now We asked Ruth what excites her about training now. She said, "The understanding that the economic growth of this century rests on effective growth and deployment of human expertise. This provides people in our business with great opportunities to demonstrate the impact of effective knowledge management and instruction on organizational performance."

She continued, "The explosion of knowledge generation will force us to abandon for the most part the labor-intensive, custom-tailored instructional design methodologies of the late 20th Century. Much greater use of 'templating' will enable subject-matter experts to build training and convert much of what was instructional design work into preparation, tagging, and synthesis of knowledge objects stored in the corporate data base. The work of the training or performance improvement specialist will shift from design of custom training to defining the interventions that best leverage organizational expertise, including training and knowledge management strategies."

Leaving the new technologies aside for the moment, what are the essential elements for a successful training program? Clark responded, "Unfortunately, there is no simple answer here, as the essential elements needed to promote learning effectively and efficiently will vary according to cognitive features of the learners and the performance requirements of the job." She recommended that training professionals consider what she calls the "four architectures" when designing training and instruction (see Clark, 2000).

Clark elaborated: "Traditional behavioral rule-example-practice types of instructional designs are well-suited for learners who are novice to the skills being trained or lack good meta-cognitive skills and for the instruction of procedural skills. In contrast, a more constructivist design, such as situated guided discovery, lends itself more to learners with some experience in the domain, with good meta-cognitive skills and for the instruction of principle-based tasks that require worker judgment to perform."

Clark believes that for training programs to be successful, specific cognitive events must occur. She said, "The learner must encode new information into working memory and rehearse it there in such a manner that it gets encoded into long-term memory. For working memory capacity to rehearse effectively, cognitive load must be managed. To ensure transfer at the psychological level, the cues inherent in the work must be embedded into the instructional environment. Thus, a more situated instructional environment in which learning occurs in job-realistic settings is essential."

Clark believes that meta-cognitive control is the key to managing these processes, whether it is activated in learners or supplemented in instruction. She said, "The type of instructional interface to support these cognitive processes will vary as a function of prior knowledge of the learner, learner aptitude, and learner motivation and meta-cognitive skills."

Training Challenges We asked Clark where training programs fail. She replied, "Everywhere. Training is not seen as a professional endeavor. The prevalent assumption is that if you know about something, you also know how to transfer that expertise to others. Thus, content is delivered to learners either on Web 'page turners' or in classroom lectures."

She believes that faulty assumptions are part of the problem: "Learning is assumed to happen in a sponge-like absorption process. It is assumed that if a high-tech delivery strategy is used, the instruction is effective." Another reason that training programs fail, according to Clark, is that evaluation efforts are inadequate. Most often, training is evaluated to find out how learners felt about a program, and rarely on the actual outcomes of training. As a result, "There are few opportunities to quantify learning outcomes and thus no basis for improvement."

Is Training Dead? Clark was direct: "I hope so. With any luck the training that is dead is all the training that never had any impact on organizational performance. Hopefully, the training that is dead is training that is an event rather than a means to improve organizational outcomes. The shift to performance means that training for the sake of training is dead in lieu of knowledge management strategies that enable that expertise to be linked to the bottom line of organizations."

The Future Clark had advice for training professionals as they prepare for the future. She said, "Learn, practice, and evaluate core strategies needed to define how human expertise can be grown and transformed into organizational bottom-line outcomes." To make her point, Clark suggested the following strategies for training professionals who work with line clients:

- Assess the barriers to achieving bottom-line work performance using techniques such as interviews, work observations, and comparing exemplary with average performers
- Artfully deliver the message to decision makers who would prefer a silver bullet training solution

- Creatively educate your line clients in the difference between training and performance

Rosalynne Price

As the manager of diversity for a large media conglomerate, Rosalynne Price has the opportunity to consult on a variety of issues, in many settings, with clients whose expectations diverge widely. This has honed her ability to observe, react, synthesize, and sell. Packaging performance technology so that everyone can use it is her prime challenge because "from the newspapers to radio stations, from telecommunications systems to car auctions, peak performance is the critical variable all the businesses seek."

Price's personal vision centers on the potential inherent in every individual.

Exciting Aspects of Training Price explained that she is excited about training now because we now know more than ever about how people learn and we can use this knowledge to design better training. Specifically, Price said, "We know that people learn in different ways, or have what Gardner called the 'Seven Intelligences.' They are kinetic, spatial, musical, intrapersonal, interpersonal, linguistic, and mathematical. Training professionals can use this information to design learning experiences that touch a variety of people in the many ways that they learn." She believes the best way to tap into every channel is to integrate a variety of activities into all training and instruction.

Essential Elements for Successful Training According to Price, the components of successful training programs are interaction, guidance, and "doing" in a way that allows people to work from their strengths. She explained, "If, for example, you are a verbal person and you need to hear something twice and you don't hear it twice, then the instructor has missed an opportunity to capitalize on your strength and you have missed an opportunity to learn."

Feedback is also essential to effective training programs, feedback from teacher to student and student to teacher. Price said that she gets feedback from her students in a couple of ways. Eye contact, for example, tells her when an audience is engaged, bored, or lost: "If I see one person's eyes are glazed over, you can bet that the person sitting behind him or her feels the same way." When this happens, Price stops what she is doing and tries a different approach.

Price also gets feedback by reaching out to her audience and asking for it with questions such as, "How am I doing?" or "Do you understand?"

According to Price, observation is also an important source of feedback. She uses group activities as an example. She can tell whether an activity is working by how engaged the learners are with one another and by the activities they share. If an activity is going well, a group will come up with three or four approaches to a problem or challenge. If they produce only one solution, Price is concerned that the members did not work well together or were dominated by a strong personality.

Another key to successful training, according to Price, is pacing. She explained, "I don't think anyone should do anything for more than fifteen or twenty minutes. They need to stop, have a checkpoint, and test for comprehension with questions or some other means of assessment."

Price noted that positive reinforcement is also essential within training programs. She said, "When people do what you want them to, you need to let them know it by smiling, gesturing, nodding, or valuing what they said by articulating their perspective." Price said that instructors need to let participants know that what they said is important: "We need to give them 'atta boys' for what we most want them to learn."

Price believes that the most powerful training programs are those that require learners to complete an activity that tells them something about themselves. When that happens, training can be "really, really powerful." She said that something as simple as a survey that asks trainees to evaluate their communication skills or assess their interactions with others can tap into who they are personally; and when this happens, it really "hooks them into the learning."

Where Training Programs Fail Training programs fail when the initial assessment of where to begin is wrong, or when trainees and instructors are on a different wavelength. To avoid this, Price suggests having several starting points that are adjustable and finding out where to begin by conducting a "mini-assessment" of the audience. Sometimes, this means talking to members of the audience in advance. Other times, especially when the audience is a familiar one, the instructor can quickly figure it out and make adjustments once the program is under way.

Price said that another potential pothole is that many training professionals believe that there is one "right" and one "wrong" way of looking at things and that training, like life, is black and white. She uses tests as an example. Price said that different people interpret language differently, and that this can color their responses on tests. What may appear to be an incorrect response on a test may in fact be a response that is reflective of a trainee with different life experiences than that of the test's author or other trainees.

She elaborated, "There is no new knowledge, just the reorganization of the bits and pieces that we already know. People learn when they are presented with information in a way that causes them to say, 'aha,' [information] that helps them make discoveries or have new insight into what they already know. One reason that training programs fail is that they are not tied enough into people's personal experiences.

"Another reason that training programs fail is that they are too limited in their focus. They tend to be all about work, but most people have much in their life besides work." Price believes that the solution is to "tie it [training] into something in their life in addition to work, because if you do, chances are that it will stick."

Is Training Dead? According to Price, "Training will never be dead. People will always need to learn, and training will be one way—just not the only way—anymore. Each person has a way of learning best, whether it is directed learning, discovery learning, trial and error, or whatever. As training professionals, we need to account for and provide for all kinds of experiences—and support them."

Price gave an example from a training class that she had taught that morning. In the class, a man spent the whole morning pushing buttons on a computer rather than listening to the instructor. While his behavior was distracting, she understood that he was learning the way he knew best—through trial and error.

The Future We asked Price whether she had any advice for training professionals. She said, "Be more sensitive as trainers to diversity and the ways that people learn. Really think about how people relate to things, because it gives us the tools to help people learn. [One way to do this is to] spend two or three days with a group of people and listen to what they are saying. Then really think about how to package or present something many ways, and about how you can re-communicate it and attach it to something in their lives."

Price saved perhaps her best advice for last when she said, "Be very aware of your biases toward *your learning preferences*—don't just work from *your strengths*; stretch and grow."

Jack Phillips

Jack Phillips has been fortunate to experience the training and development field from several perspectives, first as a trainer and developer of training programs, then as a training manager, HR manager, and top executive. Phillips has also written or edited thirty books in the training and development field. As a consultant in twenty-five countries with hundreds of organizations, he has also helped shape many training and development departments. Presently, he is with the Jack Phillips Center for Research: A Division of the Franklin Covey Company.

Training Now Phillips described four critical trends that have provided him with a very positive outlook for training, development, learning, and education.

1. The changing role of training and development creates optimism about the future of our profession. Training and development is becoming a tool to help build competitive organizations.
2. The potential for training and development to add value is enormous. A small amount of behavior change can bring tremendous economic contribution to an organization, greatly offsetting the investment in training.

3. The need for training and development will continue to increase as knowledge industries proliferate in the new century. The need for knowledge creates a need for learning solutions.
4. The way in which training and development is delivered (on the job, through the Web, in bite sizes) is greatly changing. This is exciting.

Essential Elements Phillips believes that for a training program to be successful, "There must be a clear need identified for the training and development program and a performance gap existing between the current state and the desired state. The program must be delivered at a reasonable cost at the right time to the right audience, applied on the job and supported in the work unit, and . . . must be directly linked to one or more business measures."

Where Training Programs Fail Phillips and his colleagues have studied hundreds of training programs and found some major reasons that training programs fail:

- "The program is actually not needed in the organization, but conducted at the request of a senior executive or some other group.
- The program is not aligned with any particular business need and, consequently, is not influencing a business measure.
- The content of the program is not relevant to the actual job—covering skills and knowledge not needed at this time.
- The program did not transfer into actual application of skills and knowledge on the job. (This is usually the number one reason.)
- The training is not supported in the work environment by the manager, team, systems, processes, culture, et cetera."

Is Training Dead? Phillips supports the transition from training to performance improvement and believes that the transition is essential for training to add the kind of value it must deliver in the future. Phillips provided Table 3.5, which illustrates the shift between training and performance improvement.

Phillips elaborated, "This shift involves many elements that must be addressed, moving beyond just changing the name and adding additional solutions. The shift involves changing virtually every aspect in which a training and development function operates. These changes will present major challenges because many training and development organizations have a charter to provide only learning solutions and not other solutions. They do not have the capability of offering other solutions or even handing them off to other parts of the organization. This is slowly changing and this shift will take some time to occur."

TABLE 3.5. PARADIGM SHIFT TO PERFORMANCE IMPROVEMENT.

Traditional Training Department Characterization	Performance Improvement Department Characterization
No specific client relationship is established	A client is served throughout the process
No business need for the program	Program linked to specific business needs
No assessment of performance deficiencies	Assessment of performance and causes
Most problems have training solutions	Nontraining solutions are common
Services organized around design and delivery	Full range of services to improve performance
Specific objectives focus on learning	Program objectives focused on job performance and business impact
No effort to prepare program participants to achieve results	Results expectations communicated to participants and clients
No effort to prepare the work environment to support transfer of learning	Environment prepared to support transfer performance
Typical job title includes the word designer or trainer	Typical job title includes the words performance consultant or performance technologist
Work activities focus on preparation and teaching	Work activities focus on collaboration and consulting
Communication outside the training department is limited	Contacts outside the department are frequent and necessary
No efforts to build partnerships with key managers	Partnerships established with key managers and clients
Department structure contains narrowly focused functions, such as development, delivery, and administration	Department structure contains broad-based functions, such as analysis, consulting, design, and facilitation
Department has a training label and usually reports to a human resource executive	Department has a performance improvement label and usually reports to an operations executive
No measurement of results or cost-benefit analysis	Measurement of results and cost-benefit analyses are conducted regularly
Planning and reporting on progress are input-focused or activity-based	Planning and reporting on progress are output-focused or results-based

Source: Copyright © 2000, Jack Phillips, Ph.D.

Advice for the Future We asked Phillips whether he had any advice for training professionals. He said that in addition to learning the skills needed for the specific job or assignment, trainers must:

- "Learn the business, operations, products, and services of the organization. It is essential for all trainers to understand as much as possible about the organization.
- Align training and development with business needs. Ensure that each program will add to the business in some way—even if it is indirectly.
- Develop relationships with the key clients for training and development. This often means the manager groups. Building those relationships is critical to continued support and commitment for training.
- Collect appropriate data to show the success of training and provide the data to the various groups who need it."

Recommended Resources Phillips recommended two outstanding organizations, the American Society for Training and Development (ASTD) and the International Society for Performance Improvement (ISPI). He said that both organizations have Websites and provide excellent professional development opportunities.

As for publications, Phillips recommended the magazines that come with membership in ASTD and ISPI, *Training & Development* and *Performance Improvement,* and also *Training* magazine. Each provides excellent, up-to-date coverage of events, trends, and issues.

Phillips also recommended the following books for professionals who want to learn more about great training: *Running Training Like a Business* by David Van Adelsberg and Edward A. Trolley (1999), *Creating Training Miracles* by Allistair Rylatt and Kevin Lohan (1995), *Reengineering the Training Function* by Donald Shandler (1996), *Moving from Training to Performance Improvement* by James Robinson and Dana Gaines Robinson (1998), and *Return on Investment in Training and Improvement Programs* (1997) and *HRD Trends Worldwide* (1999) by Jack J. Philips.

The Heart of the Matter

The following slides are designed to help training professionals explain and win support for training.

Slide 3.1

Defining Great Training

Great training makes a difference in the lives of people and in the work of the organization.

Afterward, you know you've been involved with something compelling, vivid, and memorable, something you can take back to your work and life.

Presenter's Notes

Describe from your setting or your background examples of great training and their outcomes. A sexual harassment workshop that raised awareness and reduced complaints? A peer-tutoring training program that boosted productivity and promoted cooperation? Ask your audience to share examples from their own lives.

Slide 3.2

Great training. . .

- **Is about something**
- **Has a point of view**
- **Says something useful or lets learners discover something useful**
- **Gives learners something to think about and use**

Presenter's Notes

Again, point to examples from your setting and compare them to examples of not-so-great training. What made the training special? Why was the other training less so? Compare and contrast; this will make the differences stand out for your audience.

Slide 3.3

Great Training Touches Hearts and Minds

For training to be successful, our work must extend to helping employees reach beyond knowing *how* to knowing *why.* They can't do it if they don't know how. And they won't do it unless they know why, accept the rationale, and possess confidence about it.

Presenter's Notes

Describe some of the strategies for influencing attitudes from Table 3.2, such as using two-sided arguments to make points, using role models and role plays during training, and providing opportunities for early successes to build confidence.

Slide 3.4

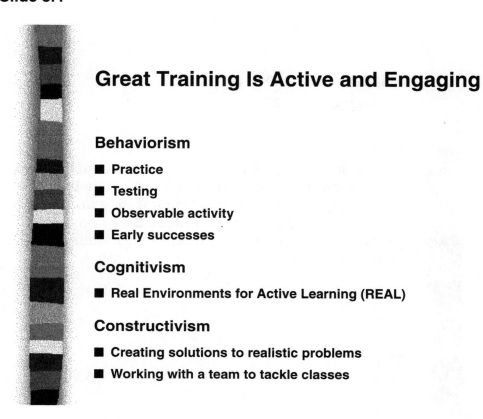

Great Training Is Active and Engaging

Behaviorism

- **Practice**
- **Testing**
- **Observable activity**
- **Early successes**

Cognitivism

- **Real Environments for Active Learning (REAL)**

Constructivism

- **Creating solutions to realistic problems**
- **Working with a team to tackle classes**

Presenter's Notes

Explain that there are many ways to make training active and engaging.

Slide 3.5

Great Training Motivates

Keller's ARCS Model

■ **Attention**

■ **Relevance**

■ **Confidence**

■ **Satisfaction**

Presenter's Notes

Great training gives learners experiences that they think are right for them; if the training is too easy, too hard, or feels useless, they will tune out or click away. Keller's ARCS model builds motivation into training.

Slide 3.6

Great Training Is Human

- ■ Great instructors; compelling media messages
- ■ Humor
- ■ War stories
- ■ Feedback
- ■ Vivid experiences
- ■ Rewarding relationships

Presenter's notes

Think about a great instructor that you had or a great class that you took. Consider dynamic on-line learning. What made the experience memorable? Stories, activities, or classmates? Tell your audience about a great learning experience that you had and why you remember it. Ask them to share their experiences, too. Discuss some of the human aspects of learning—synergy, humor, collaboration, and cooperation.

Slide 3.7

Great Training Transfers

- ■ Print and on-line materials
- ■ Job aids
- ■ Documentation
- ■ Help systems
- ■ Manager support
- ■ Supportive environment
- ■ Recognition
- ■ Rewards

Presenter's Notes

The bottom line is this: if training does not translate into improved performance, it was not successful. But there are many things that can be done before, during, and after training to promote transfer. For example, the lessons of great training can be extended beyond the classroom, if organizations provide materials that support performance at the moment of need. Examples include an EPSS system to provide help to programmers who are just learning to write XML, or an illustrated job aid to help preschool teachers give CPR in the event of an emergency.

Resources

Bednar, A., & Levie, H. (1993). Attitude change principle. In M. Fleming & H. Levie (Eds.), *Instructional message design* (pp. 283–304). Englewood Cliffs, NJ: Educational Technology.

Brinkerhoff, R. O., & Montesino, M. U. (1995). Partnerships for training transfer: Lessons from a corporate study. *Human Resources Development Quarterly, 6*(3), 263–274.

Broad, M., & Newstrom, J. W. (1992). *Transfer of training: Action-packed strategies to ensure high pay-off from training investments.* Reading, MA: Addison-Wesley.

Caudron, S. (2000, April). Learners speak out: What actual learners actually think of actual training. *Training & Development,* pp. 52–57.

Clark, R. C. (1999a). *Building expertise.* Washington, DC: ISPI Publications.

Clark, R. C. (1999b). *Developing technical training: A structured approach for developing classroom instructional materials.* Phoenix, AZ: Performance Technology Press.

Clark, R. C. (2000). Four architectures of instruction. *Performance Improvement Quarterly, 39*(10), 31–38

Duffy, T. M., & Cunningham, D. J. (1996). Constructivism: Implications for the design and delivery of instruction. In D. H. Jonassen (Ed.), *The handbook for educational communications and technology.* New York: Simon & Schuster/Macmillan.

El-Tigi, M., & Branch, R. M. (1997). Designing for interaction, learner control, and feedback during web-based training. *Educational Technology, 37*(3), 23–29.

Fister, S. (2000, April). A strategic plan and reallocation of training brings an old-line company's employee training into the 21st century. *Training,* pp. 65–70.

Foxon, M. (1997). The influence of motivation to transfer, action planning and manager support on the transfer process. *Performance Improvement Quarterly, 10*(2), 42–63.

Gagne, R. M. (1988). Mastery learning and instructional design. *Performance Improvement Quarterly 10*(1), 8–19.

Grabinger, R. S. (1996). Rich environments for active learning. In D. H. Jonassen (Ed.), *The handbook for educational communications and technology.* New York: Simon & Schuster/Macmillan.

Gayeski, D. (1998, April). Out of the box instructional design. *Training & Development.* (On-line) www.astd.org/virtual_community/td_magazine/td_0498_contents.

Hird, D. (2000, June). What makes a training program good? *Training,* pp. 48–52.

Holton, E. F. (2000). What's really wrong: Diagnosis for learning transfer system change. In Holton, E. F., Baldwin, T. T., & Naquin, S. S., (eds.), *Managing and Changing Learning Transfer Systems,* Baton Rouge: Academy of Human Resource Development, pp. 7–22.

Johnson, S. D., Aragon, S. R., Shaik, N., & Palma-Rivas, N. (2000). Comparative analysis of learner satisfaction and learning outcomes in online and face-to-face learning environments. *Journal of Interactive Learning Research, 11*(1), 29–49.

Jonassen, D. H. (1996). *Handbook of research for educational communications and technology.* New York: Simon & Schuster.

Jonassen, D. H., Grabinger, R. S., & Harris, N.D.C. (1991). Analyzing and selecting instructional strategies and tactics. *Performance Improvement Quarterly 10*(1), 34–54.

Keller, J. M. (1983). In C. M. Reigeluth (Ed.), *Instructional design theories and models: An overview of their current status.* Hillsdale, NJ: Erlbaum Associates.

Parry, S. (2000). *Training for results.* Alexandria, VA: American Society for Training and Development.

Paul, L. G. (1997). Cyber coaching for soft skills. *Inside Technology Training, 1*(8), 20–26.

Phillips, J. J. (1997). *Return on investment in training and improvement programs.* Houston: Gulf Publishing.

Phillips, J. J. (1999). *HRD trends worldwide: Shared solutions to compete in a global economy.* Houston: Gulf Publishing.

Pine, J., & Tingley, J. C. (1993). ROI of soft-skills training. *Training*, pp. 55–60.

Robinson, D. G., & Robinson, J. C. (1998). *Moving from training to performance improvement.* San Francisco: Berrett-Koehler.

Rossett, A., & Barnett, J. (1996, December). Designing under the influence. *Training*, pp. 35–41.

Rossett, A., & Gautier-Downes, J. H. (1991). *Handbook of job aids.* San Francisco: Jossey-Bass.

Rossett, A. (1997, July). That was a great class, but . . . *Training & Development, 51*(7), 18–24.

Rouzer, P. A. (2000, June). A more complex customer service relationship demands superior training. *HR Magazine*, pp. 141–146.

Rylatt, A., & Lohan, K. (1995). *Creating training miracles.* Sydney: Prentice-Hall.

Shandler, D. (1996). *Reengineering the training function.* Del Rey Beach, FL: St. Lucie Press.

Simonson, M., & Maushak, N. (1996). Instructional technology and attitude change. In D. H. Jonassen (Ed.), *Handbook of research for educational communications and technology*, (pp. 984–1016). New York: Simon & Schuster.

Smith, P., & Ragan, T. (1993). *Instructional design.* Upper Saddle River, NJ: Prentice-Hall.

Strayer, J., & Rossett, A. (1995). Coaching sales performance: A case study. *Performance Improvement Quarterly, 7*(4), 39–53.

Tyler, K. (2000, May). Hold on to what you've learned. *HR Magazine*, pp. 95–104.

Van Adelsberg, D., & Trolley, E. A. (1999). *Running training like a business: Delivering unmistakable value.* San Francisco: Berrett-Koehler.

Visser, J., & Keller, J. M. (1990). The clinical use of motivational messages: An inquiry into the validity of the ARCS model of motivational design. *Instructional Science, 19*(6), 467–500.

CHAPTER FOUR

PROVING OUR CONTRIBUTIONS

Russ: The pressure is on for sure. Maybe it's the aftermath of reengineering. Maybe it's the talk about Web training, with individual employees taking classes on their own. It's our turn to look at what difference training is making.

Sammy: I'm not surprised that people are asking. It makes sense. They know that our employees are contending with a barrage of new products, technologies, and even customers, cultures, and languages. We're doing more training to give employees the skills to handle all these challenges. And some are reaching around centralized training for classes offered on-line. Of course, someone is going to ask whether all this activity is making a difference.

Russ: They want to see the impact of training on the bottom line or on some bottom-line indicators, such as repeat business and customer satisfaction.

Sammy: Impact is not easy to prove, I know. But there is a lot we can do.

Defining Evaluation

Evaluation is the process of examining a program or process to determine impact, to establish what's working, what's not, and why. Evaluations determine the value of programs and act as blueprints for judgment and improvement.

The people who pay the bills for training, when they pause to reflect, are growing more interested in what difference the effort is making. How are training and related services contributing to what matters in the organization? Evaluation comes in many forms, some more familiar than others. The following scenarios describe typical evaluation efforts.

Did They Like It?

After customer service representatives finish a one-day workshop about plus-selling, they complete a survey about what they liked and disliked about the experience.

Did They Learn?

Data entry personnel pilot a computer-based training (CBT) module designed to help them use a new spreadsheet program. Before they begin, they take a quiz to determine existing skills. When they complete the CBT, they take a quiz to measure gains. The results help the developer of the computer module and her training manager pinpoint where the module works and where it does not.

Did Training Affect Job Performance?

Mid-level managers attend a retreat focused on improving teamwork. During the retreat, they hone group communication skills and work on conflict resolution. When they return to work, teams begin to collaborate on the rollout of a new wireless product. Throughout this five-month effort, managers provide feedback about team process and progress on the tasks. The training director then looks at that data, focusing particularly on what participants had to say about team contributions to task progress.

What Are the Strategic Results of Training?

A few months later, the training director and the executive in charge of the wireless product rollout examine the success of the rollout in light of priorities that the sponsor established at the start of the effort. They examine cycle time, requests for transfer, errors, re-work, and sales, with particular attention to exit interviews and feedback from managers. Were teaming and conflict resolution skills better? More importantly, did those better skills result in a smoother rollout?

Another way to look at strategic results is provided by looking at teachers at an elementary school after professional development about a particular approach to teaching literacy. An evaluator visits and observes at the school, in the neighborhood, and at the public library. He describes what he sees in detail, without attention to any particular checklist associated with the objectives of the program. His focus is on the many ways that literacy is taking hold in the community and on changes observed since the literacy program.

Why Does It Matter?

Organizations rely on training to keep employees' skills and knowledge current. A new product rollout? *Train 'em!* A personnel problem? *Train 'em!* New hardware or software? *Train 'em!* As noted in Chapter One, budgeted dollars for training as reported by Lakewood Training have steadily increased in the 1990s and appear to be headed on an upward trajectory in the new century.

Increasingly, professionals associated with the activity are expected to prove that their efforts made a difference.

Increasingly, professionals associated with the activity are expected to prove that their efforts made a difference. Many executives want to see a tangible return on investment (ROI) from their training initiatives.

Of course, there are those who remain satisfied with familiar metrics such as the number of "butts in seats," "hits on training Web pages," or the heftiness of course catalogues. Although those measures say something about a training department's activity level, they do not speak to the size or shape of results. In those organizations in which leadership is not yet asking questions about impact, training and development professionals themselves must raise the issue.

This push toward accountability began years ago, when executives committed to total quality management (TQM) and increased international competitiveness. The Japanese proved that TQM worked when they trounced competitors in the car manufacturing business. Since then, "quality" and related measurements have become corporate necessities in units across organizations, not just in manufacturing.

Fast on the heels of the quality movement were the radical changes associated with reengineering. Searching questions about processes and organizational structures were raised, with attention eventually turning to training and development. At the heart of reengineering was the question, "Does this process or department add value?"

The implications are clear. People, processes, and units must "add value." What is the best way to tease out that value? We believe it is from a systematic evaluation effort. If benefits are not clear, evaluation points to the places where improvements might be made.

Two Flavors of Evaluation

There are two broad approaches to evaluation, *goal-based* and *goal-free*. Goal-based evaluation is the most popular form because it responds directly to the pressures for proof of impact described here. Goal-based evaluation is used to examine training and development in light of pre-specified goals and objectives and to make judgments on the effectiveness of programs or processes. The wireless rollout example described previously was goal-based.

Goal-free evaluation, on the other hand, does not compare training outcomes to standards or criteria. Instead, goal-free evaluation describes the impact of training, without a prior agenda and with a particular interest in the unexpected. The literacy example used earlier was goal-free. Goal-free evaluation attempts to see the results of training in context by examining the effects on the larger community.

Goal-Based Evaluation

Goal-based evaluations compare training objectives with stated outcomes to determine whether programs are successful and why. The goal-based approach asks familiar questions, such as:

- "Is the training accomplishing what it promised?"
- "Did they learn what they were supposed to?"
- "When they return to work, are there more sales or fewer errors or more repeat customers?"

Goal-based evaluations are relatively straightforward. During the planning, goals are set; related objectives are written; then test or checklist items are matched to the objectives. Those items then turn into tests, observations, or questionnaires that are administered during and after the training. Trainers use the results of evaluations to examine worthy and defined performance, make improvements to ongoing programs, shape future efforts, and track individual progress.

Evaluation also tells trainers how well they are doing their jobs and tells management what they are getting for their dollars. Table 4.1 presents goal-based evaluation scenarios.

TABLE 4.1. GOAL-BASED EVALUATIONS.

Training Goal	*Outcomes*
Executives at a large wig manufacturing company are concerned about low morale, high attrition, and poor attendance. Confidential interviews reveal that employees are anxious about job security because managers criticize their job performance. To improve the situation, managers are sent to a two-day workshop on how to give effective feedback.	In response to a post-training survey, 95 percent of managers were able to describe effective feedback and how to use it for given and varied authentic situations.

Soon after training and over a two-month period, managers met with subordinates to give them their annual performance reviews. In follow-up interviews with employees, 67 percent reported that managers used effective feedback techniques during the mettings.

Six months later, analysis of company records revealed that attendance was at a two-year high, and that attrition was down 11 percent; both figures delighted managers. |
| A small engineering company buys a CAD-CAM software program. Engineers complete a mandatory computer-based training module to learn how to use the new program. | 85 percent of the engineers passed the post-training test

Supervisors were surveyed by e-mail on their observations of CAD-CAM usage. Two-thirds reported that their people had become regular users, defined as at least once per week.

In a survey completed three months after training, 72 percent of engineers reported that they were using the new software program at least twice per week and almost three quarters of the engineers say they like or very much like the new system. |

Goal-Free Evaluation

Goal-free evaluation looks at both intended and unintended effects of training. The purpose is not to compare training to an objective standard, as in goal-based evaluation, but to create a detailed description of what is happening. Goal-free studies tend to be favored by professionals whose inclinations are constructivist and who doubt the objective and external establishment of objectives and believe that individuals create their own learning and meaning. Goal-free evaluations ask questions such as

- "How do users interact with the Web prototype?"
- "Do the trainees appear to be engaged with the subject?"

- "Are the people who used the program inviting others to take a look at what they've done?"
- "Is the experience influencing the words that the team chooses to use when they talk about their global partners?"

During goal-free studies, professionals turn to observations, case studies, and immersion in the field to craft a textured picture of broad impact and trends. They are most certainly interested in questions about impact and meaning; the difference is in the serendipity of what they find and report. Table 4.2 presents scenarios in which trainers are using goal-free evaluation.

TABLE 4.2. SAMPLE GOAL-FREE EVALUATIONS.

Evaluation Focus	*Outcomes*
At a small private school, teachers attended mandatory training about classroom technology integration. Six months later, administrators want to know if the teachers have integrated technology into curricula, and in what ways.	Post-training classroom observations revealed that five of nineteen teachers were using computers for word processing and e-mail. The others made little or no use of the hardware and software. Detailed case studies of three randomly selected teachers found that the training had little impact on technology integration. Teachers appeared uncomfortable with computers and complained that computers, in general, were over-hyped. The teachers also resented the pressure to change their teaching methods, which they perceived as already successful.
Instructional designers at a manufacturing company purchased a Web-based training program about successful teamwork. Before buying a site license for the on-line program, they decide to do usability testing on the prototype. They ask six employees to pilot the training program from start to finish, while being observed and videotaped.	Five of six employees had trouble navigating within the program and repeatedly turned to the observer for help throughout. Three of six were distracted by the background music, and impatient with waiting for the pages to load. Two expressed discouragement and begged to quit prior to the end of the module. One reported that she felt more competent regarding teamwork; another reported being somewhat more competent at the close of the module.
HR professionals for a large department store chain are piloting a new customer service program at one store. Before the program is offered nationwide, trainers want to know about its impact.	Secret Shoppers "shop" at three stores in the chain. They keep detailed diaries about their experiences with store personnel and interactions they witness. These shoppers do not know which stores were involved in the customer service program and which were not. Their job is to detail their experiences and write about them, answering some broad queries.

Kirkpatrick's Evaluation Model

Evaluation is nothing new to the training profession. In fact, Kirkpatrick (1996) developed a model for evaluating workplace training forty years ago. Today, his four-level model is familiar and popular. According to many in the field, it just "feels right," although there is concern today that Kirkpatrick's first two levels dwell on matters such as fondness for the training process and butts in seats, not strategic impact.

Kirkpatrick recognizes a world divided into two realms, one associated with the training event and the other representing practice at work. This distinction has less significance in the performance and technology environment we're talking about in this book, where, for example, on-line delivery provides both education and job aids to the desktop at the moment of need. Learning and work are simultaneous. It is also less relevant when the efforts of the HR and training professionals permeate the work, including training events, coaching interactions, targeted awards, and on-line support tools. Table 4.3 presents Kirkpatrick's model.

Typically, training professionals emphasize the first two levels, with just a wink and a nod to concerns about the effectiveness of transfer of training to the workplace. Although it is important for employees to like training and to learn, the

TABLE 4.3. KIRKPATRICK'S FOUR LEVELS OF EVALUATION.

Level	Standard	Possible Measures
One	Did they like it?	Post or during training "smile" surveys; interviews; repeat "hits" on pages of a Website
Two	Did they learn what they were supposed to?	Practices throughout, pre- and post-tests to measure achievement of objectives, end-of-module scenarios to be solved by participants
Three	Did they apply what they learned?	Improved job performance, such as reduced errors, better reading scores by fifth graders, more sales of a particular product, reduced accidents
Four	Did the training translate into strategic results?	Increased market share, better products, repeat customers, more books are taken out from and returned to the local library

Source: Adapted from Kirkpatrick (1996).

goal of most training is improved job performance. Kirkpatrick's Levels 3 and 4 fit here; they are used to find out whether training did in fact result in better job performance, ideally translated into strategic results.

It is admittedly difficult to capture data about performance in the world of work; but some organizations do make that commitment, struggling to extend their measurement efforts into the field, asking difficult level three and four questions (Goldwasser, 2001). Others satisfy themselves with satisfaction and performance data more readily captured during the learning experience, whether it is in the classroom or technology-based.

Abernathy (1999) urges trainers to think outside of Kirkpatrick's "box." He makes the point that, as training has moved away from being a distinct event in time with impermeable beginnings, middles, and endings, Kirkpatrick's four distinct levels must be both respected and reconsidered.

In organizations in which proof of bottom-line impact is a priority, trainers may turn to other models, such as the Philips Five Level ROI Framework (Philips, 1997). Philips builds on Kirkpatrick's work by adding a level to determine the return on investment (ROI) associated with training. He offers a process for calculating return on investment (ROI), including formulas for converting both the tangible and intangible benefits of training into dollars and cents.

Holton (1996) draws useful attention to the human variables. He asserts that Kirkpatrick's Model is flawed because it is actually a taxonomy of training and HRD outcomes. While taxonomies can be useful, they do not account for many variables that affect training outcomes, such as motivation, "trainability," and attitude. Holton points out that, by failing to consider these "intervening variables," training professionals can't be sure why a particular training effort succeeded or failed.

Finally, while Kirkpatrick's model provides a useful starting point, training professionals should not necessarily base their efforts on Kirkpatrick's questions. A better approach is to customize and tailor evaluation efforts to answer the questions that *their clients are asking*. The tools remain the same.

Evaluation Tools

Evaluation is a search for answers to questions about learning and satisfaction, meaning and impact. There are many tools to help. Some are direct; we use them to ask people about experiences and judgments. Interviews and surveys are direct evaluation tools. Exhibit 4.1, for example, is a post-training survey from Solar

EXHIBIT 4.1. SOLAR TURBINES COURSE EVALUATION.

Solar Turbines   Technical Training Department
                                                        Course Evaluation
A Caterpillar Company

Course: _____ Date: _____

Instructor: _____ Name (optional): _____

Your opinions are important to us. Please take a few minutes to complete this questionnaire. We will use the information to ensure the quality of our training courses and to plan for future courses.

Student Experience Level

- My level of turbomachinery   ☐ less than 6 months   ☐ 1 – 3 years
  operation/maintenance experience is: ☐ 6 – 12 months   ☐ 3 years or more

For Turbotronic Control System courses   ☐ less than 6 months   ☐ 1 – 3 years
only:

- My level of experience with
  Turbotronic/PLC systems is: ☐ 6 – 12 months   ☐ 3 years or more

Course Content

- Did the objectives of this course match the course   ☐ Yes   ☐ No
  description(s) that you received before the course?   ☐ None received

  If no, please explain:

  _____

  _____

  _____

- Did the course content (subjects covered) meet your needs?   ☐ Yes   ☐ No
  If no, please explain:

  _____

  _____

  _____

- What subjects should have been covered in more detail?

  _____

  _____

  _____

- List any subjects that you felt too much time was spent on:

  _____

  _____

  _____

- List any subjects that were not covered that you would like to see discussed.:

  _____

  _____

  _____

The Instructor. . .   (Yes, excellent, agree)   (No, poor, disagree)

was well prepared to teach the course   ☐   ☐   ☐   ☐   ☐

made effective use of class time   ☐   ☐   ☐   ☐   ☐

was interested in the progress of the students   ☐   ☐   ☐   ☐   ☐

had thorough knowledge of the course topics   ☐   ☐   ☐   ☐   ☐

gave clear, understandable explanations of   ☐   ☐   ☐   ☐   ☐
course subject matter

answered student questions effectively   ☐   ☐   ☐   ☐   ☐

involved the students in class discussions   ☐   ☐   ☐   ☐   ☐
and activities

made good use of training aids (projector,   ☐   ☐   ☐   ☐   ☐
student workbook, schematics, etc.) to help
explain the material.

- Please note any comments regarding the instructor below.

_____

_____

_____

_____

Course Materials

The workbook for this course. . .   (Yes, excellent, agree)   (No, poor, disagree)

- is organized in a way that makes it easy to   ☐   ☐   ☐   ☐   ☐
  locate information on a specific topic

- contains clear, understandable descriptions   ☐   ☐   ☐   ☐   ☐
  and explanations

- contains drawings that are clear and easy   ☐   ☐   ☐   ☐   ☐
  to read

- contains photographs that are clear and   ☐   ☐   ☐   ☐   ☐
  easy to read

The illustrations and words that the instructor ☐   ☐   ☐   ☐   ☐
projected on the screen were large enough
to see and read clearly.

What *one thing* could be done to improve this course?

_____

_____

_____

Please note any additional comments about the course

_____

Source: Copyright © 1999, Solar Turbines Incorporated. Used by permission.

Turbines, headquartered in San Diego. More inferential or indirect tools for evaluation are tests, rubrics, observation, checklists, work data, diaries, and journals. Exhibit 4.2 is an example of a rubric designed to evaluate performance on an assignment. Table 4.4 presents some widely used evaluation tools and on-line examples.

Evaluation is a search for answers to questions about learning and satisfaction, meaning and impact.

Questions and Answers

Table 4.5 presents typical questions about evaluation and strategies for answering them.

Evaluation in a Hurry

How can busy trainers bring themselves up to speed on evaluation? Table 4.6 presents resources for professionals to learn more about evaluation—whether they have an hour, a day, or a week.

EXHIBIT 4.2. DRAFT RUBRIC FOR EVALUATING WEBQUESTS.

	Beginning	*Developing*	*Accomplished*	*Score*
Overall Aesthetics				
Overall visual appeal	0 points Background is gray. There are few or no graphic elements. No variation in layout or typography. OR Color is garish and/or typographic variations are overused and legibility suffers.	1 point There are a few graphic elements. There is some variation in type size, color, and layout.	2 points Appealing graphic elements are included appropriately. Differences in type size and/or color are used well.	(2)
Grammar and Mechanics				
Organization	0 points Organization is weak	1 point Somewhat organized	2 points Strong organization	(2)
Spelling and grammar	0 points There are several spelling and/or other grammatical errors.	1 point There are few spelling and/or grammatical errors.	2 points There are no spelling and/or grammatical errors.	(2)
Introduction				
Motivational effectiveness of the introduction	0 points Introduction is purely factual, with no relevance or social importance.	1 point Introduction relates somewhat to the learner's interests and/or describes a compelling question or problem.	2 points The Introduction draws the reader into the lesson by relating to the learner's interests or goals and/or engagingly describing a compelling question or problem.	(2)
Cognitive effectiveness of the introduction	0 points Introduction doesn't prepare the reader for what is to come or build on what the learner already knows.	1 point Introduction makes some reference to learner's prior knowledge and previews to some extent what the lesson is about.	2 points The Introduction builds on learner's prior knowledge by explicitly mentioning important concepts or principles, and effectively prepares the learner for the lesson by foreshadowing new concepts and principles.	(2)

continued on next page

EXHIBIT 4.2. (*CONTINUED*)

	Beginning	*Developing*	*Accomplished*	*Score*
Task (*The task is the end result of student efforts . . . not the steps involved in getting there.*)				
Cognitive level of the task	0 points Students are only asked to use lower levels of Bloom's taxonomy. They basically find information and write it down.	3 points Students may be required to transform some of what they are learning for presenting, but transformation is not explicitly required as part of the task.	6 points Explicit use of transformation is built into the task. Students are asked to evaluate, synthesize, and analyze.	(6)
Technical sophistication of task	0 points Task requires simple verbal or written response.	1 point Task requires use of word processing or simple presentation software.	2 points Task requires use of multimedia software, video, or conferencing.	(2)
Process (*The process is the step-by-step description of how students will accomplish the task.*)				
Clarity of process	0 points Process is not clearly stated. Students would not know exactly what they were supposed to do just from reading this.	1 point Some directions are given, but there is missing information. Students might be confused.	2 points Every step is clearly stated. Most students would know where they were in the process and what to do next.	(2)
Richness of process	0 points Few steps, no separate roles assigned.	3 points Some separate tasks or roles assigned. More complex activities required.	6 points Lots of variety in the activities performed. Different roles and perspectives are taken.	(6)
Roles	0 points No roles	2 points Well-defined roles, but little or no interaction.	4 points Clearly defined roles with conflicting motivations for completing the task.	(4)

EXHIBIT 4.2. *(CONTINUED)*

	Beginning	*Developing*	*Accomplished*	*Score*
Resources (Note: you should evaluate all resources linked to the page, even if they are in sections other than the Resources block. Also note that books, video, and other off-line resources can and should be used where appropriate.)				
Quantity of resources	0 points Few on-line resources used.	1 point Moderate number of resources used.	2 points Many resources provided, including off-line resources.	(2)
Quality of resources	0 points Links are mundane. They lead to in-formation that could be found in a classroom encyclopedia.	2 points Some links carry information not ordinarily found in a classroom.	4 points Links make excellent use of the Web's timeliness and colorfulness.	(4)
Learning Outcomes				
Correlation with standards	0 points There is no link to district course outlines or state standards.	2 points There are no overt references to district course outlines and/ or state standards, but an experienced teacher could identify potential standards-based learning outcomes.	4 points There are explicit references to district course outlines and/ or state standards.	(4)
Clarity of evaluation criteria	0 points Students have no idea how they will be judged.	1 point Criteria for success are at least partially described.	2 points Criteria for grada-tions of success are clearly stated, perhaps in the form of a rubric for self-, peer-, or teacher use.	(2)
Total Score				**(42)**

Source: Courtesy of San Diego State University's Bernie Dodge and ACT Now!

TABLE 4.4. EVALUATION TOOLS.

Definition	*Sample Uses*
Interviews are an excellent but time-consuming way to gather information. They can be formal or informal, conducted "on the fly" or arranged in advance. Interviews can be conducted one-on-one or in focus groups. Interview questions are based on information needed for a particular situation	A Website to support performance analysis (www.jbp.com/rossett.html) is available. An evaluation for that site asks registered visitors to be "interviewed" on-line: 1. Do you like it? 2. What did you like best? 3. What do you remember about the site? 4. Will you visit again? 5. How did you use the site? 6. What would make it more useful?
Tests should be based on objectives. They may be print based or on-line, depending on available technology and the proximity of trainees. Tests given before training assess existing skills, while post-training tests measure learning. Pre- and post-training tests also shed light on individual growth, and the strengths and weaknesses of training programs.	Safe telephone pole climbing has many objectives associated with it. At the end of the climbing class, phone repair people are asked to get on the pole and demonstrate that they can do each of those tasks. A nifty tool for generating exercises and test items is Hot Potatoes from the University of Victoria, Canada. Visit http://web.uvic.ca/hrd/halfbaked/
Surveys ask respondents questions. They may include multiple choice questions, open-ended questions that gather opinions, or both. Well-designed survey questions can be recycled and used in combination with questions tailored to specific training efforts. Like tests, surveys can be print-based or electronic.	To see examples of on-line surveys, visit The Perseus Development Corporation's Website at http://www.perseusdevelopment.com /fromsurv.htm. Another option for online surveys is www.zoomerang.com
Rubrics are charts or tables that describe and assign value to a range of performances. Trainers use rubrics to define desired performance and then to evaluate it. Trainees may use rubrics for self-assessment and to guide their efforts. Rubrics are also widely used in schools to assess academic achievement and to guide student efforts. Rubrics clarify expectations and are powerful guides for self-assessmant and review of others' work.	The rubric, http://edweb.sdsu.edu/Courses /EDTEC540/Syllabus/Buffy/analysis_rubric .html, was used for a writing assignment at San Diego State University. The rubric was meant to shape and improve report writing. It was then used for anonymous peer grading, giving students exposure to three more opportunities to think about analysis reports, all in light of key criteria established in the rubric. If you want to create a rubric, the following sites, created by Nancy Pickett, are very helpful. Creating Rubrics http://edweb.sdsu.edu/triton/july/rubrics /Rubrics_for_Web_Lessons.html Guidelines for Rubric Development http://edweb.sdsu.edu/triton/july/rubrics /Rubric_Guidelines.html Rubric Template http://edweb.sdsu.edu/triton/july /rubrics/Rubric_Template.html

TABLE 4.5. QUESTIONS AND ANSWERS.

What I Want to Know	How I Will Find Out
What happened to people who participated in the training?	I could conduct in-depth studies with just a few attendees, observing, interviewing, talking perhaps to customers and supervisors. This will help me understand the intended and unintended effects of the training. I could also e-mail participants and ask directly.
Should I fix any components of the safety program?	I will identify strengths and weaknesses by comparing their post-test scores with their pre-tests. I'll also wait a few months and see if accidents on those pieces of equipment are reduced.
Did participants enjoy it?	I will give attendees a "smile sheet" survey. If they did not enjoy the program, I will conduct follow-up interviews to find out why.
How can I show management how much we're accomplishing?	At the get-go, ask sponsors what matters to them. What indications and proof of impact will speak to them? What data, such as profits and attrition rates, suggest effectiveness? I will ask participants' supervisors about their satisfaction with the effort. What were the issues and concerns that brought the sponsor to training in the first place?
	Communicate this information at every opportunity.
Should I hire this vendor again?	I will review program objectives and exercises to make certain that this vendor is teaching outcomes that our organization endorses and seconds. I don't want to be surprised by what their priority outcomes are.
	I will ask for and use pre- and post-training tests, surveys, and interviews.
Did they learn what they were supposed to?	I will give attendees pre- and post-training tests to measure learning. I will follow up with observations some months later, to find out if they are applying what they learned to their jobs. I will interview supervisors and customers to determine their satisfaction.
Should we buy an on-line version of the program?	I will interview subject-matter experts after they have reviewed the program. I will observe intended users as they attempt to use the program. I will seek out data from the e-learning vendors regarding outcomes and communicate with others who have used their programs. I will examine reviews at www.Lguide.com to compare that program with others on the same topic. I will ask the IT department to conduct a technology platform review, to see if the program is compatible with our system, computers, and software.

TABLE 4.6. RESOURCES.

Time	Resources
"I have an hour"	Marguerite Foxon's on-line article, "In defense of post-course evaluations: Going beyond the smile sheet," is an excellent discussion of surveys. http://cleo.murdoch.edu.au/gen/aset/ajet/ajet8/wi92p1.html
	A frank discussion about what works—and what doesn't—when it comes to soft skills training: Georges, J. C. (1996, January). "The myth of soft skills training." *Training,* 48–54.
	Kirkpatrick discusses his famous model, nearly forty years after he created it: Kirkpatrick, D. (1996, January). "Great ideas revisited." *Training & Development,* 54–59.
"I have a day"	Visit the Government Performance Information Consultants (GPIC), an impressive collection of Web links on evaluation, organized by area of interest (business, education, and so on). http://www3.sympatico.ca/gpic/gpichome.htm
	The ERIC Clearinghouse on Assessment and Evaluation features a "How to" series, an on-line library, recent articles, and more. http://ericae.net/main.htm
	Is this course instructionally sound? A guide to evaluating on-line training courses: Nilson, Carolyn (Ed.). *Training and Development Yearbook 1998* (pp.5.49–5.58). New York: Prentice Hall.
"I've got a week"	Join the American Evaluation Association and attend a conference. http://www.eval.org)_and_attend
	Kirkpatrick, D. L. (1996). *Evaluating training programs: The four levels.* San Francisco: Berrett-Koehler.
	A new approach to evaluation for the 21st Century: Patton, M. Q. (1997). *Utilization-focused evaluation: The new century text.* Thousand Oaks, CA: Sage.
	A practical guide to evaluation for training professionals: Phillips, J. J. (1997). *Handbook of training evaluation and measurement methods: Proven models and methods for evaluating any HRD program* (3rd ed.). Houston: Gulf Publishing Company.
	Another useful guide to evaluation, based on success stories: Russ-Eft, D., and Bassi, L., (Eds.). (1997). *What works: Assessment, development and measurement.* ASTD Publications.

Spotlight on People

Marguerite Foxon

Dr. Marguerite Foxon is a principal performance consultant and evaluator with Motorola University, headquartered in Shaumburg, Illinois. She has authored many articles and studies about evaluation, particularly about transfer of training to the workplace.

On Evaluation Foxon believes that evaluation is a necessity, not an optional extra. She noted, "We are professionally obligated to evaluate training, to find out if it is having any effect. Another reason to evaluate is that it is a wonderful marketing tool. Evaluation gives us evidence that training is having an impact on customers, employees, and the organization."

She also believes that evaluation gives trainers valuable insight into the training itself and points to post-training surveys as an example. It is not unusual for surveys to reveal that instructional designers and learners do not always think alike. This information can be used to make improvements to existing or future training programs. Foxon also uses post-training surveys to promote the transfer of training to the workplace, asking questions that force participants to think about how they will use what they learned, such as, "What is the most useful thing you learned today? Explain how you will use this to improve your performance in the workplace."

Foxon noted that evaluation is a "must" when training is expensive or highly visible. She said, "For training that is offered repeatedly or on a regular basis, it simply isn't practical to evaluate every course. Instead, I evaluate new courses the first four or five times they are offered and watch for patterns to emerge. After that, random evaluations are adequate."

Over the years, Foxon has developed her own framework for evaluation (Table 4.7), which consists of a series of questions and strategies for answering them.

Evaluation Challenges Foxon was direct: "Evaluation is hard because it is difficult to show the impact of training on an organization. I don't believe that you can do return on investment [evaluations] in any but a few cases. I agree with Kirkpatrick when he says that you should shoot for proof but, if you can't get it, settle for evidence and tell everyone! Evidence of the impact of training is everywhere, but proof is difficult (if not impossible) to provide."

Foxon noted that there is often no money for evaluation and little support. Evaluation efforts have to be sold to customers, like any other program. She reminded us to use the language of the particular business to persuade stakeholders that it is important to evaluate. At Motorola, for example, Foxon says that metrics are very important. If you want people to support evaluation, use the language of metrics to get them to listen.

Foxon gave Motorola's Global Organization Leadership Development (GOLD™) Program as an example. This program took groups of high-potential, mid-level

TABLE 4.7. FOXON'S EVALUATION FRAMEWORK.

Question	Strategy
Evaluation Focus What do I want to know? Why?	The first thing that I do is to brainstorm. I write down everything that comes to mind, then I ask myself, *Why do I need to know that? What will I do with the information?*
Evaluation Sources Where will I go to find the information?	Possible sources include the learners themselves, their managers, subordinates, colleagues, the instructors, customer data, and so on.
Evaluation Tools How will I gather the information?	I can use surveys, observations, or interviews, or examine records, reports, sales figures, and other published data to get what I need.
Evaluation Utilization What are the outputs and who gets the feedback?	At this stage, I make strategic decisions about who will get the feedback. Better to share it with one *well-placed* person in a position to help the training department than to send it in an e-mail to the CEO. I also like to share the information with the learners, who are interested in whether their reaction to the training was the same or totally different from their colleagues.

Source: Copyright © 1990 by Marguerite J. Foxon. Used with permission.

managers from Asia, Latin America, the United States, and Europe and put them through an accelerated development process. The goal was to develop a cadre of senior leaders by the year 2000. One aspect of the program was to put the managers on "Challenge Teams" and give them strategic challenges that took many months or even years to come to fruition.

One team took on a European business challenge, and their efforts (coupled with many other people in the organization) eventually resulted in a win for Motorola, worth more than $10M. While Foxon cannot quantify how much of that money was a direct result of the GOLD program, she is confident that the training contributed significantly to the win. She said, "Can I prove that the training resulted in this huge gain for Motorola? No, but it wouldn't have happened without the Challenge Team's work; as an evaluator I'm quick to point out the positive impact our training made."

Marci Bober

Marci Bober is an assistant professor of educational technology at San Diego State University. She teaches a six-unit graduate seminar on the subject of evaluation and is an experienced evaluator focusing particularly on the impact of technology on K–12 public education.

On Evaluation Before undertaking any assessment effort, Bober urges evaluators to conduct an *evaluability assessment,* to determine if the time is right for evaluation. In some cases, the effort is premature or would result in findings that could be misconstrued or taken out of context. For example, assessing a long-term training program after eight weeks is probably a waste of time and effort. Evaluating that same program after six or twelve months would likely result in useful, actionable information.

Bober emphasized the importance of customer education in evaluation: "A good evaluator will also try to determine what the client and key stakeholders know about evaluation to ensure that everyone continually speaks the same language and shares a common base of understanding about how the process unfolds."

Presenting Results Bober believes that there are no "hard and fast" rules about reporting evaluation results. Most often, results are first given to the client who commissioned the evaluation or to the people who met regularly with the evaluator during the process. Representatives of key stakeholder groups may also be briefed, even if they were not directly involved with planning and guiding the effort. Bober added, "It's also good form to make study results available—albeit in summary form—to those who participated in the data gathering, since they are impacted by what the evaluator concludes and recommends as next steps."

She emphasized that these are just guidelines and that what happens in any evaluation effort is client-specific. The one hard-and-fast rule that applies to every evaluation effort, however, is the need to protect the privacy of respondents at all costs by keeping proprietary information private.

Evaluation Trends Bober is familiar with both traditional and emerging approaches to evaluation. She noted, for example, that "an evaluation must be tailored to serve the needs of those who have requested it. If the structure is imposed from without . . . if the evaluator generates the questions or issues independently and in isolation . . . no one has really been served or assisted." Table 4.8 presents what Bober calls typical "potholes" or "problems" with evaluation.

TABLE 4.8. POTHOLES AND PROBLEMS WITH EVALUATION.

Pothole	*Strategy*
All settings have some political overtones; this is especially true when clients want to use evaluation for political ammunition—to support, for example, elimination of people, positions, departments, projects, and so on.	Before committing to any assignment, evaluators should be aware of a setting's potential for becoming volatile and discuss concerns with appropriate people.
Some *evaluators* come into a project with preconceived ideas about what they will find and report.	Evaluators must be neutral; their job is to report "what is"—not what "should be."
Some *evaluators* believe that somewhere in the world there exists the "perfect" data-gathering tool that they can use over and over again— without any modification or customization.	Good evaluators know that no one tool works in every situation. Modification is typical, including getting permission to do so, when that is called for.
Some *evaluators* lack the requisite skills to do the job well—and aren't learning the tools of their trade, such as evaluation planning, needs assessment, instrumentation, data analysis, and interpretation.	Evaluators have a responsibility to self-evaluate their skills and limitations. Can you learn what you need? Can you team with someone who knows? Often, the responsibility for this problem can be traced back to project stakeholders—who are more interested in saving money and getting a job done quickly than gathering and reporting quality data.
There are evaluators who rush to collect and report data.	Good evaluators know and promote the idea that their work is premised on a well-constructed plan. Evaluation plans usually include a thorough description of the evaluative setting or context, identification of stakeholders/audiences, an overview of the study's underlying evaluation frameworks or approaches, identification of major issues to be investigated, and detailed plans for data collection, analysis, and reporting. Starting an evaluation project by designing and administering instruments is like buying the materials for a new home (or remodel) before finishing the architectural plans and submitting them for approval—a waste of time and money!
Unfortunately, some *evaluators* don't adhere to professional standards associated with utility, feasibility, propriety, and/or accuracy—standards available on-line from the American Evaluation Association at http://www .theriver.com/aea/Evaluation Documents/aeaprin6.html	Charlatan evaluators are as bad for assessing a project's success as quack doctors are for treating serious illnesses. Such imposters are easy to recognize—they focus on quick fixes and ways to cut corners; they promise positive findings; they over-delegate evaluation tasks to poorly paid (and unprepared) subordinates; they provide boilerplate reports.

At the Heart of the Matter

The following slides are designed to help training professionals explain and win support for evaluation efforts.

Slide 4.1

What Is Evaluation?

Evaluation is the process of examining a program or process to determine what's working, what's not, and why.

Evaluations determine the value of programs and act as blueprints for judgment and improvement.

Presenter's Notes

Note that evaluation represents a "win-win" situation for training people, management, and employees. Trainers benefit from actionable feedback on their efforts, management finds out what it is getting for its training dollars, and employees benefit from better training. The important thing is to sell evaluation in terms that resonate with your audience—if management is concerned about money, talk to them about ROI.

Slide 4.2

Why Does It Matter?

- ■ It's a quality check
- ■ It shows how and where to improve efforts
- ■ It solicits involvement and feedback
- ■ It grounds programs in real impact and strategic directions

Presenter's Notes

Again, the point is to sell evaluation in terms that your audience understands. Use examples from your setting. Was there a recent training program that would have benefited from evaluation? An expensive disaster? A shining success? Link evaluation to company goals. Evaluation means knowing how to achieve better training, better performance, better results.

Slide 4.3

Kirkpatrick's Levels

In the class

- Did they like it?
- Did they learn?

At work

- Did they apply what they learned?
- Did the effort translate into business results?

Presenter's Notes

Describe evaluation tools (surveys, interviews, observations, rubrics, and so on) and their usefulness. Point to real examples where you used them, or could have. Note that evaluation efforts vary and are shaped by the answers you need, particularly those driven by the ways that the customer defines success. Sometimes a "smile sheet" survey is sufficient; on other occasions, a major quest for indications of impact will be necessary. Here is where you engage colleagues and sponsors in conversations about extending measurement into the workplace.

Slide 4.4

Is Our Program Producing Results?

■ After completing basic Internet training, you ask the new employee to send you an e-mail. Can she do it?

■ Customer complaints were way up this year, so employees received customer service training. Have complaints dropped?

Presenter's Notes

Again, the key is to make your case with real examples from your setting. Surely management wants to know whether employees are using new skills and knowledge in the workplace. Is training affecting competitiveness, profitability, and market share? Without evaluation, there is no way of knowing what difference, if any, training is making. Note that evaluation makes good business sense and should be part of training and performance efforts.

Slide 4.5

Establish Key Goals

Sell your audience on evaluation by asking, "If you invested in a training program, would you want to know if it met its goals?" Evaluation can answer your questions and also serve as a blueprint for improvement by telling you what's working, what's not, and why. Think of training as an investment and of evaluation as a way to find out whether it is "paying off" by producing results. You probably check on and monitor your other investments regularly; why not training? Focus conversation on the problems and opportunities that resonate for them.

Presenter's Notes

The slide says it all.

Resources

Abernathy, D. J. (1999, February). Thinking outside the evaluation box. *Training & Development,* pp. 19–23.

Bassie, L. J., & Van Buren, M. (1999, January). Sharpening the leading edge. *Training & Development,* pp. 23–33.

Barron, T. (1999, February). When things go haywire. *Training & Development, 53*(2), pp. 25–27.

Carey, R. (1995, March). Coming around: 360 degree feedback. *Performance Improvement Quarterly,* pp. 58–60.

Foxon, M. (Accessed Oct. 16, 2000). In defense of post-course evaluations: going beyond the smile sheet. (On-line) www.cleo.murdoch.edu.au/gen/aset/ajet/ajet8/wi92p1.

Georges, J. C. (1996, January). The myth of soft skills training. *Training,* pp. 48–54.

Goldwasser, J. C. (2001, January). Beyond ROI. *Training, 38*(01), 82–90.

Holton, E. F., III (1996). The flawed four-level evaluation model. *Human Performance Improvement Quarterly.7*(1), 5–29.

Kirkpatrick, D. (1996, January). Great ideas revisited. *Training & Development,* pp. 67–71.

Kirkpatrick, D.L. (1996). *Evaluating training programs: The four levels.* San Francisco: Berrett-Koehler.

Kiser, K. (1999). Measuring up. *Training & Development, 36*(1) 78–82.

Nilson, C. (Ed.). *Training & Development Yearbook 1998* (pp. 5.49–5.58). Englewood Cliffs, NJ: Prentice Hall.

Parry, S. B. (1993, April). How to validate an assessment tool. *Training.* Retrieved on-line at www.trainingsupersite.com.

Patton, M. Q. (1997). *Utilization-focused evaluation: The new century text.* Thousand Oaks, CA: Sage.

Philips, J. J. (1997). *Return on investment in training and performance improvement programs.* Houston, TX: Gulf Publishing.

Philips, J. J. (1997). *Handbook of training evaluation and measurement methods.* Houston: Gulf Publishing.

Rossett, A. (1998). *First things fast: A handbook for performance analysis.* San Francisco: Jossey-Bass/Pfeiffer.

Russ-Eft, D., & Bassi, L. (Eds.). (1997). *What works: Assessment, development and measurement.* Alexandria, VA: ASTD Publications.

Ulrich, D. (1998, January/February). A new mandate for human resources. *Harvard Business Review,* pp. 125–134.

Weiss, C. (1998). *Evaluation.* Upper Saddle River, NJ: Prentice-Hall.

Wikoff, M. (1994, September). The quality movement meets performance technology. *Performance and Instruction,* pp. 41–45.

Zemke, R., & Armstrong, J. (1996, August). Evaluating multimedia. *Training.* Retrieved on-line at www.trainingsupersite.com.

PART TWO

EMERGENT DIRECTIONS

CHAPTER FIVE

WHAT DOES PERFORMANCE HAVE TO DO WITH IT?

Minjuan: Look at my new business card! Three months on the job and the director just changed our titles from "training specialist" to "performance consultant." I like training. No, I *love* training. I'm not at all sure I buy into this performance thing.

Varda: Where I work we're still focused on training products and events—and moving much of what we do to the Web.

Minjuan: We should focus on the basics at my place too. But we're off on this performance tangent.

Varda: I don't think it's just a tangent. For two years we've been cycling people through classes, with no clue whether it's making a dent in what they do in the hospital. We train them and they go back into their units and then . . . Who knows? I doubt if it makes any difference at all.

Minjuan: Yes, I see your point. I guess part of my hesitation comes from my preference for the familiar things we do in training. I should look more generously at this performance thing.

Defining Performance

Many human resources and training professionals are talking about performance. The word *performance* often appears within the phrase, "the shift from training to performance." What is this performance thing to which training and trainers are being asked to shift? What does it have to do with our work? Must we leave training behind in order to embrace performance? Is the shift happening? Should it happen?

Here we are defining performance as a way of looking at the world and of approaching opportunities and problems. Trainers may retain their familiar titles or take on new performance handles. It matters not. What matters is the approach to the work. We are urging an approach that focuses on worthy results, searching analysis, and tailored systems that *might or might not include training.*

A professional who embraces performance may indeed call herself a "trainer" and buy, build, or deliver buckets of training on-line or within four walls. What we are concerned about is that she conceived that effort systematically and that she grounds and supports it within the organization. If training is one element in a performance concert, where many elements further the message and meaning, that trainer is incorporating performance perspectives. If she's playing a training solo, relying perhaps on great platform skills or a spiffy Website with animated dancing pandas, then performance is not yet her orientation.

> *A professional who embraces performance may indeed call herself a "trainer" and buy, build, or deliver buckets of training on-line or within four walls.*

In their groundbreaking *Handbook of Performance Technology*, Stolovitch and Keeps (1992) defined human performance this way: "Human is emphasized here. [What we want is to] deal with the performance of people operating in results-oriented systems. . . . The word *performance* also denotes a quantified result or set of obtained results" (p.4). They remind us that to be performance oriented, we must be systematic, systemic, grounded in empirical evidence, open to many means and media, not just training, and focused on valuable human achievements.

Stolovitch and Keeps elaborated, "HP technologists are those who adopt a systems view of performance gaps, systematically analyze both gap and system, and design cost-effective and efficient interventions that are based on analysis data, scientific knowledge, and documented precedents" (1992, p. 7). Harless emphasized the process that brings us to performance, "the process of analysis, design, development, implementation, and evaluation of programs to most cost-effectively influence human behavior and accomplishment" (Stolovitch & Keeps, 1992, p. 8). Rosenberg (1990) noted that performance thinking involves systems thinking resulting in an array of interventions, such as Web training, coaching, and recognition programs, in service to a strategic goal.

Stolovitch and Keeps add their voices to others, such as Robinson and Robinson (1995), Hale (1998), Rossett (1999), and Fuller and Farrington (1999) to focus on systems that yield estimable outcomes. What professional is not eager to contribute to results, whether in schools, government, or corporations? What educator is not frustrated by acknowledged and limited influence over meaningful outcomes, such as test scores or love of reading and learning? What e-learning developer can ignore reports of scant Web hits or flagging persistence once on-line? Who can discount the pain of building programs that sit like wallflowers on-line or in brick and mortar, irrelevant to the challenges keeping executives and colleagues up at night? Those concerns incline us toward performance.

Why Emphasize Performance?

Enthusiasm about workplace training should be tempered by skepticism about whether training in and of itself can deliver the goods—that is, worthy outcomes.

Did they like the class? Did they enjoy the on-line module? Did they find the instructor responsive? We are at a place in history where concern with those questions is good, but not at all sufficient. Those interests, all legitimate, must be bolstered by attention to what training means to the individual and organization. That meaning provides justification for doing the heavy lifting associated with incorporating performance into the work of the training and development professional.

The rebirth of the National Society for Performance and Instruction (NSPI) into the International Society for Performance Improvement (ISPI) advanced a view of training that emphasizes performance perspectives over training events and products. In 1998, the American Society for Training and Development (ASTD), the largest trainers' association, nudged the field beyond training with a major professional development initiative targeting performance.

ISPI calls it "human performance technology." ASTD calls it "performance improvement." Dana and Jim Robinson call it "performance consulting." No matter what you dub it, a performance perspective yields expanded ways of thinking about the work, summarized in Table 5.1.

This focus on performance prods the training and human resource professional toward strategy. For example, while Sally Trainer might respond to a request for a class about e-commerce by selecting an on-line vendor, Minjuan, once converted to performance perspectives, will look at the matter differently. Minjuan, because she now perceives herself as a business partner, is at the table when concerns are raised about the workforce and e-commerce. She engages in conversations about how such e-commerce views might influence the various business units. She talks with leaders and experts about e-commerce opportunities being missed and the ones they are realizing. She's asking questions all along the way, about where they need to be, where they are now, and what's likely to help move them there. While new skills and knowledge are needed here, Minjuan

TABLE 5.1. TRAINING AND PERFORMANCE.

Topic	Training	Performance
Target	Individuals	Individual and the organization
Goals	Individual learning	Individual learning and organizational results
Source of Pride	"I build great classes."	"I solve problems and realize opportunities."
People	Instructional designers, instructional technologists, production specialists, trainers, experts, developers	Analysts, relationship managers, process engineers, instruction and information designers, quality specialists, compensation experts, line supervisors, organizational developers—and trainers
Interventions	Classes, learning products, new media training, job aids, documentation, on-line help systems	Reengineered processes, job redesign, classes, coaching, employee participation, sponsorship, goal setting, recognition, incentives, policies, technology, and all the training and information resources
Evaluation	Have they learned? Did they like their learning experience?	What has changed? Is the problem solved? Has the opportunity been realized? Does the effort matter in light of organizational strategy?
Chronology of Effort	"I respond to requests for assistance."	"I anticipate what they need because I'm close to the effort from the get-go."

is aware that other factors, such as job descriptions, current references and policies, and supervisory support, are key to substantial change and performance improvement. She then uses what she has learned to customize a meaningful initiative that blends training with other interventions as well.

Where Minjuan once focused on creating and coordinating classes, now she looks to collaborate with sibling colleagues from units such as compensation, information technology, reengineering, organizational effectiveness, and research and development to construct coordinated programs with tangible results. She recognizes that great learning and information experiences are but one element in a solution system derived from performance analysis and launched and nurtured by a team with a strategic mission.

Learning about e-commerce is one goal in Minjuan's organization; assuring that the lessons translate into meaningful thinking, planning, communicating, selling, and dreaming is quite a different matter. This larger commitment necessitates collaborations that extend far beyond the people and places traditionally associated with training and development. Thus success comes from a view that punches holes in conventional boundaries and role definitions.

Is It Happening?

Unfortunately, many colleagues reside in what feels to them like great divides within organizations and between organizations and vendors or external colleagues. Rummler and Brache (1995) called those "chasms," the white space in organizations. A 1999 study by Rossett and Tobias determined that only 18 percent of professionals identified their organizations as "boundaryless," a finding that intimates how difficult it is to install cross-functional solutions that transcend classes, job aids, and documentation.

Certainly, some training professionals are working collaboratively to build solutions systems. But the numbers suggest that current practice leaves much to be desired.

Respondents in the Rossett and Tobias study reported a slightly rosier picture than did Rossett and Czech (1996) or Tovar, Gagnon, and Schmid (1997). The Rossett and Czech study identified gaps between what performance-oriented professionals viewed as critical (such as analysis and solution systems) and the reception their ideas were receiving at work. Their managers and supervisors, as reported by the responding professionals, were far less interested in performance than were people formally trained in performance and educational technology.

[M]anagers and supervisors . . . were far less interested in performance than were people formally trained in performance and educational technology.

Tovar, Gagnon, and Schmid (1997) found that just under half of their sample were engaged with non-training interventions. Rossett and Tobias identified some positive movement, with 61 percent of their sample reporting that they relied on solutions other than training, and 63 percent reporting that they typically selected interventions based on analysis. Rather than cheering these findings, however, Rossett and Tobias were concerned because their sample was significantly composed of attendees at an ISPI conference, individuals who would be expected to be at the forefront of a commitment to the concepts described in this chapter.

Even with this sample inclined toward performance, the most optimistic of results were that just under two-thirds report that analysis and data-driven solutions are typical. As if that news is not bad enough, boundarylessness and measurement of results were reported to be even less in evidence.

Why Isn't It Happening?

When you talk to professionals about their efforts to incorporate performance perspectives into their work, they often applaud the power of performance concepts, while simultaneously admitting the difficulties associated with holding hands across conventional boundaries. Pointing at hasty leadership, distracted colleagues, and ingrained habits, many are stymied. Training professionals say, "The problem is the sponsor, the customer. He's impatient. He sees it as "analysis-paralysis."

Sponsors prefer training; some could even be described as addicted to it, hoping that a training event or Web module will "work." Training professionals perceive the busy executive's hesitations regarding playing a role in performance improvement: "You do it. I can't. Take them and train them. What you're proposing lands on my already too full plate. Just do something. They like training. Do that."

When queried about barriers to performance, many in our profession suggest that it even goes beyond the sponsor to all the people surrounding them. Who are these people?

In a 1999 article in *Performance Improvement,* Rossett identified three groups with whom we must collaborate to improve performance. The people with expertise comprise the first group. They are subject-matter experts with the know-how or know-why that a sponsor is eager to capture and spread. It might be a scientist with insight into what salespeople need to understand about a new drug or target audience. Or the source could be teacher who is particularly effective at working with parents whose first language is Tagalog. Or we might be talking about several experts on local area networks, whose approaches the organization is eager to spread across the globe.

Relationships must be nurtured so that the channels of communication are open even before they are needed.

Sibling colleagues with whom training and performance development people might fruitfully cooperate to assure performance improvement are the second target group. Compensation specialists, organizational effectiveness experts, re-engineers, information technologists, and others, inside or even outside the organizations, are our likely counterparts. Relationships must be nurtured so that the channels of communication are open even before they are needed.

Those who are the focus of the effort are the third critical group. We intend to help them serve or sell or repair or write or listen better. Just about anybody could be the focus of this attention, from engineers maintaining sonar buoys to customer service reps in the automotive industry to teachers of English as a second language.

Directly related to worker efforts are the people to whom our targets report. Successful performance improvement programs involve managers and supervisors; they are a source of success or failure. Allyne Beach, formerly education director for OCSEA/AFSCME Local 11, a 38,000-member state employee union, and now executive director of the Public Sector Labor Management Committee of the AFL-CIO, provided an example about a life-or-death matter. In addition to helping individual members, she believes that how OCSEA/AFSCME approached the situation also enhanced the value of the union to the state of Ohio and strengthened the prison system.

Beach described the situation this way:

"OCSEA/AFSCME represents approximately 10,000 employees in the Ohio Department of Corrections. Gangs, now recognized as strategic-threat groups, have long been a problem in correctional facilities. When OCSEA/AFSCME raised concerns with the Ohio Department of Corrections about corrections officer safety because of increased gang activity, the Department initially dismissed our concerns. Union concern increased in the summer of 1993, when an African American corrections officer was killed by the Aryan Brotherhood while investigating drug activity at Mansfield Correction facility, the institution where *The Shawshank Redemption* was filmed.

"The OCSEA/AFSCME Education Department went to work to bring independent expertise into the picture. We held a conference with gang experts from Ohio State and Cleveland's Task Force on Violent Crime to learn about the extent of activity, how to identify and decipher gang graffiti, and strategies to deal with gang activity. Management was invited to this conference and some did attend.

"Six months later, Ohio's biggest prison riot exploded. The Lucasville riot raged for two weeks, leaving a prison in ruins and several people dead, including an OCSEA/AFSCME steward.

"Once the media spotlighted the magnitude of the human and property damage and the involved groups, the role of strategic-threat groups could not be ignored. OCSEA went on the offensive to deliver information to union members. Individual union activists began gathering what information they could at each institution and sharing it among other bargaining unit members. They attended regional conferences on the issue at local union expense. The OCSEA/ AFSCME Education Department hosted a specific conference on the three strategic-threat groups that were responsible for Lucasville.

"Management then came on board. Within three months, a joint labor management training was held with the key gang expert from the Federal Bureau of Prisons. The union asked hard questions, admitted to gaps in their expertise regarding gangs, and reached out for growth strategies. Eventually, the critical collaboration with management occurred."

We can work most effectively with colleagues, experts, or employees and supervisors by highlighting what we have in common: (1) concern about outcomes; (2) eagerness to serve by addressing key concerns or opportunities; and (3) shared systematic strategies to find and execute for the organization and its people.

Doing the Work with Performance in Mind

Rummler and Brache (1995) offer critical guidance for training professionals who are concerned with performance and results. They present six factors associated with performance improvement: (1) establish clear expectation for the work and role; (2) devote the necessary resources; (3) establish clear consequence for doing things in the desired way; (4) provide prompt feedback about performance; (5) recognize that individuals come to their work with individual capacity and motivation; and (6) support the acquisition of the necessary skills and knowledge.

Table 5.2 offers suggested performance improvement resources. They are keyed to the time readers have available to invest.

Now let's look at a simplified approach to incorporating performance perspectives into training and development. It is not meant to replace any of the sources detailed in Table 5.2 or to define a rigid way of doing things. Rather, it is intended to suggest ways in which performance can enrich professional practice and organizational results. Four concepts can help us do the work with a performance perspective. They are examined in the following text.

1. Use Data as the Basis for Decisions and Recommendations

Data is how we figure out what to do. From data, such as that gleaned from sales figures or letters from customers or test scores or focus groups with practitioners, professionals can make decisions about how to add value in the organization.

We seek data for two purposes: planning and judging. Planning is typically associated with analysis efforts, just as we discussed in Chapter Two. Judging is what evaluation is all about, occurring when we gather data to enlighten decisions about the programs, processes, or participants we *already* have. In Chapter Four, we focused on evaluation.

TABLE 5.2. RESOURCES.

Time	Resources
"I have an hour"	Read Rosenberg (1990, February). Performance technology working the system, *Training, 27*(2), 42–48.
	Read Rossett (1997, July). "That was a great class, but . . ." *Training & Development, 51*(7), 18–24.
	http://www.astd.org/CMS/templates/index.html?template_id=1 &articleid=10988
	Skim the table of contents for Stolovitch and Keeps's *Handbook of Human Performance Technology.*
	Visit http://edweb.sdsu.edu/edweb_folder/pt/PTModel.html for a quick tour about performance concepts.
	Visit www.ispi.org, the International Society for Performance Improvement.
"I have a day"	Read chapters one, two, and three in Stolovitch and Keeps (1999) *Handbook of Human Performance Technology.*
	Learn more about change strategies by reading Roger Chevalier (1990), "Systematic Change," *Performance and Instruction, 29*(5), 21–23.
	Visit Websites that will introduce you to sibling interventions, such as http://www.epssinfosite.com/newlinks.htm
	http://www.performancesupport.com/
	http://www.learnativity.com
	http://www.nwlink.com/~donclark/hrd/hrdlink.html
	http://www.phios.com/about_approach.htm
	http://defcon.sdsu.edu/3/objects/km/
"I've got a week"	Read Judith Hale's *Performance Consultant's Fieldbook.*
	Read Allison Rossett's *First Things Fast: A Handbook for Performance Analysis.*
	Read Dana and Jim Robinson's books about performance consulting.
	Visit more related Websites:
	http://motivationmining.com/
	http://www.sims.berkeley.edu/courses/is213/s99 /Projects/P9/web_site/about_km.html
	http://www.km-review.com/knowledge/articles/01.htm#3
	http://www.nwlink.com/~donclark/hrd.html
	http://itech1.coe.uga.edu/EPSS/EPSS.html
	http://www.ott.navy.mil/

When we do analysis, we're taking a *fresh* look at the situation in order to figure out what we ought to do. Minjuan, for example, was asked to create an initiative that would help employees to better understand e-commerce. However, if we were gathering data for an evaluation, we would be looking at the effectiveness of *existing* efforts, such as on-line modules, classes, or documentation. Data gathered during an evaluation, such as participant satisfaction with a Web module, and data gathered during an analysis, such as interviews with customers, can be used interchangeably for planning or evaluation purposes.

Our purpose here is not to talk about *how* to gather the data. Rather, we're focusing on *why*. For a training and development specialist, the best reason to gather data is because it grants another view of the situation and then enables us to use that data-based vantage to argue for cross-functional approaches.

Here Orin demonstrates one kind of responsiveness, one that is both familiar and oblivious to data for planning or judging:

Louise: Two years ago we launched that initiative on team selling, and I don't see much team selling happening in EMEA [Europe, Middle East, and Africa]. Every one of our reps has been to at least one class, and some have taken two on team sales. We need to seek out a new vendor or look at some multimedia training.

  Orin: Do you have a particular program or vendor in mind?

Louise: No, I'll leave that up to you. I think we should switch from the ones we've been using.

  Orin: I'm on a training listserv. I'll put it out there and see whether anyone has a recommendation. When do you want us to start scheduling the classes?

Note Orin's response. What value is he adding here? How is the service he's providing in any way enlightened by the fact that he, too, works for the organization and knows much about its people, products, and context? Couldn't Orin, as we see him in the dialogue above, be readily replaced by an outside vendor or even an on-line learning portal? Now let's watch Orin handle it better. Watch how he uses data and the promise of data to contribute.

Louise: Eighteen months ago we launched that initiative on team selling, and I don't see much team selling happening in EMEA [Europe, Middle East and Africa]. Every one of our reps has been to at least one class, and some have taken two. Still not much teaming. We need to seek out a new vendor or maybe look at some multimedia training.

  Orin: How do you know team selling isn't happening?

Louise: Oh, you should see the sales reports. Prior to the team initiative, 93 percent of all sales were by individual reps, with only 13 percent identifying secondary and tertiary roles for other sales professionals. Our customers confirmed that view. Since the team sales initiative, those numbers haven't moved, except in Brussels. With our complex products, it's impossible to imagine that any one rep knows enough to close the sales.

Orin: I had a feeling this was going to be an issue, so when I was in Eastern Europe last month, I talked with about a dozen reps in two different locations. I asked about team selling, and they agreed that it is disappointing. When I asked why, they said the incentive structure is the main problem. They also said team selling is difficult in areas with geographical and cultural barriers, that team expectations imposed in Atlanta and Toronto don't always make sense in Johannesburg and Warsaw.

Louise: They said that? Interesting. What do you want to do?

Orin: I want to take a look at the feedback we received on the classes they did take. Did they like them? Could they locate appropriate resources? Did they see possibilities for shared roles? And I want to see what their supervisors say about all this. I think we need to spend a few days finding out *why* it isn't happening before we switch vendors and schedule any training. Also, why is Brussels more successful? Might be a lesson there for us.

When Orin comes back to Louise next week, he'll have a better sense of the quality of prior team selling training and what else it might take, besides or in addition to training, to effect this important change. The data he gathers in EMEA will help him define and sell Louise on a solutions system customized for this environment, not just a quick fix.

Table 5.3 compares the way hidebound trainers might talk about things and the way performance-oriented professionals would. The differences are exaggerated to make the point.

2. Establish Solutions Systems That Cobble Together an Array of Interventions Appropriate to the Challenge

Bringing critical changes to an organization necessitates eschewing silver bullets, *listening* to many sources of information, and then birthing customized solution systems.

What is a solution system and how do we get there? Solutions systems are *integrated approaches to accomplishment.* As you saw in Chapter Two, Figure 2.1, many people and approaches must come together to achieve worthy results.

Bringing critical changes to an organization necessitates eschewing silver bullets, listening to many sources of information, and then birthing customized solution systems.

What approaches might work? Well, many are possible, from large-scale training or

TABLE 5.3. TRAINING TALK VERSUS PERFORMANCE TALK.

Training Talk	Performance Talk
"What kind of training do you fancy?"	"Training looks like it would be very helpful here, especially for the supervisors. I'd like to make sure to bring people together to create opportunities for practice and feedback, since the topic is tricky."
"How many people do you want to cycle through the classes?"	"I used our on-line assessment and it appears that most of the skills and knowledge gaps are among employees who have been with us for more than a dozen years. That's 855 people. Shall we start there?"
"We can teach it in class or on-line. Which do you want?"	"We piloted with a group in Dusseldorf, and it appears that they very much liked the on-line offering, even better than the class we compared it to. And it will save us some money that I'd like to use to brief and involve supervisors and for an incentive program. I'm going to talk to Mick in HR about that."
"That instructor always gets them all excited about it."	"That instructor always gets them all excited about it. Just want to make sure that the excitement lasts and that we follow up with additional messages from managers, execs, and even related policy changes."

coaching programs to small, single-purpose job aids or to redesign of jobs and work processes and creation of incentives programs. Two important aspects are (1) that the nature of the solutions flows from data collected during analysis and evaluation and (2) that the interventions are integrated with each other in service to the goal.

An example of the integration issue follows. Here's the challenge: *develop a program to help teachers use technology in their classes.* After an analysis that gathered data from school leaders, technology integration experts, and teachers who do and teachers who don't yet use technology, it is time to generate a solution system. Revisit Table 2.4 in Chapter Two, where the relationship between analysis and an array of interventions is presented.

Rather than starting and stopping with in-service education about technology, as is typical, perhaps commence with redesign of jobs to free up a few teachers to serve in technical assistance roles with neophytes or to create dyads that pair people with more experience with those with less. Create a recognition program for teachers who experiment. Reward the support staff and technical associates for helping out. Make hardware and software readily available. Measure results as you go along, so that teachers can see the benefits of the stretch they've undertaken. Someone must monitor the consistency of the messages and ensure that each of the interventions is, in fact, being delivered.

A performance view honors the systems in the organizations, focusing attention on the individual, the work unit, and the larger organization. While training typically attempts to influence individual employees, say through a class on teaming, new job descriptions and articulated work expectations reach beyond the podium to influence the sales team. New gain-sharing incentives might actually influence what the sales force chooses to do.

Solution systems recognize that complex problems and opportunities demand high-octane solutions. It's almost laughable to imagine you can effect global teaming or appreciation of diversity by offering a class. More is required, including efforts that recognize that single people are part of unit and organizational cultures and systems. A conventional view of training asks them to change, regardless of what surrounds them. That's a lot to ask.

Thus the topic of change management becomes a key aspect of what we do. Chevalier (1990) notes that the interventions we use can be parsed into those that are participative, such as training and job aids, and those that are directive, such as incentives or executive sponsorship. Chevalier, in a presentation to the 2000 ISPI conference, noted that, "Participative change . . . will be effective only with those who are ready to change and will return to an environment that will support the change. This is a 'bottom-up' approach in which we use involvement to gain the commitment of those who must change." On the other hand, directive change is top-down, derived from leadership initiatives.

Chevalier noted the importance of synchronizing the two approaches: "Many effective change strategies involve the use of both position and personal power. The directive part of the strategy overcomes inertia and creates some movement toward the desired change, while the participative part of the strategy involves training the target group, adding new knowledge to affect attitudes."

3. Establish Relationships and Policies That Encourage These Boundaryless Collaborations

Let's revisit Figure 2.1. As you can see, no training and development professional is an island. A commitment to performance highlights that reality—one that will ring true to training and human resource professionals devoted to making a difference in the organization.

Langdon (1997) emphasized the concept of a performance change network consisting of performance-oriented professionals. Who are they? They are sibling interventionists in fields such as organizational effectiveness, reengineering, change, compensation, quality, and training. Langdon noted, "Their togetherness begins at analysis and extends to selecting the right combination of interventions" (p. 9). In addition, Langdon (1999) emphasized that it is critical to go beyond selection to execution. Here are some strategies to encourage boundaryless collaborations:

- Don't assume that training and development people are the only ones with an interest in the issue. If accidents are happening or customers are griping, or scrap rates are up, many in the organization are concerned. Bring those people together to facilitate a systemic approach.
- Ask the sponsor how she intends to bring resources from across the organization together in service to the issue. Plan strategies for the sponsor to bring the urgency of the issue to the organization. Anticipate resistance and work with executives and the main sponsor to make certain that colleagues are ready and able to play their roles.
- When the inevitable heel dragging occurs, what policies or pointers do you have to demonstrate how important this effort is and how committed your sponsor is?
- Involve siblings across the organization early in the process. Share data with resonance when those finding emerge. For example, if global participants are complaining about software that hasn't been installed, let MIS know about the grumbling. If incentives don't match goals, inform colleagues from human resources so that they can work to improve alignment.
- It's easier to solicit involvement from people you already know and with whom you have an ongoing relationship. Establish collegial relationships before you need them; then use those existing ties to attempt the hard work involved in working across the white space.
- Recognize individuals who have hopped across organizational divides to add their energy and expertise to solution systems. Make heroes of people who focus on worthy accomplishments, not familiar job titles or turf.

4. Position Training as One Likely and Often Critical Aspect of the Effort, but Certainly Not the Only Method or Means

Rossett (2001) expressed concern about what she called "performance prudery." Rather than raising expectations about moving *beyond* training, *from training to performance,* as it is often proclaimed, Rossett urged that we embrace training as potentially critical to most initiatives. It's hard to imagine an initiative that includes not one single sweet spot for education, training, or information support.

She admits, of course, that there are some. In those instances where performance analysis suggests that no education, training, or information is necessary, note it and then point to prior efforts where training made no dent in the situation and was money and time wasted. Also, remind colleagues and customers that unsupported training creates cynicism rather than accomplished performance. Training isn't the culprit; training in isolation from other supportive interventions is. The goal is to move from training to training *and* performance, to training as part of a solution system.

Consider ways to be in the training and the performance worlds simultaneously. Rossett (2001) advised that, given the reality of current practice and unfavorable collegial response, we emphasize strategies associated with transfer of training. Transfer of training seems to enjoy a better reception in the organization than the more abstract performance technology or performance consulting. Because transfer takes us in directions that neatly match performance priorities, it makes sense to use that strategy. Table 5.4 reviews key aspects of transfer.

TABLE 5.4. TRANSFER AND PERFORMANCE.

Principles	*Discussion*
Let the message be proclaimed far and wide, high and low, and repeatedly.	The influence of a dynamic instructor or dazzling Website must be extended by other elements within the organizational system.
Make certain that every training event and product is perceived as a system, with efforts made to prepare and follow up on the learning experience.	What happens before? How do participants know what's to come and why it matters? What happens afterwards? How is what they learned insinuated into the fabric of their work? Brinkerhoff and Montesino (1995) found that supervisory conversations with their people increase transfer.
Establish contracts that detail expanded roles for sponsors and managers.	A financial-services company uses this strategy well. At the get-go, they define roles that create a system, so that the sponsor says why she's sponsoring it, and the manager talks about it at work.
Create an active and honored role for the manager or supervisor.	The line manager is the key figure in transfer. How will you make certain that he or she is on board and aware of how to contribute? One pharmaceutical company includes a coaching guide for managers with every course delivered to employees.
Manager and peer support influence transfer.	Marguerite Foxon's 1997 dissertation research supported the strong influence of the perception of managerial support on transfer. Xiao (1996) found that peer support also influences transfer.
Describe the value of the training for the individual and the organization.	This may sound obvious, but it does not always happen. WIFM (what's in it for me?) and WIFO (what's in it for the organization?) should be included in every event, whether situated in brick and mortar or on-line.

Questions and Answers

Table 5.5 presents typical questions that might be raised by sponsors and executives confronted with performance improvement perspectives, and suggestions for responding to their concerns. Use this table to craft responses tailored to your context.

TABLE 5.5. QUESTIONS AND ANSWERS.

Questions	Answers
Our people like training, not all this other stuff.	Of course they like training. We work hard so that they will feel loyal to our classroom and on-line opportunities. But we all know training can take us only so far. We must design jobs and processes to help people do their work. We need to provide technology support for their efforts. We need incentive programs that tell employees that these efforts are important. The "other stuff" is what helps the training contribute
What you're saying seems to shift responsibility for the success of the training to me. Is that my job or yours?	It's OUR job. We can put on a great training event, of course. That's on us. But for that event to influence performance back on the job, you and your managers must be involved. Training lessons must be seconded on the job and integrated into the work. We need you to be very clear about expectations, for example.
I don't see how we can expect our managers to do all this.	We must expect it. They are critical. In fact, one study found that managers' conversations with their employees made a big difference. They must talk about it before training, ask about it afterward. And we need to think about building structured ways for them to give their people a chance to practice.
But training is so familiar and such a popular intervention.	Of course it is. We're not trying to take training away from the workforce. What we want to do is offer the right training, to select those elements that are most appropriately covered in the training, and to do those things that will make the training have more impact on what they do at work.

Spotlight on People

Russell Alan Davidson

Russell Alan Davidson is a lieutenant commander in the U.S. Coast Guard, assigned as a performance consultant at Coast Guard headquarters in Washington, D.C. He works in the Office of Training and Performance Consulting, under the director of reserve and training, who reports to the Coast Guard's assistant commandant for human resources.

Davidson provides performance consulting services to the Coast Guard's operational program managers on ways to enhance human performance and organizational effectiveness. His primary clients are the managers who manage maritime law enforcement, cutter and boat operations, search and rescue, intelligence, and aviation.

Davidson's background includes over eleven years of Coast Guard service, including various operational and staff assignments as a commissioned officer, a bachelor's degree in management from the USCG Academy, and a master's degree in educational technology from San Diego State University.

Training and Performance We asked Davidson how performance has changed the work of the training professional. He replied, "We have responsibility for a much broader spectrum now, and the people in the Coast Guard want that. But at the same time that it's neat, it's not easy. We cobble together training and non-training solutions that affect and require the support of other programs—recruiting, selection, assignment, leadership, workforce planning, acquisitions, systems and logistics—lots of things outside of our own office, and even outside the HR office. So it requires us, as practitioners, to be even more knowledgeable of the entire organization—not just of our own world as we used to envision it. That means understanding the programs, the performances, the power, and the political realities."

He continued, "I think we have also acquired responsibility to educate others about what it is we do and how we do it. Human performance technology should not be the exclusive domain of the performance improvement group. Solving others' problems for them breeds dependency. We need to equip leaders and managers at the front line—those who can in turn use it to solve problems wherever they are."

Davidson added, "We influence performance by educating and influencing others about performance and then by helping them do just that. We partner with others to generate understanding about what's getting in the way of the performance we want and then select, design, and implement interventions to rally performance in the positive direction. In the Coast Guard, we are seeing fewer habitual reaches for the 'training hammer' when having problems setting a sheet metal screw into drywall. We are working with the sheet metal workers, the drywall folks, and the building contractors. It's no longer just about training. We've made great strides."

Difficulties Davidson said, "In our organization it's particularly tough. We have a huge job—work that's tremendously important to the nation. We are, however (and it has taken some time to publicly admit and acknowledge this), inadequately staffed and resourced.

"And we are a service of leaders . . . who want to be regarded as 'do-ers' and 'fixers,' not 'studiers.' The other factor at play is that we shift jobs often, typically within two to four years at the helm. So there's not a lot of patience or support at times to engage in lengthy analysis—even for complex matters. These factors add up to a lot of fixing going on at times. Unfortunately, most of the fixing seems to focus on low-hanging fruit—the easy, quick, non-system fixes. The tendency is to opt for the symptomatic solution, not the fundamental one. So we often seem to 'fix' things that we just 'fixed.' That makes it quite a challenge for us at times, as 'professional fixers.'"

Davidson described how he figures out what to do for his customers: "Usually, I begin by asking some pretty direct questions to drill down further into the nature of the problem and attempt to determine what it is that dissatisfies the client. Questions such as 'Can you tell me what it is about the small boat coxswain performance that isn't acceptable?' 'What is it that they are doing now that you don't want them to do?' 'What is it that you'd rather they do?' 'Do you suspect that they know what to do?' Usually my performance analysis leads to (1) a light bulb lighting as the client begins to sense what to do and it seems reasonable or at least worthwhile or (2) a bilge alarm triggering as the client begins to sense that what I will figure out is not necessarily what they had in mind at the get-go.

"Specifically, with regard for the shift from training to performance, we have some elaborate paradigms to overcome. Ours can be a cumbersome and often slow to change culture, successfully handed down for over two hundred years. But we are getting there."

Davidson knows there is progress because: "More and more, we see folks come to the door asking 'Can you look at this for us?' instead of stating 'I need a class.'"

Performance at Work For Davidson and many colleagues, performance improvement in the Coast Guard could almost be described as patriotic activity. He put it this way: "The flag officers promote human performance technology routinely. It has become a matter of business. They specifically check to make certain that projects, initiatives, or developments have been given the 'stamp of approval' by Coast Guard human performance professionals.

"We've enjoyed some success in some notable areas: changing the way we bring in and then train recruits, mentor petty officers, senior enlisteds, and junior officers; how we more appropriately define the world of work at small boat stations; how we crew our cutters, staff our operations centers, acquire new ships, planes, boats, and systems; and in how we develop specific areas of specialty, such as what we've done for rating master chiefs and surfmen."

A Success Story Davidson described the way performance perspectives contributed to the Coast Guard: "A good example might be a recent analytical look that we took at a new Coast Guard acquisition—the deployable pursuit boat. With some anti-drug money provided to us by the Clinton administration, we purchased a number of high speed, high performance, and offshore intercept boats to counter the threat posed by drug traffickers using 'go-fasts' in the southern latitudes. This boat was all new to us so we examined it, the expected and required performance, the would-be performers, and the contexts in which the boat and its people would find themselves. We even had a human factors/ergonomic specialist look at the boat to recommend adjustments. We developed an instructional outline and learning objectives for a training curriculum, and we addressed motivation/incentive and environmental factors with the potential to influence performance. The program seems to be pretty successful so far. Sure, we did training, but not as much as in the past. A combination of communication (clear expectations), training, and performance support was a stronger solution."

Recommended Resources Davidson remains a student of the field. Here is what he suggested for others: "Organizations like ASTD and ISPI are a great start. And ISPI's publication *Performance Improvement* and any selection from their 'book store' are relevant, of course. I'm also a fan of *Training* and of *Training & Development.* Depending on where you work and what you do, *Business Week, Fortune,* or *Fast Company* might make good night table reading. Probably the best related book I've read within the last three years was Tom Stewart's *Intellectual Capital.* I also enjoyed Alan Briskin's *The Stirring of Soul in the Workplace* and Alan Cooper and Ayman Sawaf's *Executive EQ.* Other authors to consult, beside Rossett, are Senge, Argyris, Langdon, Stolovitch and Keeps, Drucker, Rummler and Brache, Robinson and Robinson, Clark, Keller, Kaufman, Dick, Gilbert, and Mager. There are gobs of good, intelligent on-line resources available today. I periodically check Edweb at San Diego State, www.edweb.sdsu.edu, and the associated links posted there. Otherwise, a keyword search through a search engine has always taken me where I've wanted to go, and then some."

Davidson advised: "Keep reading, writing, and honing your skills. Don't allow yourself to become complacent. Just when you think you've figured it all out, the trouble sets in. And allow yourself adequate time for reflection. But most of all have fun. If you aren't, then something is wrong."

Roger Chevalier

Roger Chevalier is an independent consultant who specializes in integrating training into more comprehensive performance improvement solutions. He specializes in leadership, coaching, change management, sales, sales management, and customer service performance improvement.

Chevalier is a former vice president of Century 21 Real Estate Corporation's Performance Division and a former training director for the U.S. Coast Guard's west coast training center. He has more than twenty-five years in the performance improvement business.

Chevalier has earned a Ph.D. in applied behavioral science as well as two master's of science degrees in personnel management and organizational behavior. His previous education includes bachelor's and master's of arts degrees in English literature. He is a faculty member for the International Society for Performance Improvement's Human Performance Technology Institute and is the human performance technology forum editor for ASTD's *Performance in Practice*.

How We Influence Performance Chevalier said that the most powerful and most underutilized tool in instructional systems design (ISD) is evaluation. He believes that evaluation is the link between training and performance improvement, noting that "If trainees and their managers know that performance will be evaluated, they are more likely to use what they learned." Chevalier offered a formula for successfully influencing performance, "Training plus evaluation equals accountability."

He provided an example of how measurement, evaluation, and accountability can influence performance. Some years back, he was in charge of twenty-four Little League coaches, where the stated goal was to develop children, not win games. After experiencing one too many problems with aggressive coaches who attempted "to win at any price," Chevalier decided that is was time to hold coaches accountable for their behavior.

Prior to the beginning of the season, he held coaches' clinics, during which he emphasized the need to play all players fairly and to strive for each player to play at least half of each game. To back up the training, he showed the coaches a survey that would be used to evaluate their performance. The form was very simple. Parents would evaluate the coach's performance on a five-point scale by indicating the degree of their agreement with four statements. Space was provided below each statement for written comments. The statements were:

1. "My child increased his/her knowledge and skills in baseball."
2. "My child increased his/her knowledge and skills in team play."
3. "My child was treated fairly by the manager and coaches."
4. "This baseball season was a good experience for my child."

This simple survey communicated and measured organizational values. At the end of the season, the coach who had won the championship series had the worst evaluations. He did this by playing only his best players, eventually forcing his weaker players to quit. At the end of the season, he had only his nine best players and easily beat the other teams in the playoffs against coaches who were still playing all thirteen of their players.

As a result of the survey and direct observation of the coach at games, the manager of the championship team was not allowed to coach again. Chevalier said, "When the word 'hit the street' the following year, all managers played their players more fairly and focused more on development and skills than wins and losses. As you can see, while we tend to think of evaluation as a complex task, the best measurement systems are simple and to the point."

Describing and Selling Performance Improvement Chevalier believes that the best way to sell performance improvement is to talk to clients about how to assure return on investment for their projects. He believes an important way to improve ROI is by creating a work environment that supports performance improvement through systematic assessment and continuous improvement.

He said, "Performance improvement does not usually happen as a result of training alone, no matter how great the training." Chevalier cited another example of a major real estate franchise organization implementing a new sales training program to be delivered to over fifteen thousand new salespeople each year: "The first step in implementing the new sales training program was to create an environment that would support the training. Before an office was allowed to send new salespeople to the training, the broker was required to attend a one-day program on ways to support the training."

Another example Chevalier gave of how training should be supported by management systems started as a result of a request for sales training: "A software company had developed a new product line and had formed a sales department to bring the products to market. While there were obvious knowledge and skill deficiencies in this new sales team, something more than training was needed.

"Fortunately, the sales manager was open to a more systemic approach. Two sales management systems were put in place to track the progress of prospects in the selling process and to provide feedback to each salesperson from their prospects with a customer satisfaction survey. The training then was used to impart new knowledge and skills *and* to introduce the sales force to these sales management systems."

These examples support the messages presented in this chapter regarding the critical role of the manager and supervisor.

Chevalier went on to say, "If the environment doesn't support training, implementation of what was learned will be left to chance." He noted that training professionals need to advise their clients that if they really want performance to improve, they must have systemic approaches that create an environment in which the student will be encouraged to use what he or she has learned.

How Our Responsibilities Have Changed Chevalier has provided leadership in linking the work to change initiatives. In his article "HPT: The Power to Change" (Chevalier, 2000), he stated, "We are being drawn into the realm of human performance technology (HPT) as our traditional roles as trainers and facilitators are being expanded into true change agents. While our attraction to HPT is found in the broader base of available interventions in our tool kits, our challenge is to move from partici-pative interventions, such as providing training and facilitating group decision mak-ing, to more directive change strategies, such as changing measurement and reward systems."

Chevalier doesn't mince words. He remarked that the new emphasis on perfor-mance also means, "If training professionals don't become performance improve-ment specialists, they will end up working for one."

Performance Improvement Systems at Work Chevalier described his work at the Coast Guard Training Center in Petaluma, California. By approaching the challenge as a system, rather than as a training problem, he was able to develop a highly effective and efficient organization. The key to this improvement process was an evaluation of all courses by surveying all graduates and their supervisors three to six months after they had completed the training.

Feedback was received as to how frequently the respondents practiced the desired behavior, how well they were able to do it, and how important it was to their organization. Following the mantra of "systematic assessment and continuous im-provement," Chevalier's staff was able to improve the quality of training provided while reducing direct training costs from $9 million to $6 million in five years for the twenty-five courses they provided for four thousand students each year.

Chevalier and his staff did this by developing systems for curriculum design and development, by changing personnel management systems, and by altering the re-ward systems (performance evaluations, medals, promotions).

The roles of course designer, developer, and evaluator were elevated as more im-portant than the instructor's. It was decided that a good course designer shaped the future and impact of the training program, whereas the instructors only influenced the students in their classes.

By changing the overall evaluation system, they went beyond measuring class-room satisfaction to determining whether or not the training was, in fact, contribut-ing to the organizational mission.

Chevalier said that experience has taught him that "What gets measured gets done" and that evaluation should not be viewed as "optional equipment" in the in-structional systems design process, but rather as a necessary part of the overall im-plementation strategy.

Recommended Resources Chevalier recommended *Smart Training* by Carr, *Man-agement of Organizational Behavior* by Hersey and Blanchard, and *The Handbook of Human Performance Technology* by Stolovitch and Keeps.

At the Heart of the Matter

The following slides are designed to help professionals explain and win support for their efforts to integrate performance perspectives into their work.

Slide 5.1

Defining Performance

"HP technologists are those who adopt a systems view of performance gaps, systematically analyze both gap and system, and design cost-effective and efficient interventions that are based on analysis data, scientific knowledge, and documented precedents."

(Stolovitch and Keeps, 1992, p. 7)

Presenter's Notes

Stolovitch and Keeps offer a familiar definition that emphasizes worthy outcomes, systematic strategies for arriving at these outcomes, and an array of cost-effective interventions, not just training.

Slide 5.2

Huh? What Is It Again?

■ **Here the focus is on training and development *with a performance perspective***

— **Decisions based on data from analysis and evaluation, not title or habit**

— **Solution systems that are tailored to the situation, where training is one aspect**

— **Strategic results linked to organizational purposes**

Presenter's Notes

While it is typical to talk about the *shift from training to performance,* here we are proposing that training and development professionals look at it a little differently. Think about training *and* performance, or training *with* a performance perspective.

Slide 5.3

Training *and* Performance

Training

- **Goal is individual learning**

- **Classes are output**

- **We do training, job aids, documentation**

Training and Performance

- **Goal is individual learning and organizational change**

- **Results are output**

- **Interventions of many kinds are tailored to the need**

Presenter's Notes

A performance perspective softens our training bias. Instead, the approaches we take are based on analysis and evaluation, on taking a fresh look at the situation. This results in increases in learning and in organizational change.

Slide 5.4

With Performance in Mind

- **Search analysis to find fresh, systemic solutions**
- **Focus on strategic outcomes, business partnerships**
- **Anticipate needs**
- **Collaborate with colleagues in areas such as information technology, organizational effectiveness, quality**

Presenter's Notes

In a study for a financial services company, we found that throwing out the training titles and switching to performance handles was a mixed blessing. Customers didn't get it. Colleagues remained confused. Here we are not urging trainers to give up their training handles, but rather to approach them with a performance perspective. Training remains what we do, but training that is carefully selected and supported in the organization.

Slide 5.5

When Sponsors and Executives Support Performance

- **Ask hard questions about what it will take to achieve performance outcomes**
- **Note that training is one component of the solutions, typically, and not the whole enchilada**
- **Bring sibling interventions together to collaborate on achieving outcomes**
- **Measure success on outcomes, not butts in seats or hits on sites**

Presenter's Notes

If you are a training and development professional, this is what the performance perspective looks like in brief. What role should the customer play? Here are a few critical things we need to ask for. Of course, they are not easy to accomplish, but they need to be presented, so that movement can commence.

Slide 5.6

Use Transfer of Training Strategies to Get at Performance

- **Focus on the role of the manager—his or her support influences transfer from training to the workplace**
- **Increase supervisory conversations to second training messages**
- **Establish contracts that define active roles for managers, sponsors, and colleagues across the organization**
- **Establish relevance for employees**

Presenter's Notes

Transfer of training is close kin to performance. Use it to garner support for these concepts, because most customers are eager for the training to make a difference.

Resources

Brinkerhoff, R. O., & Montesono, M. U. (1995). Partnerships for training transfer. *Human Resource Development Quarterly, 6*(3), 263–274.

Briskin, A. (1998). *The stirring of the soul in the workplace.* San Francisco: Berrett-Koehler.

Carr, C. (1992). *Smart training: The manager's guide for improved performance.* Highstown, NJ: McGraw-Hill.

Chevalier, R. D. (1990). Systematic change. *Performance and Instruction, 29*(5), 21–23.

Chevalier, R. D. (2000). HPT: The power to change. Online at www.ispi.org/services/ culturechange/concurrent.htm.

Cooper, R. K., & Sawaf, A. (1997). *Executive EQ: Emotional intelligence in Leadership and Organizations.* New York: Grosset/Putnam.

Foxon, M. J. (1997). The influence of motivation to transfer, action planning and manager support on the transfer process. *Performance Improvement Quarterly, 10*(2), 42–63.

Fuller, J., & Farrington, J. (1999). *From training to performance improvement: Navigating the transition.* Washington, DC: International Society for Performance Improvement.

Hale, J. (1998). *Performance consultant's fieldbook.* San Francisco: Jossey-Bass.

Hersey, P., & Blanchard, K. H. (1988). *Management of organizational behavior: Utilizing human resources.* Englewood Cliffs, NJ: Prentice-Hall.

Langdon, D. G. (1997). A look into the future of human performance technology. *Performance Improvement, 36*(6), 6–9.

Langdon, D. G. (1999). *Intervention resource guide: 50 performance improvement tools.* San Francisco: Jossey-Bass.

Mager, R. M., & Pipe, P. (1984). *Analyzing performance problems.* Belmont, CA: Pitman Learning.

Robinson, D.G., & Robinson, J.C. (1995). *Performance consulting.* San Francisco: Berrett-Koehler.

Rosenberg, M. J. (1990, February). Performance technology: Working the system. *Training, 27*(2), 42–48.

Rossett, A. (1987). *Training needs assessment.* Englewood Cliffs, NJ: Educational Technology Publications.

Rossett, A. (1987). What your professor never told you about the mundane practice of instructional design. *Tech Trends, 32*(1), 10–13.

Rossett, A. (1996, March). Training and organizational development: Siblings separated at birth. *Training, 33*(4), 53–59.

Rossett, A. (1997, July). That was a great class, but . . . *Training & Development, 51*(7), 18–24.

Rossett, A. (1999). *First things fast: A handbook of performance analysis.* San Francisco: Jossey-Bass/Pfeiffer. www.jbp.com/rossett.

Rossett, A. (1999, January). Understanding the people in the organization who aren't us: Communication strategies for analysis. *Performance Improvement Quarterly, 38*(1), 16–19.

Rossett, A. (1999, May). Knowledge management meets analysis. *Training & Development, 53*(5), 62–68.

Rossett, A. (2001). Beyond performance prudery. In R. A. Reiser & J. Dempey. *Trends and issues in instructional design and technology.* Upper Saddle River, NJ: Merrill/Prentice Hall.

Rossett, A., & Czech, C. (1996). They really wanna, but . . . The aftermath of professional preparation in performance technology. *Performance Improvement Quarterly, 8*(4), 115–132.

Rossett, A., & Tobias, C. (1999). An empirical study of the journey from training to performance. *Performance Improvement Quarterly. 12*(3), 31–43.

Rummler, G. A., & Brache, A. P. (1995) *Improving performance: How to manage the white space in the organization.* (2nd ed.). San Francisco: Jossey-Bass.

Stewart, T. A. (1997). *Intellectual capital: The new wealth of organizations.* New York: Doubleday.

Stolovich, H. D., & Keeps, E. J. (1992). What is human performance technology? In H. D. Stolovich & E. J. Keeps (Eds.), *Handbook of human performance technology: A comprehensive guide for analyzing and solving performance problems in organizations* (pp. 3–13). San Francisco: Jossey-Bass.

Strayer, J., & Rossett, A. (1994) Coaching sales performance: A case study. *Performance Improvement Quarterly, 7*(4), 39–53.

Tovar, M., Gagnon, F., & Schmid, R. (1997). Development of a consultation profile of interventions perceived as successful by human performance technology consultants. *Performance Improvement Quarterly, 10*(3), 67–83.

Watkins, R., Leigh, D., Platt, W., & Kaufman, R. (1998, September). Needs assessment—A digest, review and comparison of needs assessment literature. *Performance Improvement, 37*(7), 40–53.

Xiao, J. (1996). The relationship between organizational factors and the transfer of training in the electronics industry in Shenzhen, China. *Human Resource Development Quarterly, 7*(1), 55–73.

CHAPTER SIX

WHAT ARE OUR TECHNOLOGY OPTIONS?

Jill: Why is everyone talking to me about technology? I work in human resources, not information technology. My classes are full, and employees like them. Do you think all this tech talk is a fad?

Jose: I don't think so. I'm not saying that classroom training will disappear, but technology can do things we've always wanted to do—and for hundreds and even thousands of employees at once, not dozens. Think about the problems we're always having with travel budgets. Remember how impossible it is to keep our materials up-to-date. And that doesn't even include the ugly fights about classroom space.

Jill: With classroom training, I have my arms around what is possible. We touch people in real ways. We look 'em in the eyes. With these technologies, I'm less certain about the impact—what we can accomplish.

Defining Technology-Based Training

Technology-based training is any training that is delivered partially or entirely through electronic hardware, software, or both. Computers, audio- and videotapes, CD-ROMs, and the Web are some of the technologies used to deliver training and information now.

Why Technology?

Whether Jill is ready or not, technology is here—and in a big way. ASTD studies have found HRD executives to be enthusiastic about the shift to technology-based delivery of training. Confirming this upward trajectory, *Training* magazine cited an International Data Corporation (IDC) prediction that technology-based training will grow at an annual rate of more than 50 percent between 1996 and 2002. The investment firm W.R. Hambrecht & Company has initiated coverage of e-learning stocks, firms devoted to technology-based learning for K–12, higher education, and workplace learning (www.wrhambrecht.com/research/index). Public education, too, has climbed on board in a big way. *The New York Times* (McGeehan, 2000) noted that Merrill Lynch has sized the K–12 e-learning market at $1.3 billion in 1999, with projected growth to $6.9 billion in 2003.

[T]echnology-based training will grow at an annual rate of more than 50 percent between 1996 and 2002.

Training and HR professionals, like radiologists, architects, and loan specialists, are wise to ponder the impact that technologies will have on the ways they work and on what their customers will expect from them. The situation presents opportunities for both excitement and caution. The purpose of this chapter and the one that follows it is to tour the technology and training terrain.

The Possibilities

Chapter One introduced our view of what is happening in the field of training and development. One massive force is technology. On its own, that's not the most intriguing thing to us. Far more interesting is what the technology means to the way we now can deliver programs and services.

Let's look at the ways technology influences the approaches that were highlighted in Table 1.2, in Chapter One. In Chapter Seven, we'll focus on the Web and its implications for the purposes and roles identified in Tables 1.1 and 1.3.

Expanding Approaches to Training and Development

Technology, in general, creates options for training and development. Messages can be delivered in many ways, repeatedly, across great distances, and with continuing availability for reference. In our business, those are very big benefits indeed. Let's look at the way technologies can and do influence our work.

Systems. In the past, training was too often a moment in time, or a week perhaps. With technology, a message about ethics or diversity or new software can be repeated as a mantra. Before class, perhaps, participants listen to an audiotape explaining the purposes for the class and how to scan the environment in preparation. The class may be interspersed with video snippets that focus on the ways that equipment problems typically manifest themselves and how to check for problems. After class, the instructor may engage the participants and their supervisors in asynchronous on-line chats.

Convergence of Learning and Work. So much of contemporary work relies on computers. Shouldn't training and support be there, right next to the application programs? A program designed for site acquisition specialists is an example. After a detailed analysis, it was clear to the planners that fewer moments of classroom time were required. What most users wanted were tools to help specialists pick sites, negotiate contracts, and win contracts. The on-line resource features examples of forms, reports, proposals, briefings, and contracts, enriched by commentary in pop-up boxes, loaded on the portable PC, to help the site specialist do the job and learn more about it simultaneously. Next up—some videos with sample briefings for use by city councils, with snippets illustrating best practices.

Learner-Centered Delivery. Executives are clear that they want employees to grow to match emergent challenges. They are, however, less eager to pull them off the job and put them in classrooms to accomplish this goal. Technology provides options here. A tax consultant seeks information about a new piece of tax legislation? Put it on-line. Concerned about the related issues keeping high-net-worth customers up at night? Distribute audiotaped briefings about the new legislation that are replete with their comments and questions. Want to hear what corporate leadership in Atlanta is saying about the thrust of tax legislation? Schedule a satellite broadcast. Learner-centeredness and learner responsibility go hand in hand. Tax consultants need to know what they need to know. Then they must set aside time to read, listen, reflect, and apply. That's the opportunity and the rub.

Authenticity in the Classroom. Although technology will increase the amount of individual and independent learning that occurs, let's not forget that it can do wonderful things within the classroom too. Technology brings what's outside the classroom inside. Real people and real problems are right where instructors and students are. Through audio and video, the voice of the customer can be brought inside. Do you want a help desk specialist to deal with a modem problem for the first time on the job, when an irate buyer calls it in? Of course not. Simulations are another example. Do you want your pilot to practice handling wind shear at 34,000 feet or in a simulator?

Instructor-Led and Self-Instruction Together. In the old days, training professionals had to choose. Will it be a classroom experience or will it be delivered via self-instruction? Now technology makes it possible to do both. Commence, for example, with a classroom orientation, and then move to independent experiences such as videotapes, satellite broadcasts, and on-line chats for participants, no matter their geography or line of business. There is also the opportunity to repurpose elements of the class for wider distribution and subsequent independent review or reference. The challenge of teaching children to read provides an example. Video examples enrich teacher training classes and can be distributed to neophytes so that they can view them at home, as they prepare lessons, and just prior to classroom interactions.

In the old days, training professionals had to choose. Will it be a classroom experience or will it be delivered via self-instruction? Now technology makes it possible to do both.

Turn of the Century Training Technologies

HRD and training professionals have many choices for technology at the turn of the century, from low-tech options such as audiotape to pricier solutions via satellite. Familiar technologies are described below, followed by tables that summarize each option. In Chapter Seven, we'll look closely at the technology that is grabbing the most attention, the World Wide Web.

Audiotape

Although audiotape is not new or high-tech, it is a viable and powerful training technology. Audiotapes effectively deliver lecture-based training and reinforce print materials. They bring content to life with music, narration, and sound effects. Audiotapes also convey characters and interactions, materials that are often at the heart of the work. Trainees can anticipate customer concerns and hear the perspectives of subject-matter experts, star performers, and colleagues. When a real estate company, for example, wanted to prepare employees to do sales listing presentations, they provided examples and commentary on audiotape, so that trainers could deliver authentic messages and agents could listen in their cars later, immediately prior to their meetings with homeowners. Table 6.1 gives some characteristics of audiotape.

TABLE 6.1. AUDIOTAPES.

Technology	Pros	Cons
Audiotape	*Affordable:* Tapes are inexpensive to produce, reproduce, and distribute.	*Nonvisual:* Content is limited to sound.
	Convenient: Trainees can listen at home, at work, or in their cars.	*Inflexible:* Learner has no control over or interaction with content.
	Portable: Truly "anytime, anyplace" learning as trainees can take tapes anywhere they go.	*Restrictive:* There are no opportunities for practice with feedback or assessment.
	Repeatable: The tapes can be revisited by rewinding and replaying.	*Disposable:* They have limited shelf life because they are not updatable.
	Accessible: Access to tape players is nearly universal.	
	Powerful: Tapes can effectively teach interpersonal or "soft skills," convey emotions.	
	Popular: Strong acceptance and familiarity by users.	

Videotape

Videotape is a tried-and-true technology that typically ranks at or near the top in frequency of use in Billcom's (*Training* magazine's) annual census. Video is used in training classes to teach things that are hard to describe, to demonstrate procedures, to encourage soft skills, to model performances, and to present "guest speakers." Video can also travel to where trainees are, delivering "lessons" to employees who are too busy or too distant to attend classes. Employees can watch at their convenience, at home, at work, or anywhere with access to a VCR.

Training videos can be engaging, motivating, and informative. For example, a vendor wanted to tackle the issue of sexual harassment in a way that would define this complex concept. The trainer used videotape to present examples that vividly illustrated the attributes of sexual harassment and provided trigger scenarios so participants could practice identifying instances of sexual harassment. Table 6.2 shows some characteristics of videotape.

TABLE 6.2. VIDEOTAPES.

Technology	Pros	Cons
Videotape	*Affordable:* Videotapes are inexpensive to copy and distribute.	*Expensive:* Production costs are potentially high.
	Cost-effective: Training classes can be delivered live once, then replayed endlessly.	*Didactic:* They are useful for lecture or presentation only.
	Convenient: Trainees can watch at home or at work.	*Inflexible:* Learner has no control over or interaction with content.
	Portable: Truly "anytime, anyplace" learning as trainees can take tapes anywhere they go.	*Restrictive:* There are no opportunities for practice with feedback or assessment.
	Repeatable: Users can revisit training by rewinding and replaying as often as they need to.	*Disposable:* They have limited shelf life because they are not updatable.
	Accessible: Access to tape players is nearly universal.	
	Popular: There is strong acceptance and familiarity by users.	

Videoconferencing

Videoconferencing brings people in two or more locations together, face-to-face, in real time. Room-sized or desktop videoconferencing units with monitors and high-speed, high-capacity transmission lines allow participants to see, hear, and talk to one another in real time. Human resource professionals now use this technology to deliver training to employees around the world.

Videoconferencing is similar to classroom instruction, because trainees can listen to lectures, ask questions, participate in discussions, view video clips, tour Web sites, and even share documents. Videoconferencing is moving to the World Wide Web via vendors such as Placeware, Centra, and Liveware 5.

For example, at San Diego State University, graduate students on and off campus who wanted to study performance technology were offered a class via videoconferencing. This created a larger community of health practitioners and campus-based graduate students, united by team assignments, videoconferences, and their shared interest in performance improvement. Some pros and cons of videoconferencing are shown in Table 6.3.

Computer-Based Training

Computer-based training (CBT) is a term that describes any training delivered by a computer, including CD-ROM, Digital Video Disks (DVD), and on-line training. *Training* magazine reported that CBT is a very popular delivery medium, and with good reason. Computer-based training can reduce or eliminate the costs associated with classroom training, including lost productivity while sitting in

TABLE 6.3. VIDEOCONFERENCING.

Technology	Pros	Cons
Videoconferencing	*Interactive:* Trainees can ask questions, participate in discussions, and share documents.	*Expensive:* Videoconferencing technology is expensive, and maintenance can be an issue.
	Multimedia: Instructors can play videos, tour Websites and walk users through computer programs.	*Unreliable:* The technology is not yet "plug and play," and technical problems are common.
	Repeatable: Videoconferences can be recorded and replayed.	*Nonintuitive:* Videoconferencing requires specialized skills that many training professionals do not yet have.
	Assessment: Trainees can practice skills and receive guidance and feedback from instructors.	*Compatibility:* This is a major issue, because videoconferencing units have to connect at the same "speed" or rate of transmission per second (kbps).
	Familiar: It mimics classroom and meeting formats that are comfortable for participants.	

class, stale materials, travel costs, and instructor fees. Computer-based training, once built, can be repeatedly used both for instructional and reference value. Unlike an instructor, who is prone to road weariness, CBT doesn't fatigue, except perhaps in its content. Computer-based training is also convenient, because it allows employees to participate whenever and wherever they wish, at home, at work, or on the road. They can also practice and hone new skills in private and revisit lessons as often as they elect. Global rollout of a new pharmaceutical product has been accomplished by CBT, with salespeople getting to know new drugs, features, and disease states wherever they are, through their computers. Some features of CBT are shown in Table 6.4.

CD-ROM

CD-ROMs, or read-only computer disks, deliver multimedia training programs to the desktop or wherever a CD player is located. They offer more tailored training possibilities, transcending the capacity of linear videotape by enabling multiple paths and languages. CD-ROMs often include audio, video, graphics, and animation. Responsive and interactive, CD-ROM enables users to engage text and print-based material, as well as dynamic audio or video interactions. CD-ROMs give trainees control over their learning experience, while still providing guidance and structure. Training delivered on CD-ROMs may include exercises, tests, and authentic scenarios that allow trainees to practice and hone their skills, test their knowledge, and receive immediate feedback. Many vendors now provide soft-skills training in CD-ROM formats that give interactions, characters, and unresolved problems and cases—critical approaches to topics such as communications, coaching, and supervision. Some characteristics of CD-ROM training are presented in Table 6.5.

Digital Video Disks

Digital video disks (DVD) have all the capabilities of CD-ROMs and more. They hold up to twenty times more data. DVD drives can be installed on computers or hooked up to televisions, in the way that we attach VCRs to TVs. This flexibility represents a definite advantage over CD-ROMs and other training technologies. DVD technology is also "backwards compatible," meaning that CD-ROMs can be played on DVD players. This is good news for companies that have CD-ROM-based training libraries and are considering upgrading to DVD technology. Existing CD-ROM software will remain useful to the organization. New computers

TABLE 6.4. COMPUTER-BASED TRAINING.

Technology	Pros	Cons
Computer-based training	*Convenience:* Employees can complete training wherever they have access to a computer.	*Expensive:* Computer-based training can be expensive to develop and deliver, particularly if the technical infrastructure (computers, networks) is not yet in place.
	Richness: Computer-based training may feature text, graphics, audio, video, and animation.	*Challenging:* Many training professionals do not yet have the skills necessary to develop computer-based training.
	Interactivity: Trainees can take tests, complete exercises, and respond to challenging, realistic scenarios; they can also monitor their own progress and performance during training.	*Timeliness:* CBT takes time to develop, and the danger is that by the time the training is ready, the information may be outdated.
	Repeatable: Employees can revisit training as often as they wish, converting lessons into reference materials.	
	Assessment: Trainees can practice new skills, take tests, and receive immediate feedback and guidance.	
	Learner control: Trainees have control over their own training; they complete it at their own pace, on their own schedule, in a private, risk-free environment.	

TABLE 6.5. CD-ROMS.

Technology	Pros	Cons
CD-ROM	*Convenience:* Employees can complete training anywhere they have access to a computer with a CD-ROM drive.	*Expensive:* CD-ROMs tend to be expensive to produce.
	Richness: CD-ROMs may feature text, graphics, audio, video, and animation or a combination of these media.	*Nonintutive:* Multimedia production requires specialized skills that many training professionals do not yet possess.
	Interactive: Trainees can take tests, complete exercises, respond to challenging, realistic scenarios; they can also monitor their own progress and performance during training.	*Timeliness:* CD-ROM production takes time, and the danger is that by the time the disks are ready, the information may be outdated.
	Engaging: At its best, CD-ROM-based training is effective, entertaining, and engaging.	*Disposable:* CD-ROMs cannot be updated once they have been produced and distributed.
	Repeatable: Employees can revisit the program as often as they wish, converting lessons into reference materials.	
	Portable: CD-ROMs can go anywhere that employees do.	
	Assessment: Trainees can control tests and exercises, and receive immediate feedback and guidance.	
	Learner control: Trainees have control over their own training; they complete it at their own pace, on their own schedule.	

are being built with DVD drives, increasing the attractiveness of this powerful technology, the characteristics of which are shown in Table 6.6.

Wireless Technology

Wireless technology is generating a lot of excitement currently because it is at the heart of "mobile training." Wireless personal communication devices (cell phones) and personal assistants (Palmtops, Gameboy, and OmniSky) are 100 percent battery powered. Free from the constraints of wires, cords, and cables, wireless technology is small, portable, and convenient. Wireless devices are carried by the user, facilitating access and communication anywhere, any time. Perhaps the biggest differences between wireless technology and its predecessors are the graphic user interface (GUI). With wireless, users interact with the technology by pushing buttons on a miniature keypad; there is no mediating device such as a mouse, remote control, or a keyboard.

Wireless technology holds promise for people in our field because it accelerates the shift from memory to reference and from placebound to mobile options.

Wireless technology holds promise for people in our field because it accelerates the shift from memory to reference and from placebound to mobile options.

Telephone numbers, calendars, job aids, policies, procedures, and notes will be available at the moment of need. We asked some experts their opinions of wireless technology.

Marty Murillo, a sales training manager at iPlanet (a Sun/Netscape Alliance) believes that wireless technology is of interest because "Individuals would have access to information regardless of what device is used. This has more to do with just-in-time decision making than the technologies involved . . . we will care more about the content than the way we get it and the enabling technologies."

Brett Clapham, a project manager at AMERANTHÆ Technology Systems Inc., although very enthusiastic about wireless, did point out some drawbacks of the technology. First, he pointed to the most obvious problem: the size of the display. There's not much real estate, and only Web pages or other inputs that are the same size can be displayed. Clapham also thinks that wireless technology might accentuate impulsiveness because it provides instant gratification. He explained, "In the past, you would sit down and write a letter, then reread the letter. Then you would put the letter in an envelope and mail it sometime after that. You had to really want to communicate with someone to go to that trouble, and then you could tear the letter up if you changed your mind. With wireless, you have an urge to call or write someone, and you just do it."

Some characteristics of wireless technology are summarized in Table 6.7.

TABLE 6.6. DIGITAL VIDEO DISKS.

Technology	Pros	Cons
DVD or Digital Video Disks	*Convenient:* Employees can complete training anywhere they have access to a DVD drive. DVD drives may be hooked up to a TV or be installed on computers. *Compatibility:* DVD drives are "backwards compatible," meaning that they can also play CDs as well as DVDs. *Richness:* DVDs may feature PC files, feature-length films, text, graphics, audio, video, and/or animation. *Interactive:* As with CD-ROMs, trainees can take tests, complete exercises, respond to challenging, realistic scenarios and monitor progress and performance during training. *Repeatable:* Employees can revisit the program as often as they wish, converting lessons into reference materials. *Portable:* DVDs are small and portable. *Assessment:* Trainees can complete tests and exercises, and receive immediate feedback and guidance.	*Expensive:* Like CD-ROMS, DVDs can be very expensive to produce. In addition, the cost of DVD drives must be factored in to any DVD-based training. Because the technology is new, few organizations have it. *Nonintuitive:* Multimedia production requires specialized skills that many training professionals do not yet have. *Timeliness:* Just as with CD-ROMs, it takes time to produce training on DVDs, and the danger is that by the time the disks are ready, the information may be outdated. *Disposable:* DVDs cannot be updated once they have been produced and distributed.

TABLE 6.7. WIRELESS TECHNOLOGY.

Technology	Pros	Cons
Wireless communication devices and personal assistants	**Portable:** Wireless devices are small, portable, and most often carried on the user.	**Tiny:** The screen is small and much of what people want to look at isn't.
	Interactive: Some wireless devices facilitate two-way communication with other people and the Internet. Users can send and receive e-mail, visit a Website, or create sites and home pages.	**Expensive:** Wireless technology is still expensive, although experts predict that the prices will drop eventually. Cell phones are particulary expensive because they can't be used without a service provider (such as Sprint or PacBell) and monthly charges.
	Efficient: Wireless technology saves time because it can be used anytime and anywhere. Users can communicate, get help, advice, or information as needed.	**Unreliable:** WML is harder to program than HTML, because it is translated into binary code before it is sent through or to wireless equipment. This can cause "mutations" or errors, making it an unstable programming language.
	Intuitive: Wireless devices are easy to use because they build on familiar technologies, including telephones, computers, and the Internet.	**Compatibility:** Many wireless Internet sites are not yet compatible with some cell phones This is a major problem that experts predict will not be solved until the year 2002 (Pringle, D., 2000).
	Multimedia: Wireless devices like Game Boys feature interactive, multimedia games, which can be educational and/or entertaining.	
	Learner control: Users have complete control over their interaction with wireless devices; they can use them whenever and wherever they like.	

Web-Based Training

Web-based training (WBT), also known as e-learning and on-line learning, is training that resides on a server or host computer that is connected to the World Wide Web (WWW). Employees can use WBT with any computer with Web access and a browser program, such as Netscape or Internet Explorer. Like CD-ROMs and DVDs, Web-based training can feature text, graphics, audio, video, and animation. At its best, WBT is interactive, both individualized and communal, and offers authentic, challenging opportunities for practice and assessment.

Web-based training is appealing because it offers features unmatched by any other medium. Materials that reside on the Web can be updated quickly and cheaply. They can be delivered anytime, any place, to people all over the world, no matter the time zone. Much to the delight of many employers, many on-line training programs track trainees' progress, persistence, and performance in astonishing detail. In addition to presenting ideas, examples, and cases, on-line training may engage participants via e-mail, chat rooms, knowledge bases, and discussion forums, offering opportunities to establish communities of practice that transcend geographical and even organizational boundaries.

E-learning enables access to all of the resources that reside on the larger World Wide Web as well as those on an organizational Intranet, including information, directions, tutorials, policies, expert advice, databases of best practices and lessons learned, an encyclopedia, and dazzling graphic illustrations. In Chapter Seven, we will tout a big-tent definition for e-learning, one that encompasses training, reference, information, and support tools. Table 6.8 shows features of Web-based training.

Technology-Based Training in a Hurry

How can busy training professionals get up to speed on technology-based training? Table 6.9 contains resources for professionals to go further with this topic — whether they have an hour, a day, or a week.

TABLE 6.8. WEB-BASED TRAINING.

Technology	Pros	Cons
E-learning	*Cost effective:* When the technological infrastructure already exists, on-line training is cost effective. It also saves on travel and distribution costs, as well as instructor fees.	*Sluggishness:* On-line training that features graphics, audio, video, or animation downloads slowly for all but the fastest connections.
	Convenient: Training is delivered to the desktop and can be completed at home, at work, or wherever employees have access to a computer and a connection to the Internet or intranet.	*Expense:* The initial costs of developing on-line training can be high, as are maintenance costs. Providing universal access to computers and connections to the Internet or intranets is also expensive. Intranets are costly to develop and maintain.
	Richness: On-line training may feature text, graphics, audio, video, and/or animation.	*Nonintuitive:* On-line training requires specialized skills to design and develop, and basic computer skills to access and complete.
	Interactive: Trainees can take tests, receive feedback and matched tracking, complete exercises, respond to challenging, realistic scenarios, and monitor their own progress.	*Unsystematic:* Reliance upon portals or on-line programs can distract from organizational systems. Once contracted to provide WBT, how will the organization support it and further messages?
	Engaging: At its best, on-line training can make you smile or even laugh out loud.	*Not invented here:* Much of what people are learning on-line is produced outside the organization. Does it reflect key messages? Will it attract support from supervisors? Is it WBT tailored to the context?
	Updatable: A huge plus. Easily updated and disseminated.	
	Accuracy: On-line training is accurate and up-to-date when it is regularly scrutinized and maintained.	

TABLE 6.9. RESOURCES.

Time	Resources
"I have an hour"	Web-based training information center. A great place to learn about Web-based training, on-line learning, or distance education. Featuring discussions, resources, surveys and a WBT primer. http://www.filename.com/wbt/index.html
	Inside Technology Training. Read the latest issue on-line, join a discussion forum, or subscribe to this very readable magazine. Articles by notables like Brandon Hall. http://www.ittrain.com/
	The Technology Source. Features cutting-edge articles on integrating technology and teaching in organizations. http://horizon.unc.edu/TS/
	Visit the American Museum of the Moving Image at http://www.ammi .org, a gorgeous site that uses motion to illustrate complex concepts.
"I have a day"	Join the Association for Educational Communications and Technology (AECT). Brings together professionals who are interested in instructional technology. http://www.aect.org:80/
	The Masie Center: The learning and technology think tank. Features articles and resources, and the TechLearn bookstore. http://www.masie.com
	The Journal of Technology Education provides a forum for scholarly discussion on topics relating to technology education. Complete issues on-line, dating back to 1989. http://scholar.lib.vt.edu/ejournals/JTE/about_jte.html
	Read Marc Rosenberg's new book, *E-Learning: Strategies for Delivering Knowledge in a Digital Age.* McGraw-Hill, 2001.
	Take a look at www.Lguide.com, a portal that provides reviews on WBT products.
"I have a week"	Attend ONLINE LEARNING, Lakewood Publishing's technology conference. Check out ASTD's technology conference. Also, don't miss www.influent.com, another source for technology training and conferences.
	Consider joining Computer Using Educators (CUE), a national association for educators who use technology in schools, http://www.cue.org/
	Read back issues of *Training* and *Training & Development* devoted to learning technologies.

Spotlight on People

Carla Fantozzi

Carla Fantozzi joined the Museum of Television and Radio in July 1996 as the education manager coordinating school and family programs. She is currently deputy director of the museum. For the previous eleven years, Fantozzi was on the staff of the City of Los Angeles Cultural Affairs Department as museum education director at Barnsdall Art Park and later as the manager of the Office of Youth Arts and Education. One of her current activities is a distance learning project that brings the museum's education classes to students across the United States.

Videoconferencing Fantozzi had several great reasons for being excited about videoconferencing:

Reach Distant Audiences She said: "Our collection has traditionally been accessible only on-site. Now, with this technology, we can present our collection and programs to students and teachers around the country. This enables us to broaden our audience and offer our unique programs to many more students and teachers than we would otherwise be able to do."

Acting on Teachable Moments Fantozzi said that with a collection of over 100,000 programs, the museum has developed a unique approach to the analysis and critical study of radio and television, one that allows the staff to teach to almost any curriculum area. They do this by selecting a subject, then developing classes that demonstrate the impact that television or radio has had in that specific area.

She explained that she and her colleagues in the museum's education department tend to "focus our efforts on those areas where television or radio has had the greatest impact. For example, we look at the Civil Rights Movement . . . and reflect on the significant role television played in accelerating the movement by broadcasting injustices against African-Americans in the south to millions of households across the country."

Fantozzi believes that because educators can connect with the museum precisely when they are teaching a particular unit such as civil rights, they "can act on teachable moments in a more spontaneous and direct way."

Making Connections with Other Content Providers Fantozzi pointed out that videoconferencing also "fosters collaborations between collections and content providers." For example, classes studying civil rights can not only connect with the museum, but can later connect with "the Civil Rights Museum in Birmingham, Alabama, or meet with one of a number of civil rights leaders."

First-Hand Experiences with Experts Expert presentations are one of the most exciting opportunities presented by video conferencing, in Fantozzi's opinion. She said, "Meeting an astronaut or scientist from NASA can be a moving as well as informative experience. Students don't have to leave their classroom, take buses, or just read about people or ideas—they can have first-hand experiences with what they are studying. Videoconferencing brings the experts into the classroom."

Using Videoconferencing to Teach and Train
Fantozzi said, "Connecting with content providers is just one way videoconferencing is enhancing education today. Videoconferencing is also a great educational tool when connecting classroom to classroom or teacher to teacher. The intimate environment of a videoconference allows students and teachers from different areas of the world, country, state, or town to come together; students can share projects, make presentations to each other, and gather/collect information for each other; and teachers can model teaching practices and plan and develop joint programs, et cetera."

Vivid Examples
Fantozzi was happy to provide some vivid examples. She said, "Among the hundreds of videoconferences that the museum has conducted in the last three years, two programs stand out for me as exemplifying the power and potential of videoconferencing as a teaching tool.

"In February of 1999, the museum presented our most popular Black History Month program, the 'Civil Rights Movement and Television,' to two classrooms, sixth graders from PS 183 in Brooklyn, New York, and eighth graders from Castaic Middle School in San Diego, California. We came together to explore the roles television played in the Civil Rights Movement.

"What was most exciting was the communication between the two classrooms. By the end of the videoconference, the students were asking questions of each other, discussing the issues presented in the program; and the eighth graders even showed a video of their school for the students in Brooklyn. Not only were the students and teachers taking advantage of a teachable moment, but the students were connecting with each other, an all too rare occurrence today."

She continued, "Another exciting program was when a teacher on the listserv asked if there was anyone who could teach animation to her third graders in Erie, Pennsylvania. The museum offered to develop a special program for her that integrated an existing museum animation class with an expert presentation by Van Partible, the creator of the cartoon series *Johnny Bravo*. Mr. Partible, a good friend to the museum, offered to come in and meet with the students. The videoconference was broken down into three segments: viewing and discussing clips, question and answer with the artist, and drawing heroes.

"The students had prepared questions for Mr. Partible, and they quickly learned the steps of how a cartoon is made. But the most exciting part of the program was when the students took out their sketch pads and began drawing. In his discussion Mr. Partible explained how to develop a hero for a cartoon series, exaggerating features, et cetera. The students drew and, using a document camera, shared their drawings with Mr. Partible. Mr. Partible quickly re-sketched their drawing and showed them how to exaggerate features, et cetera. The students were thrilled! And all of Mr. Partible's sketches were sent to the students by mail."

The Power of Videoconferencing We asked Fantozzi what videoconferencing can do that other technologies cannot. She said, "Videoconferencing allows for intimate and personalized teaching and immediate communication between groups and content providers. It also allows presenters to test comprehension on the spot with questions, and to encourage group interaction by doing group presentations."

Drawbacks to Videoconferencing Fantozzi said that the main drawback is the tendency for teachers to become "talking heads." She explained, "As an instructor, it is sometimes just easier to keep talking than to engage students and teachers in a discussion. One of the ways that I have ensured that the museum instructors don't fall into this trap is to develop classroom management strategies that encourage all students to speak up during a videoconference." Fantozzi and her staff encourage participation by providing classes with subject-matter outlines and questions to think about before videoconferences and group activities to complete during the sessions. The materials serve two functions: they let students know that they are expected to participate, and they make it easier for them to contribute because they are already familiar with the material.

Fantozzi said that the other major drawback to videoconferencing is the technology itself. She said that the transmission technology is changing, fueling an ongoing discussion among school technology directors about "what will be the next/best delivery system for videoconferencing." She said that the museum is excited about the changes that technology will bring, including streaming video and wider bandwidth, but in the meantime, "We are experimenting and perfecting content for whatever the next delivery system will be."

Recommended Resources Fantozzi said that, although books and articles about videoconferencing are available, the best thing to do is to just talk to people who are already doing it. She explained, "Videoconferencing is so new that all presenters are learning, developing content and presentation formats. Everyone is willing to share successes and failures."

She said that the Videoconferencing Collaboration Collage (www.kn.pacbell .com/wired/vidconf/ed1vidconf) hosted by Pacific Bell's Knowledge Network Explorer, is the "most useful tool we have as we develop content," and she suggested that people visit the site.

Barry Shelton

Barry Shelton has worked in the wireless industry since May 1998, when he designed the initial server infrastructure for Qualcomm, for what later became Wireless Knowledge, a separate, joint venture between Qualcomm and Microsoft. Wireless Knowledge provides wireless carrier neutral and airlink neutral applications for wireless devices of all types. Shelton is currently the vice president of operations and oversees the quality assurance, IT, systems engineering, technical support, and technical documentation groups and also serve as patent counsel for Wireless Knowledge.

Excitement About Wireless Technology Shelton said that after years of unfulfilled promises, wireless data networks are finally materializing, and wireless carriers have learned what subscribers are willing to pay "dearly" for wirelessly enabled enterprise applications and not for sports scores and weather. He explained, "The ability to access corporate data in real time from outside the office extends that information in a powerful way. The common example of this new paradigm is a mobilized sales force that can keep up with the office while they're in the field selling." In this way, wireless technology allows employees to "reap the benefits of both environments."

Shelton said that this is why wireless devices from data browser phones to Palm Pilots to Microsoft Windows CE and Pocket PCs are becoming so popular. He believes that the introduction of third-generation (3G) networks represents the next evolutionary stage of wireless devices. These networks will "foster streaming multimedia capability, greatly enriching the content viewable on wireless devices. Moreover, advances in wireless device processors and memory will make the devices faster and capable of more sophisticated operation."

What Wireless Can Do Shelton said that the clear advantage that wireless has over other technologies is mobility, or the fact that it frees users from the confines of the office or the home. Another advantage of wireless devices is flexibility. He explained, "Cellular and digital phones have become ubiquitous in our society; wireless technology makes it possible to use the same phone . . . to trade stocks, check e-mail, and order flowers.

"Historically, wireless networks were slow and suffered from high latency [network delay] compared to terrestrial or wired networks. Advances in digital wireless networks and breakthroughs in 3G airlinks will largely negate those deficiencies."

Drawbacks to Wireless Shelton said that wireless technology is improving every day, but admitted that there are still some kinks to be worked out. He explained, "Like any wireless system, wireless data networks are dependent on adequate reception of a radio signal. As any mobile phone user knows too well, dropped calls are as much a part of the experience as any other facet. Understandably, users expect widespread data network coverage, minimum latency, high throughput, and high availability. Just as in the early days of both AMPS and digital voice networks, conditions improve on a weekly basis, but for some users the pace is not fast enough."

Shelton said that security is also a major drawback to wireless technology, but not for the reasons that most people believe. He explained, "Perhaps the single greatest threat to wireless data adoption is the perception that data sent over the air is naturally susceptible to eavesdroppers. While it is true enough that the very nature of wireless data networks allows unintended receivers to receive the signal easily, there are hurdles that an eavesdropper has to overcome.

"First, depending on the wireless standard, it requires considerable sophistication to decode the signal received. CDMA, for example, has 4.4 trillion codes that it chooses from to encode each individual session or conversation. The requests and responses that are encoded are typically previously encrypted with a higher layer security protocol, which might require years to decrypt, depending on the power and number of computers able to be put to the task.

"Then, presuming that the signal is decoded and then decrypted, the original requests and responses have to be analyzed to determine the content. So it is commercially impracticable to break the security of a wireless data session, yet the perception that it is an insecure medium persists nonetheless."

The Power of Wireless Technology We asked Shelton to describe the benefits of wireless technology to organizations. He said, "Reduced cost of doing business and a greater ability to communicate with a distributed workforce." He explained, "At Wireless Knowledge, employees are able to access their e-mail, contacts, and calendar information from anywhere within the corporate headquarters or without. It is common for employees to be alerted to high-priority e-mail or calendar changes wirelessly, and without voice calls. Gone are the days of being out of touch because you aren't sitting at your desk."

Benefits for Employees Shelton said that wireless technology benefits employees because it frees them from being tied to a traditional office. He explained, "In the past, being out of the office for any reason meant being cut off from what was going on. Now, with wireless data capabilities, employees are plugged in to what is happening, regardless of their physical location. It is an especially important advantage for employees who travel frequently or otherwise spend significant amounts of time out in the field. With wireless data applications, these employees are as connected to the pulse of the organization as someone physically located within the building, indeed maybe more so. It has often been said in the last few decades that our workforce is transitioning from predominantly service-based to one characterized mainly by information handling. Whether this is true or not, it seems clear that well-informed employees are happier and more productive as a result."

Recommended Resources Shelton said that there are surprisingly few books and magazines on wireless data networks and their market impact, but "there are a number of magazines like *Wireless World* and many Web-based wireless periodicals out there. The Wireless Application Protocol (WAP) Forum is an international industry-based consortium that would be a good place to start, particularly for the more technical aspects of wireless data architectures, found at www.wapforum.org. This year's PC Expo actually had much more to do with wireless data devices than PCs, a first. The largest wireless data show in the United States is CTIA (Computer Telephony Industry Association), which is held in the spring."

Bob Hoffman

Bob Hoffman is an associate professor of educational technology at San Diego State University. He teaches educational multimedia design and development, including workshops in reusable learning objects, learning management systems, sub-laptop mobile computing devices, and educational video development. His research is in educational applications of virtual reality and interactive multimedia. Current grant projects include a CD-ROM virtual reality California mission for the National Endowment for the Humanities and a digital culture resource for the U.S.-Japan Friendship Commission in Washington, D.C.

Exciting Aspects of Technology Hoffman said that he's excited about technology for communication and transportation. He explained, "By communication I mean that the new media, including e-mail, the Web, video and audio conferencing, electronic forums, and all the rest that facilitate people communicating with one another. Education is a communal process. Even those who claim to be largely 'self-taught' almost always read books written by others or follow models built by others.

"In any case, most effective educational approaches involve teaching and learning, communication between teacher and students, among students, or between students and content experts. The new media broaden the pool of both students and content experts; they help bridge barriers of time and space; they support additional styles of communication and, therefore, learning."

He continued, "Transportation means movement from one place to another. New modes such as multimedia and virtual reality bring exotic or specialized environments closer to students in support of higher fidelity representation, more frequent and realistic practice and feedback, and more authentic assessment."

Technology and Teaching We asked Hoffman to provide a vivid example of how technology can be used to teach or train, and he described a recent project that he developed with graduate students at San Diego State University. He said, "In the Mystery of the Mission Museum [www.mystery.sdsu.edu], fourth-grade students practice to serve as docents in a CD-ROM virtual reality California mission. They learn about and develop authentic characters, reconstruct relationships among Spanish padres and soldiers and Native Americans, and interpret daily life in their presentations and reenactments. They research authentic sources and process what they learn by writing, drawing, and presenting their findings."

Drawbacks of Technology Hoffman said that a major drawback of technology is that most are not designed specifically for learning, but instead begin with designs based on commercial needs, such as facilitating communication and transportation (as described above). In spite of this, Hoffman said that new technologies, including personal data assistants, global positioning satellites, and wireless Web, often lend themselves to educational applications. He said that "the drawback is that it takes extra effort to figure out how to turn these new technologies to educational purposes."

Hoffman added that he believes that technology *never* gets in the way of learning, but that the poor use of technology, including "drill and kill" and unstable technology, does. He concluded, "But [when technology is] properly used for communication and transportation, how can that be bad?"

Enriched Learning Experiences Hoffman pointed to the mission museum project again as an example of how technology enriches learning experiences. Yet when it comes to cutting-edge technologies such as wireless, he said: "Who knows? We're just beginning to experiment. But ideas that are floating around involve delivering job aids in the field at the instant needed, using wireless to feed data to a remote brain and receive appropriate, customized feedback, directions, or heuristics, and to provide simulation 'in-box' data for learners in real environments instead of virtual ones." In other words, the possibilities for using wireless to enrich learning experiences are plentiful and exciting at this point in time.

Recommended Resources We asked Hoffman what resources he would recommend for someone who wants to get up to speed on wireless technology in a hurry, and he said that the best are on the Web right now: Phone.com (www.phone.com/index) and Anywhere you go.com (www.AnywhereYouGo.com/ayg/ayg/Index.po?).

Resources

Colvin Clark, R. (1994). *Developing technical training.* Phoenix, AZ: Performance Technology Press.

Desmarais, N. (1997). Innovations affecting us: Technology to learn anytime, anywhere. *Against the Grain, 9*(4), 84–91

Driscoll, M., & Alexander, L. (1998). *Web-based training: Using technology to design adult learning experiences.* San Francisco: Jossey-Bass.

Espinoza, S., & Zhang, Y. (1998). Relationships among computer self-efficacy, attitudes toward computers, and desirability of learning computing skills. *Journal of Research on Computing in Education, 30*(4).

Glennan, T.K.A.M. (1996). *Fostering the use of educational technology: Elements of a national strategy.* Santa Monica, CA: Rand Institute.

Jonassen, D. H. (1996). *Handbook of research for educational communications and technology.* New York: Simon & Schuster.

March, T. (1996). Working the web for education: Theory and practice on integrating the web for learning. Retrieved March 30, 1999, from the World Wide Web: www.nwlink.com/~donclark/hrd/glossary.

McGeehan, P. (2000, August 17). Technology briefing: E-commerce; Merrill shutting shopping sites. *The New York Times,* Business/Financial desk.

Moore, M. G., & Kearsley, G. (1996). *Distance education.* Belmont, CA.: Wadsworth.

Pringle, D. (2000). WAP standard runs into trouble with incompatible technologies. Retrieved May 15, 2000, from the World Wide Web: www.interactive.wsj.com/articles/SB957807830719193619.htm).

Rosenberg, M. (2001) *E-learning: Strategies for delivering knowledge in a digital age.* New York: McGraw-Hill.

Web-based training boom ahead (1999, August). *Training, 36*(8),16.

CHAPTER SEVEN

WHAT ABOUT THE WEB?

Rudy: Myron just told me that 50 percent of our compliance training needs to be on-line by December. How are we going to do that?

Ella: You know why he's pushing us there, don't you? There's big executive pressure to move to e-learning. What concerns me is that all this hurry is keeping us from making judicious decisions about how and when.

Rudy: Yes, I heard that one company is mandating a move of 80 percent of what they do to e-learning. Which 20 percent won't go? Why? Why 80 percent, not 75 percent or 90 percent? Whole classes or just parts?

Ella: I can see why there's excitement, sure. The Web is not any one medium. It delivers many media. And you can find what you need when you want it. Just last week, we wanted to find some options to help our people learn a new software package. We looked at www.lguide.com. In ten minutes, I found several options and credible reviews. Oh, we'll review the programs ourselves, of course, but it's a start. The Web helped us there—and fast.

Defining Web-Based Training

Web-based training is any training that is delivered partially or entirely through the World Wide Web.

"The Internet is the single most important development since the IBM PC"
[Bill Gates, Microsoft internal memo, 1995].

Like the PC before it, the World Wide Web is revolutionizing modern business—and along with it, the business of training and development. How so? What are the possibilities? What are the realities? Where should we exercise caution? We introduced the Web in Table 6.8. Now, let's use some of the concepts from Chapter One to look at the Web for learning and performance improvement.

A Place for Individual Memory

Training professionals know how important it is to monitor individual progress in light of some shared standards. The Web offers a great leap forward in this area. What skills have been acquired? What goals remain unmet? How has a particular employee or group done at mastering a domain? Where do needs reside?

Saba (www.saba.com) and Click2Learn's Ingenium are two examples of learning management systems (LMS). With Saba, learning infrastructure is the heart of the business. Ingenium is a key aspect of the many things that Click2Learn (www.click2learn.com) brings to the marketplace. The growth of these two companies and others, such as Docent, signal the importance of tracking individual progress. Even enterprise management system SAP is establishing a learning management system.

A Place for Organizational Memory

"If HP only knew what HP knows." That quote, attributed to David Packard, articulates the case for organizational memory and the concern about how much organizational wisdom and knowledge is frittered away. Enter the Web, knowledge management, and database technology.

The emergence of the knowledge worker attracts attention to what employees know and on how to collect, stir, store, and refresh that knowledge. The effort to do this is known as *knowledge management* (KM), a strategy to make best practices and ideas widely available. While training is an event scheduled for a single place or date, KM is a system that permeates the organization. The goal is to get the right knowledge to the right people at the right time through organizational policies, technologies, and tools. Chapter Nine is devoted to KM and training.

Even though KM's most obvious contributions are as a rich repository of organizational lessons and materials, it also provides new ways of approaching employee development and performance support. A small initiative at San Diego State University provides an example. Two new faculty members joined the Department of Educational Technology in August 2000. One challenge that would surely vex them was time management. We could, of course, have sent them to a time management class. But KM offered another approach that would yield resources of interest to junior faculty in the future. Graduate students Barbara Gruber and Simine Dadgar collected time management ideas, examples, and anecdotes from current faculty members and housed them in a database structured by the new professors' likely concerns and questions about managing time. Worried about e-mail? See how four faculty members handle it. Pondering alternatives for how to approach office hours? Five faculty members have ideas about that challenge.

Will formal training be needed for the new faculty members? Perhaps. What is certain is that the new faculty members possess an on-line resource tailored to the mundane issues that will try their patience and waste their time. And it couldn't happen without the Web.

Lifelong and Independent Learning

E-learning enables lifelong learning. If an employee wants to learn a new skill, become more familiar with a country or culture, pursue a hobby, or keep abreast of trends, the Web provides rich options that by-

E-learning enables lifelong learning.   pass inconvenient, unresponsive, or geographically undesirable training schedules.

For example, one Argentinean professional recognized that he was behind when it came to e-commerce. Although his global company offered courses in that area, he wanted to make progress on his own before he attended class. He went on-line and for $7.95 U.S., he got a head start on the topic from ElementK (www.Elementk.com).

The opportunities, of course, do not stop with development associated with employment. The American Association for Retired Persons (AARP) provides modules to help seniors get up to speed on the Internet, for example, at www.aarp .org/expedition/mod01_0.

Instant Updates and Distribution

An appealing benefit of the Web is that on-line training and support can be updated and distributed quickly and easily. No more wondering and worrying about whether employees are using the most current information. No more concerns about whether the three-ring binders have been updated to reflect the newest systems and prices. At one pharmaceutical firm, for example, when government regulations change, as they are wont to do, materials are updated online. Employees concerned about compliance are then notified automatically and electronically. And the company can keep track of the diligence with which individuals scrutinize updates.

This update feature also creates opportunities for another kind of professional, a person Oracle Computers has dubbed a "cybrarian." This is the person who assures that on-line programs, documentation, and knowledge bases reflect relevant and current needs and thinking.

Content Galore

Cybrarians also review, collect, and organize Web resources into on-line libraries and databases on topics as diverse as health, law, veterinary medicine, and public school curriculums.

Blue Web'n, shown in Figure 7.1, is an award-winning collection of excellent education sites on the Web. Updated weekly, this site rates and reviews Websites

FIGURE 7.1. BLUE WEB'N.

of interest to students, teachers, parents, and librarians. The site, www.kn.pacbell .com/wired/bluewebn is organized by subject area and lesson types, such as tutorials, lessons, references and tools, etc.

The American Society for Training and Development's (ASTD) Website, www.astd.org, is a good example of plentiful on-line resources directed at the interests of training and human resource professionals. Imagine that you are tasked with writing your own job description. You might post a question about it to the ASTD Website. Some will respond, yielding an array of useful and not so useful options for how to describe the work.

There is no end to the information available on-line. A search on the Web might lead to an on-line course, a virtual library, an expert on the other side of the world, or a listserv shared by people fascinated with the challenges of supporting call center personnel or caring for pigs as house pets. A search on a corporate intranet might provide sample sales presentations, enabling a busy and mobile sales professional in Peru to tailor an existing presentation made by a colleague in Costa Rica.

Providing Access to Multiple Perspectives

Visitors to on-line learning modules and knowledge bases are exposed to a variety of perspectives and ways of doing things. In contrast to classroom training, where classroom content typically highlights the views of a single instructor or course developer, the Web enables the presentation and contemplation of many views.

An example is the Doctor's Dilemma: Medical Ethics on-line, as seen in Figure 7.2, which presents "cases" that physicians must decide how to handle. As they work on cases that present ethical dilemmas, doctors are exposed to the perspectives of other doctors, a lawyer, a psychologist, and an ethicist, as well as regulations tailored to the particular U.S. state in which they reside. The site parallels the ethical dilemmas confronted by physicians at work, encouraging reflection and research. You can visit the Doctor's Dilemma by going to its parent site, Integrated Medical Curriculum, www.imc.gsm.com, and registering for free.

Accommodating Individual Preferences

For many decades, the training profession has expressed interest in matching learning strategies to individual learner preferences. The Web provides an opportunity to begin to do that because it is a distribution channel for many media, including text, audio, video, and graphics.

The Web example shown in Figure 7.3 illustrates the possibilities. Seattle's Experience Music Project, www.emplive.com, allows maximum choices, as each visitor's experience permits casual browsing or drilling down to prose and visual

FIGURE 7.2. THE DOCTOR'S DILEMMA: MEDICAL ETHICS.

details about American music. Eventually, although certainly not at this time, the browser might learn how you prefer to experience museums or music or math online and tailor subsequent visits to prior choices and performance.

Enabling Vivid Interactive Experiences

While some Web programs include gratuitous graphics and animation, others delight through authentic scenarios, such as the Medical Ethics example in Figure 7.2. In that program, the voice of the patient's wife moves us as she seeks a miracle for her comatose husband.

The University of Colorado's Physics 2000 offers another example of a vivid on-line experience (Figure 7.4). It uses text, graphics, and animation to teach the basics of physics, a subject that has proved challenging for many students. On this

FIGURE 7.3. EXPERIENCE MUSIC PROJECT.

Source: Copyright © 2000 by Experience Music Project. All rights reserved.

FIGURE 7.4. PHYSICS 2000.

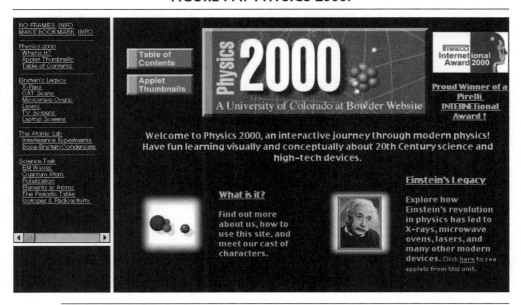

Source: Copyright © 2000, University of Colorado at Boulder. Used by permission.

site, www.Colorado.EDU/physics/2000, abstract concepts, such as evaporative cooling, make sense when they are presented through appealing movies or gorgeous graphics.

Learner Control and Guidance in the Same Place

On-line programs can offer users control over their own experiences, while simultaneously providing guidance for next steps.

An example of this, shown in Figure 7.5, is *First Things Fast: A Handbook for Performance Analysis*, a Web tool (www.jbp.com/rossett) based on the award-winning book of the same name. The site provides a definition of performance analysis, then gives trainees opportunities to apply new knowledge to realistic workplace challenges and conversations. Visitors may elect to follow the guided tour (upper-right column) structured by the authors or to make their own choices via three different navigational menus.

FIGURE 7.5. FIRST THINGS FAST.

Source: Rossett, A. *First Things Fast* Website. Copyright © 1999, Jossey-Bass/Pfeiffer. Reprinted by permission of John Wiley & Sons, Inc.

Networking

The Web enables electronic learning to be continuously convivial. For example, relationships that span the globe are initiated at Accenture's three-week, brick-and-mortar training; they are cemented on-line and often continued throughout long careers.

Other examples are that teachers of English as a second language gather at www.eslcafe.com to share ideas, concerns, and research; new parents are welcomed at www.babycenter.com, where women are linked by their due dates. The Web creates a way to find and feel involvement in communities that have nothing to do with where one lives.

The boundaries that once distinguished between formal and informal learning, classroom and work, instructor and teacher, and novice and veteran are blurred by the Web.

The boundaries that once distinguished between formal and informal learning, classroom and work, instructor and teacher, and novice and veteran are blurred by the Web.

Systems On-Line

The Web makes good sense as a component in a performance system. Let's use a safety training program as an example. Employees targeted for training might first receive an e-mail that defines upcoming instructor-led training. They are then directed to a Website with a site safety checklist so that participants come to class primed to focus on their own work situations. After a class that has focused on site safety challenges, a Web-based conversation focuses on follow-up and follow-through, so that classroom content transfers into a safer environment.

Too Good to Be True

"The Internet, everyone tells us, is an amazing thing. It's a technological marvel with a common touch: a neural network spanning the world on which computers send vast amounts of information to each other, but that any carbon-based life form with a Web browser or an e-mail program can tap into" (Ganzel, 1999, p. 50).

There is no question that the Web holds great promise for training and HR professionals. Is it too good to be true? Perhaps. An issue that must grab our attention is the problem of persistence. The freedom to go on-line to learn or to check out a knowledge base is also the freedom to skip it. Rossett (2000) described herself as a Web dropout—and one you wouldn't anticipate. Motivated to sign up for an investment class, after three of six modules, she quit. The rest of her life was more compelling than the class. Rossett pondered how the Web could hold viewers' attention. Some call this "stickiness," and it is no small matter for training professionals.

Another concern with on-line classes is download time. Before we get too excited about on-line graphics, audio, animation, and video, we need to consider that the letters, "WWW" might just as well stand for World Wide Wait, for users not connected via speedy devices such as cable modems or T-1 or T-3 lines. This is also true for training that is delivered via intranets. For all but the high-speed connections, many big files download slowly and consume disk space once they are transferred. Although the future promises better, such as dynamic HTML and streaming video, speed remains a key concern for professionals who develop or depend on e-learning. Has your organization committed to a shared, global, and appropriate technology platform? We've been surprised at the organizations who are excited about the Web for learning and performance support, but not willing to allocate necessary resources.

Iplanet's Marty Murillo noted that we too often forget the significant costs associated with infrastructure and maintenance. The tradition in training departments is to determine the costs of development without focusing on what is to come. When on-line learning and support are involved, this becomes particularly painful because the best maintenance and content updating should be done very close to where the work gets done. That means significant organizational collaboration and alignment.

Still another critical issue is that the Web is bursting at the seams with unappealing content. Many sites resemble junk mail. While there are many fine Websites, including those cited earlier in this chapter, they are currently the exception, not the rule.

Web-based training and knowledge bases are so new that "best practices" are still emerging. Currently, there is a tendency to put existing materials and classes on-line without adapting them for the Web. According to Hall (1997), because of this reliance on legacy CBT, some will spend hours reading from a computer screen, with interactivity limited to clicking a mouse or scrolling down a page.

A review of a corporate sales Website provided an example of the heavy burden that legacy courses place on Web training. The developers had conceived an on-line system to serve as both training and support, available as needed by salespeople and offering classes, databases, and job aids. When we looked more closely at the on-line classes, however, we found that the test item questions were derived directly from the older CBT; thus they assumed that the user was expected to memorize the information. Testing more appropriate to the possibilities afforded by the Web would have asked the salesperson to use the site and its rich resources as references, supporting him as he attempted to answer. Instead, the prior model lingered, pressing salespeople to regurgitate a memorized answer about parts and compatible peripherals.

Web-based training, like its classroom kin, is too often subject-matter and information driven, rather than focused on the functional needs of participants. Other drawbacks include the risk of cognitive overload, as trainees tend to get lost and distracted in cyberspace, digress by following an interesting link, or aimlessly wander the Web, like visitors to an art museum whose visit is pleasurable rather than purposeful.

Table 7.1 catalogues lingering concerns about the Web for training and performance improvement. Consider these concerns prior to allowing enthusiasm for the Web to distract you from good sense and planful design and execution.

How the Web Changes What We Do

One of the authors visited a large global consulting firm to talk about the impact of the Web on the way we do our work. The purpose was to discuss the contributions that the Web might make to training and development people and the units they serve. Look back at Table 1.3 in Chapter One and use it to consider the possibilities.

From Developer to Broker. The Web enables the creation of a system that envelops the employee, one that potentially serves up instruction, information, decision support, performance support, knowledge bases, and performance tracking. Development and maintenance of these elements is not for the faint of heart. Can you author? Should you author? Do you have a preference for XML or HTML? For Dreamweaver? For Toolbook II? For Flash? Can you call on experts in these areas? Can you discern critical from gratuitous graphical elements? Can you keep your eye on strategic purposes while juggling technical details? Many internal training professionals will find themselves working with producers, vendors, and portals, serving as a broker between line organizations and external resources, all in an attempt to tailor offerings and achieve cost efficiencies.

From Deliverer to Consultant. The talk about the shift from training to performance consultant may finally come to fruition because of the Web. Portals like Smartforce, Learn2.com, ElementK, and Click2Learn present rich options for lessons about software, hardware, business, and interpersonal skills. Skillsoft, NetG, Ninth House, and PlaybackMedia, for example, have worked hard to produce content that tackles thorny challenges presented by soft skills development. But who among us believes that an on-line product, any more than an isolated class,

TABLE 7.1. CONCERNS ABOUT WEB-BASED TRAINING.

Concern	Discussion
Lack of individual persistence	The freedom to choose the Web is also the freedom to depart or to pay perfunctory attention. Hits on a Website do not guarantee quality engagement with the material, of course.
Is anything happening?	Some training professionals wonder how they can measure learning when training is Web-based. For example, Sexual Harassment in the Workplace (www.sexualharass .com) includes a quiz, but the scores are not saved. The training director who points an employee to this site has no way of knowing if the material "stuck." Learning-management systems, such as Saba and Ingenium, respond to this concern.
Vendor compatibility	Web-based training is so new that there is little agreement as to which systems, software, platforms, and vendors are best. The result is that some prefer Softskills classes, while others like Playback Media and still others prefer Element K products or NetG. Consider the challenge to a large company when employees elect to learn from so many and varied products.
Vendor tyranny	Outside vendors, such as NetG, Gartner Group, CBT Systems, Digitalthink, and many, many others, are having a large say in what employees learn. The dilemma is that organizations can only buy what vendors have created, materials not typically tailored for individual settings. This represents a worrisome shift away from customized, tailored training and toward a generic, "one size fits all."
"Just give me the answer. I've got no time for a class."	The Web encourages the human tendency to favor a quick fix over the effort involved in understanding the subject.
Everyone is an expert	The World Wide Web is very democratic, as all opinions and options appear equal and accurate. A lab tech from Boise or Bangledesh can put a brain-surgery class on-line. How will users assure accuracy and currency?
Promises, promises	The First Amendment rules on the Web, resulting in Websites that make extraordinary promises. For example, www.realeducation.com promises to create a campus and courses in just sixty days!
There is a pile of inaccurate stuff on-line.	The very richness and democracy of the Web leads to valid concerns about junk on-line. See www.fathom.com and www.epinions.com for strategies to add authentication to materials that appear on-line.

will transfer to performance—without aligned organizational systems? This effort, the fertilization, matching of opportunities to needs, and follow-up and follow-through, is critical work for the professional.

More Measurement. The Web makes it easier to know who is doing what. Earlier in this chapter, we talked about Ingenium, Docent, and Saba. Obviously, they make it possible to keep track of individual progress. Without committing to any particular LMS, there are many "hit-tracking" systems that can give a training professional a sense of what employees are up to, where they visit, how long they linger, if they return, and where they go from the site. This insight into employees' choices is potentially rich. Haven't you often wondered what was going on inside employees during a class, whether they're thinking about the class or lunch, if they'd choose to be there if they could find a way out the door? Web tracking, available from organizations such as Webside Story, can be helpful in providing measurement and insights. The purpose, of course, is not to violate privacy but rather to use the intelligence to provide better programming.

An Expanded Opportunity to See and Communicate. The Web enables more people to have immediate and continuous access to information. Supervisors can scrutinize what their employees select. Executives can examine sign up, completion, and persistence patterns. Employees can review customer satisfaction data or sales data as it happens, influencing their choices about what to study, examine, and improve. Sponsors can make choices about the allocation of resources after reviewing on-line feedback from students and their supervisors. There is much more transparency now for employees and leaders, and there are opportunities to wrap messages and meaning around the data.

More Development for Some. Although most training professionals won't find themselves developing Web programs, some will, particularly for proprietary internal material or when they are employed by Web content developers such as NetG and ElementK. What's most interesting is that the nature of the Web programs is expanding, parallel with a grander and more strategic view of our business. We'll see on-line materials that teach, coach, collaborate, nudge, and inform. The fleet-footed developer will produce "objects" that can be repurposed as lessons, practices, examples, customer support materials, and even job aids. These topics are treated in greater detail in Chapters Nine and Ten.

A Seer of the Future. Unlike instructor-led training, which can be modified on the fly when the instructor perceives blank stares, Web training today is notoriously immutable during instruction. That makes planning even more important.

The savvy Web developer must see into the future, into the skills, interests, and concerns of users who might come from organizations and cultures very different from her own.

Parallel Programs. Every training professional has a story to tell about supervisory resistance, about great programs that were wasted because managers failed to second the messages taught in class or on-line. Here is our opportunity to build for both audiences, for supervisors and job incumbents, with prior and follow-up modules making certain that lessons learned do in fact transfer to the workplace.

Objections and Counters

Table 7.2 lists some concerns from the training and performance improvement community. We also present strategies for responding to these objections when they come from others—or even from ourselves.

Screening Strategies for E-Learning Readiness

Although planning is an important part of any training program, it takes on particular importance for Web training. Why? So much enthusiasm, so little prudence! As Ella said at the start of the chapter,

So much enthusiasm, so little prudence! "What concerns me is that all this enthusiasm is pushing us away from making judicious decisions about how and when." She could add "why." There is good reason to attempt to temper the exuberance that results in mandates to switch huge hunks of training to the Web.

Are you and your organization ready for Web training? Will your people persist? The questions in Table 7.3 will help you to decide. Another resource is provided by DiamondCluster International's Marc Rosenberg at www.books .mcgraw-hill.com/training/elearning/downloads.html.

E-learning has a big persistence problem, described by Rossett (2000). Even though she sported many positive indicators for e-learning success (solid equipment, reasonably techno-savvy, strong learning-to-learn skills, volunteer student, and selecting her own topic), still she dropped

E-learning has a big persistence problem. out without finishing her on-line class.

Systems are critical, on-line or on terra firma. Leigh Kelleher, Deloitte Consulting partner in charge of their e-learning practice, put it like this, "We've found that you have to tie the completion of the training to some milestone. Some of this 'I'll get to it' mentality changes if your

TABLE 7.2. OBJECTIONS AND COUNTERS.

Concern	Counter
"Why should I embrace e-learning? It could put *me* out of a job!"	As organizations increasingly use technology to deliver training, our traditional roles are changing. For those willing to embrace it, technology represents opportunities for professional growth, as trainers increase their value to organizations by developing new skills and using existing skills in new ways. Some will learn to manage and develop in the new media. Others will focus on assuring individual and organizational readiness to use technology resources. Some will concentrate on measurement.
"Why should I embrace e-learning? It could put *our unit* out of business!"	Might just, especially if we refuse to change. If we perceive ourselves as course developers and deliverers, conventional units are threatened by portals. If we expand our function to work as brokers, in the interface between rich external resources and the organization, then we remain viable, even critical. How can we help tailor existing libraries of on-line resources to be relevant? We must engage with that question.
"Our employees view their annual training as a perk that they don't want to give up. They get to travel, stay in a nice place, and maybe learn something new—how can I persuade them that Web-based training is good for them and for the company?"	Show employees what Web-based training can do for them (help, expert advice at their fingertips, training, information delivered to the desktop when they want or need it, learner control, authentic challenges, practice, and feedback and assessment in private). Talk to management about offering incentives or compensation for the perceived "loss," until Web-based training is firmly established in your organization. Also, *note that the organization need not choose between classrooms and the Web. In most cases, systems that include both make sense.*
"I've seen Web-based training, and it was nothing more than a textbook stuck on-line."	Just as the quality of classroom training varies considerably, so too does Web-based training. And yes, many programs are old CBT that has been ported over without considering the new and numerous possibilities presented by the Web. Identify a concern or topic and look at many on-line examples. Review some of the options presented at http://www.Lguide.com. Outstanding programs can be found, with some effort. Note that much of what makes the training effective is thoughtful instructional design, not "bells and whistles" that dance around the screen.

TABLE 7.3. ARE YOU READY FOR WEB-BASED TRAINING?

Question

Do employees want to know more about the topic?

Can they explain why the topic is important, how it relates to their and the organization's strategic goals?

Do employees have hardware and software that will make access a snap or a tolerable wait?

Can employees explain why this approach to learning is valuable? Can they explain the business case for e-learning?

Have your people previously learned via technology? What happened? How have you adjusted and responded to their experiences?

Are managers and supervisors interested in this topic and in the goals associated with these on-line materials? Have they conveyed their enthusiasm to their employees?

Will employees swiftly experience success? What have you done to make the materials friendly, to make it easy for them to find what they need?

Does the program offer clear guidance about how to use the software, about learning and reference paths? Will it track where they are and where they have been?

If employees have questions about the program, are managers and supervisors prepared to coach?

Will this program boost knowledge, skills, and capacity? Will it also serve as future reference?

Are the knowledge bases and on-line supports, if any, readily accessible and matched with the functional work challenges?

Has the program been updated?

Are resources allocated to assure that the program will be updated?

How will the organization track and recognize participation, persistence, and performance? What will happen if an employee drops out, fails to complete, or doesn't refer to tools and on-line resources? What is the carrot for completion?

---

bonus doesn't come 'til you complete the course, or you can't get promoted, et cetera. . . . The biggest issue is that people can't allocate quiet time to do the learning, and sometimes it's environmental issues beyond their control."

Kelleher continued, "This is one of the 'cultural' issues we address in our consulting. We're starting in some cases to have people move in their office to a learning lab where they can 'escape' the regular office environment and not get interrupted by their boss, the phone, et cetera. . . . They still don't have to travel for their classes, but they are out of their normal environment. When you are in that protected area, it's like being in a library—it means 'Quiet, I'm working.'"

Web-Based Training in a Hurry

How can busy training professionals get up to speed on Web-based training? Table 7.4 contains resources for professionals to go further with this topic—whether they have an hour, a day, or a week.

TABLE 7.4. RESOURCES.

Time	Resources
"I have an hour"	Visit the Web-Based Training Information Center. A great place to learn about Web-based training, on-line learning, or distance education. Featuring discussions, resources, surveys, and a WBT primer. http://www.filename.com/wbt/index.html
	Inside Technology Training. Read the latest issue on-line, join a discussion forum, or subscribe to this very readable magazine. Articles by notables such as Brandon Hall. http://www.ittrain.com/
	The Technology Source. Features cutting-edge articles on integrating technology and teaching in organizations. http://horizon.unc.edu/TS/
"I have a day"	Join the Association for Educational Communications and Technology. Brings together professionals who are interested in instructional technology. http://www.aect.org:80/AECT.htm
	The Masie Center: The learning and technology think tank. Features articles and resources, and the TechLearn bookstore. http://www.masie.com
	The Journal of Technology Education provides a forum for scholarly discussion on topics relating to technology education. Complete issues on-line, dating back to 1989. http://scholar.lib.vt.edu/ejournals/JTE/about_jte.html
"I have a week"	An excellent starting point for anyone who is interested in Web-based training is B. Hall's (1997) *The Web-based Training Cookbook.* New York: Wiley Computer Publishing.
	Attend ONLINE LEARNING, Lakewood Publishing's technology conference at www.billcom.com.
	Consider Computer Using Educators (CUE), a national association for educators who use technology in schools, http://www.cue.org/
	Best new book: M. J. Rosenberg's *E-Learning: Strategies for Delivering Knowledge in the Digital Age,* New York: MacMillan.

Spotlight on People

Marc Rosenberg

Marc Rosenberg is a senior principal at DiamondCluster International, Inc., and the distinguished author of many influential articles and a new book, *E-Learning: Strategies for Delivering Knowledge in the Digital Age* (McGraw-Hill, 2001). Rosenberg advises companies on knowledge management and building a sustainable digital learning strategy.

Web-Based Training Rosenberg said that his clients are asking about e-learning, and no wonder. Web-based training is "changing the whole paradigm of learning" because content can be delivered and updated instantly.

Ready— Or Not? How can training professionals decide whether Web-based training is right for their organizations? Rosenberg suggested they consider several variables: "First, examine the culture of the organization. Is there evidence that they will support an innovative solution? High-level support is critical to the success of any initiative, particularly one that is potentially costly."

Rosenberg said that another important consideration is the existing corporate infrastructure. Do employees have computers and Internet access? Do computers already play an important role in the business? If so, Web-based training should be considered.

Perhaps the most important consideration is the learners themselves. Rosenberg emphasized that training professionals must consider the audience and ask themselves, "Can they do it? Do they have the skills and resources? Employees who are ready for Web-based training are comfortable with the Web, use it regularly, leave time during their workday to learn and are encouraged to do so." Finally, he noted that they must be self-motivated or really want to learn.

The final consideration, according to Rosenberg, is the content or curriculum. Trainers need to consider learners' entire development path—what they will do during training, from the first day to the last. They should consider different strategies for different curriculum chunks, keeping in mind the bottom line, that is, "What do they need to be able to do?"

Potholes Rosenberg is familiar with obstacles that Web-based training initiatives face. He noted, for example, that many managers prefer to send employees away to training, one reason that a supportive atmosphere is so important. Another problem is that employees may not see the relevance of Web-based training to their work, but wonder, "Who decided that I need to learn this?" According to Rosenberg, this lack of acceptance could mean that they have been exposed to training that is not pertinent to their work and/or lacks authenticity. One of the other dangers of irrelevant or inaccurate training is that students might actually believe and act on it. Rosenberg describes this type of training as "Garbage in, gospel out."

Sometimes the primary obstacle to Web-based training, according to Rosenberg, is the content itself. While the Web is very good for delivering what Rosenberg called "pre-skill-based content," such as facts and rules, it is less than ideal for teaching some skills. Rosenberg used CPR as an example. Although trainees can learn *about* CPR on the Web, can learn the steps to take in the process, and might even be able to participate in a simulation of the experience of giving CPR, they cannot practice or demonstrate the actual skills, at least not yet. Some skills can only be learned when trainees are exposed to live, authentic experiences and have opportunities to practice those skills under the watchful eye of a good coach or teacher.

Finally, Rosenberg said that, as HR and training professionals, "We often look at the Web as an on-line classroom, and that may be the wrong metaphor . . . a better metaphor is a library." He believes that knowledge and information is available in all forms—from courses to knowledge management to performance support. The key is being able to select the right type of resource for a given learning need. He explained, "This is what libraries do. Search engines are the card catalogs, and Websites are the stacks and shelves." He thinks that a goal of Web-based training should be to teach learners how to find and access information, not memorize it.

Web-Based Training That Works
Rosenberg said that when training professionals think about Web-based training, they need to think about learning, which he defined as "the art and science, process and heuristics of turning information into knowledge, because it should be the focus of any training initiative, not the technology. Training that is effective, which results in real learning, is comprehensive, accurate, and authentic, whether it is on the Web, a CD-ROM, or in a classroom."

Rosenberg described effective Web-based training as training that is "user friendly, not painful. It should also be interactive, but not gratuitously so. Simulations and scenarios should put training in context by realistically representing workplace challenges. Another hallmark is outstanding feedback all the time, which effectively combines feedback with coaching." Simply telling trainees that they are right or wrong, Rosenberg believes, is not enough.

Effective Web-based training also creates an environment in which it is safe to fail. Rosenberg said that one way to do this is to include stories from colleagues who have "been there." Due to the nature of the technology, stories can be added or updated regularly. Expert opinions, heuristics, and examples are also effective in creating the right environment for learning.

Rosenberg said that, once built, effective e-learning still has value because it is reusable and updateable. One way to assure its continuing value is to include resources that learners can use after they have completed training or, as he put it, "Now that you have taken the course, let me show you where to find more information on this." The resources should be original and updated regularly.

Marty Murrillo

Marty Murrillo is currently a sales training manager at iPlanet, the Sun/Netscape Alliance, with worldwide responsibilities for sales improvement solutions, program management, and instructional design. His recent work has centered on Internet delivery and testing, corporate university curriculum design, and certification programs. Murrillo's prior experience includes training, performance consulting, and strategic planning in the medical and high-technology industries.

On-Line Training Murrillo described the ideal corporate environment for on-line learning as one where the technological infrastructure is already in place. In other words, trainees should have ready access to computers and the Internet or an intranet. He said that if the content of the training were stable, then a CD-based CBT would make sense, but if the content is less stable, then WBT may make more financial sense. He also explained that it is often cheaper to deliver training on-line than by other methods. This is true because, typically, the costs of developing on-line training are high, but costs drop dramatically after delivery when compared to instructor-led training.

Good On-Line Training Murrillo was quick to describe the characteristics of good on-line training: "First, it must be engaging and relevant to the learners or they'll choose not to engage with it. Trainees should be able to answer the question, 'What's in it for me?' If they know the answer, they'll be motivated." Murrillo said that good on-line training also outlines course objectives and then presents the content. This allows trainees to set goals for their training, develop realistic expectations, and organize their efforts. Murrillo explained that content should also be "chunked" into segments that take no longer than eight to ten minutes to complete. Murrillo said that e-learning should also include multiple opportunities for practice with feedback, and he added that assessment of new skills and knowledge is critical, as are opportunities for remediation.

Pitfalls Murrillo described the pitfalls of on-line training. Sometimes, he said, it is just too expensive, so other, more affordable delivery methods make more sense. Using an iceberg as an analogy, Murrillo described the cost of on-line training. He said that design, development, and delivery represent about 20 percent of the cost, the tip of the iceberg. The other 80 percent, the unseen base of the iceberg, are the hidden costs of content maintenance, infrastructure, equipment, and content updates.

Other pitfalls include a long cycle time to develop on-line training once a need or opportunity has been identified. On-line training also requires certain expertise with new development tools that many training and HRD professionals may not have yet. Another problem he listed is the high learning curve and discipline associated with on-line training, as some trainees may not have even basic computing skills. Plug-ins can also be a problem, according to Murrillo, if trainees do not have them or do not know how to download and install them. Finally, configuration and compatibility issues (operating systems, platforms, and software) are also potential pitfalls of on-line training.

Lessons Learned As an experienced training professional, Murrillo had advice for those considering on-line training: "First and foremost, know your audience—not just their current knowledge levels, but what systems they are working on. Establish a minimum level of technical specs that you can develop to." He also advised taking a long, hard look at the costs associated with on-line training: "Consider not just the development costs, but also the hidden costs. In addition, a solid instructional design will help ensure your success. Designing for Web training is different than designing for instructor-led. Expect slippage in the development schedule; plan for it."

Murrillo also suggested talking to subject-matter experts (SMEs) in advance, agreeing on how much time they will need, and building it into the schedule: "Have them block out the review time as if it were a scheduled meeting. That way you can count on them and they are clear on the expectation. Other considerations include details like paying attention to the fine print on seat licenses. The key to success is organization, good planning, and being realistic about what it takes to develop an on-line course."

At the Heart of the Matter

The following slides were designed to help training professionals explain and win support for technology-based initiatives.

Slide 7.1

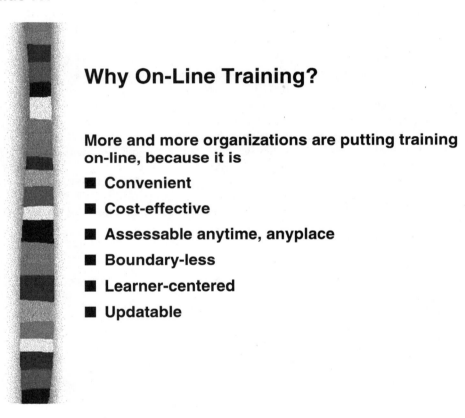

Why On-Line Training?

More and more organizations are putting training on-line, because it is

- **Convenient**
- **Cost-effective**
- **Assessable anytime, anyplace**
- **Boundary-less**
- **Learner-centered**
- **Updatable**

Presenter's Notes

Access to technology, particularly computers, is widespread. This means that many employees can access training anytime, anyplace. They can also complete training at their convenience, at their own pace; revisit training as often as they wish; and practice new skills in private. On-line training can be delivered to employees all over the globe, and can be updated and upgraded quickly and easily. On-line training also reduces or eliminates costs associated with classroom delivery, including travel costs, instructor fees, and the expense of producing print-based materials.

Slide 7.2

Web-Based Training: The Dream

Why are so many training professionals enthusiastic about on-line training?

■ **Speedy access**

■ **Can be presented to match the ways that we think about "it"**

■ **Real situations that resonate**

■ **Rich-data-based**

Presenter's Notes

But that's not all. Web-based training also allows us to do the things we have always wanted to do, such as promoting lifelong learning, delivering learner-centered training, and appealing to employees through many modes. Web-based training also exposes trainees to authentic contexts and reduces geographical distance so that employees can communicate and collaborate with colleagues all over the globe. It also nurtures interactivity and feedback, and facilitates peer and self-assessment. Web-based training exposes trainees to multiple perspectives, rather than just the perspective of a single instructor or instructional designer. What's not to like?

Slide 7.3

Reality Check

On-line training is great, but it's not perfect.

- ■ **Lots of "calories," lack of nutritional content**
- ■ **Cognitive overload**
- ■ **Weak instructional design**
- ■ **Tends to be SM/information driven**
- ■ **Hard to determine what they learned**

Presenter's Notes

With literally millions of Websites in existence and more added every day, worth-while Websites are relatively few and far between. The problem is that anyone can put up a Website and call it training. In cyberspace, democracy rules, and it can be hard to discriminate between the accurate and inaccurate when all opinions appear equal.

Resources

Beer, V. (2000). *The web learning fieldbook*. San Francisco: Jossey-Bass.

Colvin Clark, R. (1994). *Developing technical training*. Phoenix, AZ: Performance Technology Press.

Desmarais, N. (1997). Innovations affecting us: Technology to learn anytime, anywhere. *Against the Grain, 9*(4), 84–91

Driscoll, M., & Alexander, L. (1998). *Web-based training: Using technology to design adult learning experiences*. San Francisco: Jossey-Bass.

Espinoza, S., & Zhang, Y. (1998). Relationships among computer self-efficacy, attitudes toward computers, and desirability of learning computing skills. *Journal of Research on Computing in Education, 30*(4).

Ganzel, R. (1999). What price online learning? *Training, 36*, 50–54.

Glennan, T.K.A.M. (1996). *Fostering the use of educational technology: Elements of a national strategy*. Santa Monica, CA: Rand Institute.

Hall, B. (1997). *The web-based training cookbook*. New York: Wiley Computer Publishing.

Jonassen, D. H. (1996). *Handbook of research for educational communications and technology*. New York: Simon & Schuster.

Khan, B. H. (Ed.). (1997). *Web-based instruction*. Englewood Cliffs, NJ: Educational Technology Publications.

March, T. (1996). Working the web for education: Theory and practice on integrating the web for learning. Retrieved March 30, 1999, from the World Wide Web: www.nwlink.com/~donclark/hrd/glossary.

Moore, M. G., & Kearsley, G. (1996). *Distance education*. Belmont, CA.: Wadsworth.

Rosenberg, M. J. (2001). *e-Learning: Strategies for delivering knowledge in the digital age*. New York: McGraw-Hill.

Rossett, A. (2000, August). Confessions of a web dropout. *Training, 37*(8), 100–99.

Tapscott, D. (1996). The digital economy: Promise and peril in the age of networked intelligence. New York: McGraw-Hill.

Web-based training boom ahead. (1999, August). *Training, 36*(8), 16.

CHAPTER EIGHT

WHAT ABOUT INFORMAL LEARNING?

Raj: Just when our employees get accustomed to a software program, a new version comes out. We can't train them fast enough. Management buys the latest technology, but it's worthless if our folks aren't using it.

Steve: Have you thought about having them learn on their own?

Raj: Sure, but most of our employees are already working long hours and don't have the time or energy to go back to school. They're even reluctant to attend training here when we offer it at the company during regular work hours.

Steve: I wasn't talking about classroom training. People learn by making mistakes, watching others, reading manuals, chatting at the water cooler, and watching a supervisor or colleague.

Raj: You have a point, but my job is to develop and deliver training. We mostly focus on what happens in the classroom. And my group, as you know, is measured by the butts we put in seats, otherwise known as our enrollments. I can see the value in the informal and personally driven stuff, but. . . .

Defining Informal Learning

Winston Churchill said, "Personally, I'm always ready to learn, but I do not always like being taught." Informal learning happens just about everywhere, as people live their lives. It is meaningful when it occurs naturally and is knit into the fabric of people's lives.

Informal learning can take many forms, such as when employees talk to one another, search in a knowledge base, share opinions, use job aids, observe colleagues, chat over coffee, compare their efforts, and give and receive feedback. It happens at the computer, over lunch, in the lounge, and through e-mail.

Some informal learning has clear, defined goals, such as getting up to speed on a new software package or learning to use a particular tool. At other times, informal learning may be directed at more diffuse outcomes, such as understanding corporate culture, getting the feel of a new role, or learning how the group approaches audits.

While informal learning typically happens outside classrooms and training programs, it can and should be jump-started, encouraged, systematized, and enhanced by training and development professionals. That's why we write about it here.

Examples of Informal Learning

From chatting to teaming, from mentoring to coaching, informal learning takes many forms. Some are familiar, others less so.

Teaming

After a glowing review by a local food critic, a small family bakery cannot meet demand for its unique breads. They hire new bakers to boost production, but soon receive complaints that the bread just doesn't taste as good as it did before. The family wonders, "How could this be? The recipes haven't changed in 125 years!" They decide to team new bakers with family members to upgrade the novices' efforts.

Observation

Kara writes for a small company. She loves her job, but hates the new word processing program. Whenever she tries to make tables, define styles, or do just about anything, she runs into problems. Frustrated, Kara keeps hollering for help from

Stu, the resident expert. Eventually, Kara notices that Stu relies on the on-line help system to answer his questions about the software. She begins to do the same.

On-Line Community

Leslie wants to know how much to charge for a consulting job. She underbid on her last contract and ended up with an hourly rate that felt obscenely low to her. In a message to her on-line community, www.trainingsupersite.com /community, Leslie admits to blowing the estimate and asks for advice. The responses tell her about estimation; she also receives sample contracts, tax information, and queries about her availability for other opportunities.

Mentoring

Adelado is an intern for a live, local television show. His responsibilities include shelving and dubbing tapes, greeting guests, and answering phones. Gradually, Adelado develops the beginnings of a friendship with Greg, the host of the show. Over coffee and an occasional lunch, they share opinions and discuss story ideas. Adelado benefits from Greg's many years in the business, and Greg learns how station decisions affect junior staff members and the kinds of topics that interest Adelado, a new immigrant in his early twenties.

Schmoozing

Many real estate salespeople have breakfast at the Huddle. They've been doing it for years. When a new sales professional is fortunate enough to come under the wing of a veteran, the newcomer gets invited to breakfast and, while eating, gains insights into selling into this marketplace.

Why Informal Learning Matters

The information age and global economy have transformed the business world. Change is constant, loyalty scarce, and innovation essential. In the last thirty years, "over half of all Fortune 500 companies have reorganized, downsized, or otherwise reinvented themselves" (Marsick & Volpe, 1999, p. 1).

When ideas, information, and innovation are the capital that matters, lifelong development becomes job one. Organizations and their employees have no choice but to learn continuously, to keep up or to fall far behind. Motivated to meet goals, to add value to organizations, to become and stay competitive, to hone skills and prepare for new challenges, and to respond to job demands, many individuals turn to informal learning.

Also influential is the shift within many organizations to policies that tout career self-reliance. This directive puts more of the onus for continuous development on the employees themselves. For example, a global company communicated with its worldwide employees in a way that proclaimed directions and the skills on which they'd place a premium on in the future. Then they asked for the means that employees wanted to help them stay current. Prior corporate paternalism was replaced with clear expectations and continuing resources for individual development.

Training and development departments cannot schedule sufficient training programs to address all learning needs.

Training and development departments cannot schedule sufficient training programs to address all learning needs. Finite resources limit the possibilities.

Speedy response is also an issue. Formal training and education programs, including contracts that enable employees to turn to on-line learning modules, are developed deliberately. These painstaking processes run counter to the urgency that many managers and employees perceive. People at work often feel that the learning was required *yesterday,* not next month or quarter, or after the contract has been negotiated with the instructor or e-learning provider.

Another factor is the time away from work that conventional training demands. Many managers want their people doing the work of the organization, not sitting in or traveling to and from classes. Although formal training remains a critical contributor to organizations, the bottom line is that *continuous learning does not and cannot rely on continuous training.*

"Informal Learning in the Workplace," a study by the Center for Workforce Development at the Education Development Center, made just that point. An announcement summarizing the results of the study recognized the centrality of informal learning in participating companies: "Informal learning was widespread, and served to fulfill most learning needs, perhaps as much as 70 percent of organizations' learning needs. In general, we noted that informal learning was highly relevant to employee needs and involved knowledge and skills that were attainable and immediately applicable. Informal learning also plays a critical role in how people learn to do their jobs, and results in measurable economic benefits" (Bischoff, 1998).

Informal learning turns out to be good news for the training and development professionals. . . .

Informal learning turns out to be good news for the training and development professionals whose goal is to contribute to organizational and individual development, no matter the means and no matter the amount of overt day-to-day control they exert over it.

Importance of Informal Learning

Informal learning often looks the way it sounds. It appears informal, offhand, natural. However, the way it seems from the outside does not mean that it is unplanned on the inside. In fact, there are distinct roles to be played by training professionals in nurturing and structuring informal learning.

How can we nudge more informal learning out of the organization? How can we direct more informal contacts toward critical purposes? And how can we do all this without snuffing the idiosyncrasy, immediacy, and individual agency that give informal learning its edge?

We won't look at the supervisor or operator who profits from a walk on the beach or a quiet moment contemplating the manufacturing floor, although we are aware that good comes from such moments. Our attention is on the roles of the training professional in encouraging informal learning to flourish.

Bringing People Together for Good Reasons

One critical role we play is to encourage people to work together. Johnson and Johnson (as cited in Jonassen, 1996) analyzed hundreds of studies about cooperation and achievement. Their work, although primarily focused on youth, clarified the value to be found in teams:

- More willingness to take on challenging tasks, and to persist when the going gets tough
- Better recall of what is learned
- Critical thinking and reasoning skills
- More motivation to do their jobs and spend more time on tasks than people who work alone
- Positive attitudes, which transfer to the work and to the organization
- Transfer of skills and knowledge learned in groups to individual job performance

The role of the training professional is to make certain that the following forms of togetherness happen across the organization.

Teaming. Teams bring people with complementary skills together. While accomplishing the primary task, diverse individuals grow by rubbing their skills and perspectives up against each other in service to a task. For example, recently, one of the authors joined a team with a programmer, a graphic artist, a content provider, a subject-matter expert, and a project manager to create reusable, Web-based learning objects for graduate students eager to learn more about audio. The resulting Website can be seen in Figure 8.1. Other good things happened, too, as team members learned new technology skills from one another.

Virtual Teaming. Technology enables a new kind of teaming, virtual teaming, which happens when professionals who are geographically dispersed meet and work together via shared technology and collaborative workspaces. The technology may be as simple as e-mail or conference calling, or as sophisticated as GroupWare or videoconferencing. Engenia's Unity (www.engenia.com) provides a good example. The digital dashboard accommodates time-stamped postings and threaded discussion, as well as many other forms of desktop applications. The idea is to use the technology as a gathering place, where ideas, work products, and feedback are captured and shared.

FIGURE 8.1. LISTENING AND LEARNING.

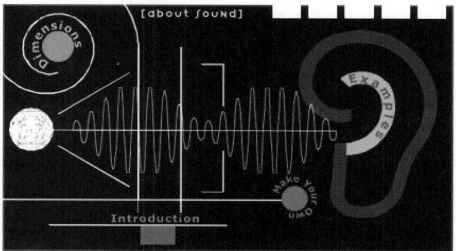

If you are a training and development professional for a global organization, virtual teaming can help you span cultures, time, and space. A San Diego Sandbox (www.sandbox.sdsu.edu) project for the U.S.-Japan Friendship Commission is an example. Productivity is enhanced, travel costs reduced, and different versions posted, examined, and revised. In the not-so-distant past, The San Diego Sandbox would have created the prototype, printed it, shipped it to Washington, D.C., and waited for feedback in the form of hard-copy scribblings or a lengthy telephone call. Then revisions would have occurred, followed by even more shipping, this time from San Diego to Japan and Washington. Technology-based teaming supports ongoing dialogue and team member development, all centered on work products.

Directing Team Attention to Real Problems

When teams at work commit to collaborating to solve an authentic problem, many call it action learning. Marquardt (1999, p.4) defined action learning as "a process and a powerful program that involves a small group of people solving pressing organizational problems, while at the same time focusing on what they are learning and how it can benefit each group member and the organization."

Action learning is a form of teaming, of course, but it differs because it emphasizes solving real problems *and* learning *and* processing the experience, all at the same time. An example of action learning is Motorola's award-winning GOLD process (Figure 8.2). GOLD prepared high-potential managers for success in a diverse, global organization. The action learning aspect of GOLD was represented by the *business challenge*. Examples of business challenges included, "Create and establish a pervasive brand identity and dominant market presence in China" and "Identify, analyze, and evaluate the factors contributing to higher manufacturing costs in the region. Then develop and implement strategies and plans which will lead to significant and timely reductions."

Marguerite Foxon of Motorola University said about the project, "In designing GOLD, we recognized that no matter how mind stretching and job relevant the content is, training alone cannot accelerate the development of a new generation of leaders. Tying the course content to the business challenges provided our managers with the perfect opportunity to put the new learning into action, real time."

Two alumni from Motorola's GOLD process had this to say about their experiences: "Leading a business challenge team on a project outside my functional skill area, with all male members from different cultures, helped me to be culturally sensitive to other people's inputs, styles, and thinking," and "When we were working hard on our business challenge, we all felt like we might actually be able to make a difference in the organization. This was different from attending other management / leadership courses where you get all pumped up during the class about the 'right' way to do things, then go back to your job but nothing changes."

Communities of Practice

Communities of practice are naturally occurring informal groups in the workplace that come together, develop, evolve, and disperse according to the rhythms and the energy of their participants.

Membership is open, structure is loose, and rules are few to none. Communities of practice lack beginning and ending dates. According to Wenger (1998), a community of practice is a different kind of entity than a task force or a team. Perhaps we could see them as the most informal of the informal learning structures.

Communities of practice come together at the watercooler, over lunch, after work, or whenever it is convenient. Participants discuss mutual interests—

FIGURE 8.2. MOTOROLA'S GOLD™ PROCESS.

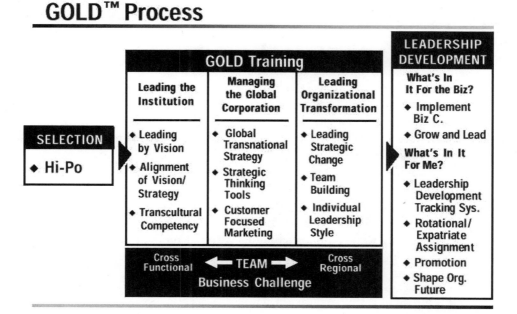

sometimes work-related, often not. These ad hoc communities form when employees find co-workers who share an interest, hobby, concern, goal, or skill and then elect to talk about them over time. For example, a group of technology buffs meets for lunch on Fridays, while a group interested in yoga meets after work, and a group concerned about social justice in the organization uses a listserv to share their concerns and projects.

In an article in the *Harvard Business Review,* Brown and Duguid (2000) highlighted the value of funky social groups. Their example came from Xerox, where researcher Julian Orr studied the services provided by reps to customers. Orr noted the divergence between the formal descriptions of their work processes and the tacit improvisations involved in handling unforeseen problems with equipment.

How did inexperienced reps learn, if the formal processes enshrined in policies and training are off base? Orr pointed to the informal aspects of their lives, elements that contribute to getting the job done. For example, the reps ate breakfast together. During the meal, they collaborated on problems and shared war stories, expanding on and enriching the formal artifacts that typically surrounded their work.

On-Line Communities

Technology provides a way for communities of practice to transcend their physical boundaries. According to Clark, in an interview presented later in this chapter, an on-line community is "a group of people who use the Internet to meet and communicate." They may be friends, colleagues, classmates, or complete strangers who decide to form a virtual community. On-line communities may be small or large, open or closed, obviously related to work or not much related at all. Each has a unique culture, similar to what you find in neighborhoods in a city. Mona Meyer, long-time member of an on-line community, noted an important distinction, "On-line communities are different [from other communities]. It is extremely easy to disentangle yourself (or distance yourself) from an on-line community. If you get sick of the vibe, just type 'unsubscribe.' I think an argument could be made that, in many ways, on-line communities are far more genuine than traditional communities, simply because their members really want to be there" (e-mail communication, March 4, 2000).

Interestingly, the on-line community is becoming a staple in many learning and knowledge enterprises because the on-line connection adds a social dimension, via threaded discussions, listservs, and chats, to distance education classes.

On-line communities are appealing because they offer instant communication, information, and companionship. For some, such as the ITForum (itforum@

listserv.uga.edu), conversation is work-related, focusing on software, training strategies, and the changes now buffeting higher education. Here is one example of a message posted on the ITForum on June 20, 2000. Andy Yip, chief inspector for the Hong Kong Police wrote: "I am a policeman responsible for instructional technology for the Hong Kong Police Force. After many [years] of struggle, we finally start to introduce computer-based training to our force. I am now preparing a paper on the culture change arise from the introduction of technology. I have done some research, and seemed more of the books I found are management books such as those talking about organization change. I would wonder if anyone can recommend any book or article about the issue on bring in instructional technology on top of instructional led training, e.g., staff resistance, management concern, technical constraint, et cetera."

Some on-line communities are concerned about important matters that go beyond work. For example, www.babycenter.com establishes that kind of community, where women at various stages of pregnancy bond to talk about their shared experiences, joys, and concerns.

[I]t's important to remember that only a small percentage of the world's population enjoys access to the Internet.

Although it is easy to become excited about on-line communities for wireless telecommunications engineers, women with breast cancer, and new employees at a New Zealand university, it's important to remember that only a small percentage of the world's population enjoys access to the Internet. As we write this book, the number of people who are on-line is at 259 million, but it is increasing at an incredible pace every minute of every day (Petsca, 1999), according to Computer Industry Almanac (www.c-i-a.com/index).

Enriching Interactions Between Two People

Just as teams and communities enable good things to happen, we're also interested in what two people can offer each other and the organization. Training and development professionals have a role to play in establishing and nurturing these pairings.

Mentoring

In the past, mentoring occurred when senior executives picked and groomed successors who were typically pretty much like themselves. In most cases, the information flowed in one direction, from the top down, and the relationships lasted for many years. Although such mentoring still occurs today, a new style has emerged, one that has the fingerprints of training and human resources on it. This more democratic version of mentoring defines, launches, and maintains pairings between people where they probably wouldn't happen on their own.

This contemporary mentoring focuses on establishing relationships between senior managers or employees and less experienced employees *not under their supervision.* In these more short-term pairings, the hope is that the benefits are mutual. Executives learn how their decisions affect employees, and how work actually gets done. Protegees tap into mentors' expertise, get advice and guidance, and imbibe lessons about organizational culture.

At a multimedia development company in Germany, for example, new employee Chris Volkl was abruptly promoted to vice president after a colleague went on leave. Although Chris possessed much of what was required to do the job, he was concerned that he wasn't sufficiently seasoned for the position. The president of the company found a mentor for the new vice president, a former CEO who had recently retired from a very successful career. Chris and his mentor met every month, discussing management, organizational culture, change, and more. The relationship provided the support that Chris needed and it continues to this day.

Peer Tutoring

Peer tutoring happens when employees teach their co-workers. Often it just happens, sometimes under the umbrella of on-the-job training encouraged by human resources and training professionals, but mostly because someone knows how to fix the jammed equipment and someone does not.

Peer tutoring may be as minimal as answering questions when they come up or as complicated as providing on-the-job demonstrations and opportunities to practice and receive feedback. Some tutors have been taught to teach; most have not. Some are paid for the additional effort involved in tutoring; most are not.

Peer tutoring is mostly good for organizations, as it can reduce training costs. Another benefit is that a person with real, contemporary experience is delivering the messages in the context of the work. A third benefit is the informality itself. Some employees feel safer with their peers at work than when attending training classes.

A drawback to peer tutoring is that tutors can and do teach some bad habits. Although we want to encourage peer tutoring, and it will happen even without professional nudging, it's important to examine the lessons that are being conveyed. As an example, a colleague at a turbine company described a critical error that was being passed from employee to employee, absent any recognition that the erroneous procedures were being disseminated as gospel.

Peer tutoring has become increasingly important to organizations, as rapid change has created a "digital divide." At San Diego-based IVID Communications, for example, peer tutoring became part of the organizational culture when professionals with different skills teamed up to develop multimedia products. Some designers were proficient with technology, while others had worked exclusively with low-tech to no-tech delivery methods in the past. During meetings, the designers with limited technology experience often had questions, but were uncomfortable asking what they feared were "stupid" questions. Those less comfortable with technology found the answers they needed from their peers during private, informal conversations as the work moved forward.

Coaching

Coaching is not so much about a program or job classification that is recognized in the organization as it is about a way that mentors and tutors, colleagues, supervisors, and even CEOs choose to communicate. It's a role that can and should be added to every job.

When managers are coaches, they are doing good things for their people and for the larger organization. Most trainers yearn for managers who will follow up with employees and offer praise, timely feedback, and advice. Consider building small and structured ways for managers to participate in critical initiatives, such as preliminary coaching and follow-up. Researchers have found that conversations between managers and employees significantly boost transfer of training outcomes to the workplace.

Salina Khan (2000) touted the unique contributions made by the CEO of the Ritz-Carlton Hotels as both a trainer and a coach: "Schulze is the gentle but demanding coach. As he tells them about the company's philosophy and goals, he stops to chide some for 'studying the ceiling.' When he spots a sleepy employee in his audience, he jokes that there are some in every class and they're always men" (p. 3B).

Century 21 International built a sales training program around the value of peer coaching. After years of attrition by new real estate salespeople, the company committed to coaching for new sales professionals. They determined from a review of the literature that successful coaches did three things: (1) trained new people on sales skills, such as selection of a "farm"; (2) integrated them into the culture of real estate sales; and (3) motivated them, even in the face of frequent rejection. Rossett and Strayer (1994) looked at the impact of this multi-faceted program. They found that the program did indeed work, boosting both sales and confidence, and that sales for the coached associates were significantly better than for associates in offices without the program and the coaches.

Training and Development Versus Informal Learning

An expanded definition of training and development allows us to perceive formal training as just one of many types of workplace education and informal learning as another. Informal learning typically springs from the enthusiasm and needs of participants and from the opportunities presented by the work.

Although informal learning cannot be scheduled in the same ways that classes are, it can be encouraged, promoted, and supported.

Although informal learning cannot be scheduled in the same ways that classes are, it *can* be encouraged, promoted, and supported. The challenge for the training and development professional is to figure out how to encourage informal learning without taking away its unique individual, social, spontaneous, and idiosyncratic aspects.

The Professional's Role

An EDC study in 1997 (Center for Workforce Development, 2001) captured media attention because participating companies were engaged in so much informal learning. In fact, the authors of the study suggested that as much as 70 percent of the organizations' learning needs were being met informally.

Find It. How much informal learning is going on in your organization? Even if you elect not to support a comprehensive study, seek examples and anecdotes of informal learning in your organization. Find the people and groups who do it and profit from it. Get a sense of the kinds of informal learning going on. Where is it happening? When? How did it start? Why does it endure? To what challenges does it contribute? In what ways is technology involved? What are the core messages?

Learn from It. What topics serve as grist for the informal learning? What materials and artifacts are being created by tutors and coaches and handed off from employee to employee? How can you leverage the impact of these informal artifacts? What topics are engaging on-line communities? What errors and misconceptions are being conveyed? How can you second key messages and correct flawed information?

If employees are chatting on-line about a customer problem or how to fix a software bug, perhaps this topic should be insinuated into formal classes or the knowledge management system. Lunch conversations about new global efforts could become the basis for an international mentoring program, whereas war stories about customer complaints could be repurposed into elements in the knowledge management system.

If employees are thriving in those situations in which they are being coached on the job, it's time to consider ways to encourage it more broadly. Can such coaching be modeled and defined in classes? As the University of Missouri's David Jonassen wrote in 1996, "We no longer teach, but rather we coach; we have moved from the sage on stage to the guide on the side" (p.184).

If employees are coming together on-line to chat informally, are there ways to seed their efforts and rivet that attention to important issues? Can you sponsor action learning groups that devote attention to key issues as Motorola did?

Honor It. There is a fine line between recognizing and valuing informal learning and changing its nature with attention and kudos. Provide examples of coaches at all levels in the organization, from the CEO mentor to the truck driver peer tutor. Consider involving informal learning leaders in formal training events. Do they want to teach? Produce videos with their ideas and stream them around the globe. Produce videos that capture informal meetings and allow others to participate. Use technologies, such as NetMeeting, to help distant colleagues communicate. Repurpose ideas and materials into knowledge bases.

Give credit where it's due, but ask first. Some informal learning participants prefer the ad hoc and sub rosa nature of their contributions and relationships. They want to decide about how much formal organizational applause they receive.

Integrate It. Is there a way to make the boundary between formal and informal learning more permeable? Can you urge instructors to become involved in an on-line community or a mentoring relationship? Can you bring a strong voice off the intranet and into the classroom? Can you pick up the homemade materials that technicians are sharing at lunch and bring them into the classroom? Can you infuse some of the classroom and on-line resources into peer tutoring?

Support It. Look for small ways to be a friend to informal learning. Can you assure space in a building? Provide a pizza? Connect the group to a person familiar with the technology that interests them? Recognize a particularly devoted peer tutor or mentor? Does the informal group want more people to know about their existence? Can you help a group in a distant land to upgrade its technology platform? Can you provide an informal guide to informal groups as part of orientation?

Launching an Informal Learning Program

You already have an informal learning program; in fact, it's likely there are many such programs, large and small. Now is the time to find and nurture what you have, to learn from these more informal interactions, and to make certain that informal learning creates readiness for all the many ways that development and performance are supported. Table 8.1 presents strategies and actions to promote informal learning in the workplace.

TABLE 8.1. STRATEGIES FOR INFORMAL LEARNING.

Strategy	*Actions*
Help employees develop goals for learning by providing vivid statements about organizational direction.	Provide a roadmap so employees can measure themselves and make good decisions about their own development. Link resources to these new goals and directions. If the company is going to commit to broadband in a big way, for example, communicate the vision loud and clear.
	Tell employees exactly what new skills and perspectives must be cultivated. Provide formal learning and opportunities and encourage the informal to bloom.
	Be clear about the shift to career self-reliance.
Block (1993) suggests shifting from "parents to partners," from paternalism to stewardship.	Engage informal learners in orientations and training. Familiarize new and interested people with the current and emerging informal efforts and configurations.
	Use classes to springboard to on-line and interpersonal informal learning.
	Create rich resources on-line that capture extant best practices and allow employees to add and use as needed.
Provide opportunities for employees to learn where work happens, when it happens, *on the job.*	Create an expectation that managers will coach. Develop coaching skills for interested managers.
	Make peer tutoring and mentoring a recognized and honored effort.
	Encourage people to talk to their colleagues about how they handle challenges and to demonstrate approaches that work as needs arise.

TABLE 8.1. (*CONTINUED*)

Strategy	*Actions*
Provide support resources.	Provide job aids, manuals, reference books, peer tutors, and coaches.
	Make sure that the orientation points people to helpful informal resources, such as existing handbooks, on-line job aids, and knowledge bases.
	Charge supervisors with maintaining these rich resources.
	Provide new software that includes useful HELP systems.
Encourage employee interaction at work, on-line, and in communities.	Provide a comfortable place where employees can informally gather during breaks, lunch, or after hours. Create on-line sychronous and asynchronous "space."
	Organize social events which bring employees together.
	Create a company listserv, which enables professionals to communicate with their colleagues.
Encourage employees to document their work. Reward employees for documenting their work and for sharing the information with others in knowledge management systems.	Reward employees who document their work.
	Create a knowledge management system in your company.
	Make heroes of individuals who share through conversations, demonstrations, and knowledge management systems.
Teach employees how to help one another.	Develop and support peer tutors, mentors, and coaches.

Questions and Answers

Table 8.2 presents answers for questions from employees and HR and training professionals about typical workplace scenarios and what informal learning might do for them. Table 8.3 presents resources for promoting informal learning, whether you have an hour, a day, or a week.

TABLE 8.2. QUESTIONS AND ANSWERS.

Question	Answer
I am a busy graphic artist. I need to update my skills, but don't have time for training. My boss is hesitant about freeing me up.	There are many ways to update skills without formal training. Take the initiative by asking colleagues for help. Work on projects with people who know more than you do. Consider joining an on-line community, community of practice, or a professional listserv; they can be a great source of help, support, and advice.
One of our programmers is really talented, but she can't seem to get along with anyone. I'd hate to let her go, but—	It sounds as if she would benefit from having a mentor, someone who is wiser and experienced in the company and work. Mentors can teach valuble lessons about organizational culture, norms, and unspoken rules, as well as specific "survival skills," such as getting along with colleagues. The mentor, in turn, can learn about new products and find out what newer hires are thinking.
The engineers all took the same Java class, but only two are using it. Should I ask the others to take it again?	You could do that, but formal training is expensive, and might not be any more effective the second time around. Before you send them back to class, why not empower the engineers who are using Java to tutor their peers, either one-on-one or with small, informal classes? Many people prefer to learn from their peers (Rickett, 1993), and employees who have incentives to become tutors (rewards, recognition) are often happy to share their expertise with their colleagues. Another way to help those who are not yet using Java is to encourage and reward employees with Java expertise to document their work. Turn this information into job aids and add it to your organization's knowledge management system. If you don't yet have a KM system, put the information on the intranet so that your engineers can benefit from their expertise.
We need the brightest and the best on this wireless database project, but they're scattered all over the globe. Travel costs are prohibitive. How can I bring them together without breaking the budget?	Thanks to technology and the Internet, the world is literally boundaryless. You can now create a virtual team to "meet" and collaborate via shared technology (videoconferencing, e-mail, conference calls, collaborative workspaces on the Web, and so on). Even the language barrier is less of a problem with Web-based services such as Altavista's Translator (http://babelfish.altavista.digital.com/translate.dyn).

TABLE 8.3. RESOURCES.

Time	Resources
"I have an hour"	Visit the Informal Learning Homepage, an excellent starting place for anyone interested in this important subject. http://www.infed.org/
	Read Rossett and Strayer's 1994 article, "Coaching sales performance: A case study." *Performance Improvement Quarterly,* 7(4).
	The report that put informal learning on the map, "The Teaching Firm" (1998). Center for Workforce Development, Education Development Center Inc., Newton, MA.
"I have a day"	Spend some time at the Training Supersite Research Center reading about informal learning in the workplace. Use the search engine to find relevant articles. http://www.trainingsupersite.com/research/index.htm
	How can I capture the outcomes of informal learning and spread them throughout the organization? Visit Knowledge Management for Training Professionals at http://defcon.sdsu.edu/1/objects/km/welcome/
	What are the benefits of a mentoring program? Does my organization need one? Why or why not? Read Margo Murray's *Beyond the Myths and Magic of Mentoring.*
"I've got a week"	Read *Action Learning in Action* by M. Marquardt (1999). Palo Alto, CA: American Society for Training and Development.
	Have you ever considered joining an on-line community? Read this engaging book first: Howard Reingold's *The Virtual Community,* available on-line at http://www.rheingold.com/vc/book/

Spotlight on People

Margo Murray

Margo Murray is president and chief operating officer of the Managers' Mentors, Inc., an international consulting firm specializing in the design, implementation, and evaluation of facilitated mentoring processes and total quality productivity performance systems. Murray founded the firm in 1974. Her 1991 book, *Beyond the Myths and Magic of Mentoring: How to Facilitate a Mentoring Program,* is a seminal work on facilitated mentoring.

On Mentors Murray noted that the word "mentor" has its roots in Greek mythology, when Odysseus asked his wise and trusted friend, Mentor, to advise, counsel, guard, and guide his son Telemachus during his absence in the Trojan War.

The role of mentor has evolved in a number of significant ways. Murray described mentors' tasks today as "advising, counseling, coaching, giving feedback, sharing experiences, providing support, and guiding the professional, and sometimes personal, growth and development of their protégés." Murray defined mentoring as "the deliberate pairing of a more skilled or experienced person with a lesser-skilled or experienced person with the agreed-on goal of having the lesser-skilled person grow and develop specific competencies" (Murray, 1991). She stressed that mentoring relationships today are often created to transfer knowledge, skills, and experiences both ways. The expert-hire mentor may bring state-of-the-art technical skills into the organization, and the protégé with longer service may provide coaching in the communication channels, politics, and culture of the organization.

In the not-so-distant past, Murray remarked, mentors were likely to be senior executives who selected protégés to "clone" into their own image. These relationships might continue until the senior executive retired and the protégé perpetuated the status quo. Performers learned to think, behave, and make decisions like their mentors. The problem with this practice, according to Murray, was that the resulting narrow sameness weakened organizations. She said that the strength of an organization comes through the diversity of its leaders and members.

On Mentoring Relationships According to Murray, the length of mentoring relationships varies greatly. The determining factors are the knowledge, skills, or experiences the protégé wants to gain and the amount of time spent on the coaching and feedback. A specific technical skill might be learned in a relatively short period of time, while the development of generic leadership skills may take longer.

Murray said that the goal of any mentoring relationship is the transfer of knowledge, skills, or experiences that the protégé requires for competent performance. A series of mentoring relationships will enrich the learning for protégés and expose them to different management and leadership styles.

Drivers for Mentoring Programs In a recent study, Murray found that 42 percent of mentoring pairs were matched to support the career development of employees; another 31 percent of pairs focused on technical skills transfer; 17 percent were paired to increase an awareness, appreciation, and valuing of diversity within the workplace; and just 4 percent were paired to support succession planning.

Murray explained that a facilitated mentoring process promotes measured growth and gain to all stakeholders in the process: the protégé, the mentor, and the organization.

Successful Mentoring Murray said that a mentoring process must be linked to the goals, needs, and opportunities of the organization: "This is as true for non-profit and community-based mentoring processes as it is for profit-based organizations. Any process or program must contribute to the results of the organization or it will not survive in lean economic times. Group processes such as training classes convey information and knowledge and seldom provide sufficient practice for skill development." Murray's research showed that about 15 percent of the content of most generic courses is relevant to any one learner, thus wasting 85 percent of the learner's time. "One-on-one learning is focused, efficient, effective, and just-in-time," Murray explained. "The protégé learns what is needed, at the time it is needed. Time and support from the organization and commitment from the matched pair are vital to the success of every mentoring relationship."

Pitfalls According to Murray, there are many challenges to implementing a successful mentoring process:

- "The relationship between supervisors and mentors can be problematic if the supervisor abdicates responsibility for helping the employee with professional development.
- Protégés may play mentors and supervisors against each other.
- Mentors and supervisors may talk about protégés, violating the confidentiality of the pair's agreement.
- Organizations may wrongly assume that supervisors and/or managers will donate their time to 'tomorrow's opportunity.'
- Organizations may not adequately reward and recognize mentors, causing them to lose interest.
- Organizations may not evaluate mentoring programs, and may eventually abandon them, breaking promises to employees and creating an atmosphere of distrust."

In Murray's thirty years of experience with designing, implementing, and evaluating mentoring processes, she has identified the following critical success factors:

- Identify needs, goals, opportunities, and readiness
- Plan and design to meet the goals

- Communicate clearly what the mentoring process is and is not
- Match on the basis of skill gaps and create workable agreements
- Orient and prepare the partners for their roles
- Create specific development plans
- Evaluate and continuously improve the process

Caleb John Clark

Caleb John Clark has been involved with net culture and Web development since 1993. His accomplishments include co-founder of the NoEnd Web Developer's group in the San Francisco Bay Area; freelance writer for *Wired* magazine, serving as professional on-line host for Netscape Inc. (prior to the AOL buyout); corporate webmaster and numerous freelance Web development projects as both an HTML/media Web monkey and project manager. Clark recently completed his master's degree in educational technology at San Diego State University, where he taught graduate-level multimedia development classes—both in person and on-line. At the time of writing this book, he was working as a project manager and on-line community director for what he described as "a crazy little Internet start-up."

On-Line Communities Clark defined an on-line community as "a group of people with something in common who use technology to communicate" and listed the essential elements as "leaders, lurkers, and posters." Clark said that the things that make on-line communities successful are the same things that make any community successful: "Good communication, clarity of purpose, shared goals, leadership with authority, filters for membership, and trials for inclusion." He added, "Communities should encourage giving before taking, personalization through identity building, and face-to-face meetings."

Homesteading in a Brave New World Clark is a veteran on-line community founder and member. He created NoEnd (www.wired.com/news/culture/0,1284,9749,00) in January of 1996, when he was the lone webmaster at a small ad agency: "I really wanted to talk to other webmasters, so I organized three of us to meet at a bar, then five came, then seven, et cetera. Within a couple of months, we got a listserv. The first members of NoEnd were a group of 'Web heads,' film students, writers, artists, industrial geeks, engineers, lawyers, and students in the Bay Area. Since then, NoEnd has grown into a powerful Web development community that was the subject of an article in *Wired* magazine."

The Purpose, the Postings Clark said that the purpose of NoEnd is "to humanize technology." Members communicate through an e-mail listserv and meet in person regularly. Postings are a funky mix of technical and personal messages, with poetry, travel essays, and opinions as likely as technical information sharing and job announcements. Clark said that in NoEnd (and other on-line communities), most messages are written by a few people and read by all.

The Problems Clark said that NoEnd has a sub-mailing list for community leaders, who deal with problems behind the scenes. The community also has a powerful listmom who can remove anyone from NoEnd at any time, no questions asked. When membership ballooned to nearly nine hundred, Clark handled it by inventing a technique he called "hot tubbing." He explained, "Hot tubbing is named after a secret hot tub in Oakland [California] that you can only get into by knowing the key code to the lock. There is no talking aloud in this hot tub, and it is free. Every once in a while some incident happens and they change the door code, passing the new one out only to a handful of the most trusted users. They in turn spread it out to friends. I hot tubbed NoEnd when the signal-to-noise ratio was too high with nine hundred people. We [the leadership] gave a twenty-four-hour notice that the list was going to disappear. Then we killed it and started it back up with no subscribers and different subscription protocols. We then had an in-person meeting, and everyone who came was given the new subscription directions. They [the members at the meeting] gave them out to close friends and like-minded artists, webmasters, and writers. Now we've stabilized at three hundred or so, with subscription being controlled by the listmom, Eric."

The Outcomes Clark says that NoEnd has resulted in the best networking in the world, because members have made a deliberate effort *not* to network. Instead, they get to know one another as they really are, without the usual artifice and trappings (name tags, slide presentations, resumes) associated with networking.

Clark believes that, as information sharing on NoEnd continues, industry news and inside information have dramatically improved as members have become more prominent in the Bay Area's high-tech industry and beyond. He continued, "NoEnd amounts to a very high quality stream of information and access to resources that provides a sort of ongoing training and development of the community as a whole. After four years, NoEnders applying for jobs now consider the years spent in the community to be worthy of an entry on their resume in the 'experience' section."

At the Heart of the Matter

The following slides are designed to help training and human resource professionals encourage informal learning in their workplaces.

Slide 8.1

Defining Informal Learning

Informal learning happens just about everywhere, as people live their lives.

It is meaningful when it is knit into the fabric of people's lives.

Presenter's Notes

Informal learning is easy to define because we all do it, all the time. Offer examples from your life, from interactions in the organization. Soon your audience will be nodding their heads, remembering examples from their own lives. "When my son was two, I joined a play group and learned a lot about being a good parent," or "My father taught me how to hang wallpaper."

Slide 8.2

What Does It Look Like?

- **Colleagues discussing wireless technology over lunch**
- **A mentor describing organizational culture to a protégé**
- **An on-line community of surgeons debating the merits of core versus surgical biopsies**
- **An expert customer service rep sharing tips with colleagues**

Presenter's Notes

In a workplace where informal learning thrives, working and learning are one and the same, as employees ask colleagues for help, talk technology at lunch, or ask members of their on-line community for advice. Learning and talking are constant, taking place in and outside the classroom, before, during, and after work hours. It's not always easy to tell if what's transpiring would be counted as learning or not.

Slide 8.3

Why Does Informal Learning Matter?

■ **It involves skills and knowledge that are directly applicable to job performance.**

■ **It meets up to "70 percent of organizations' learning needs."**

■ **It plays an essential role in how people learn to do their jobs.**

■ **It results in "measurable economic benefits."**

SOURCE: Center for Workforce Development at the Education Development Center (1998).

Presenter's Notes

A recent study by the Center for Workforce Development at the Education Development Center (EDC) found that informal learning is a major force in most organizations today. The challenge for organizations is to revise their definition of learning to include the tightly controlled versions that take place in the classroom and on-line, and the ongoing, spontaneous, and unpredictable interactions that sometimes produce tangible results—or might not.

Slide 8.4

What Drives Informal Learning?

- Lifelong growth and development are *essential* to organizations in the Information Age

- Organizations can't afford to meet the learning needs of every employee

- Employees need training *yesterday,* not weeks or months down the line

- Many employees would rather learn from peers than from instructors

SOURCE: Rickett, D. (1993). Training today—peer tutoring: Not just a low budget answer. *Training 30*(2), p. 70.

Presenter's Notes

Informal learning helps employees maintain their skills and continuously learn. The price is also right. Informal learning also offers an alternative to formal instruction for employees who are not comfortable in the classroom.

Slide 8.5

What Drives Informal Learning?

■ **Personal goals, choices, and preferences**

—**"I need to learn Java to stay competitive"**

—**"How should I handle difficult customers?"**

—**"I want to learn more about environmental engineering, but don't have time for a class."**

—**"I'd rather learn to troubleshoot by observing experts than listening to a lecture about it."**

—**"I wonder what other graphic artists charge for freelance work?"**

Presenter's Notes

Informal learning is driven by employees who want to change jobs, get promoted, and update skills or learn something new. They may want to create a Web page for the Help Desk with Dreamweaver 4 or write an independent consulting contract with MS Office 2000. There are as many reasons for informal learning as there are individuals, because informal learning is motivated by employees, not organizations.

Slide 8.6

What Is Informal Learning?

- **Working together**
  - **—Teaming**
  - **—Virtual teaming**
  - **—Action learning**
- **Communicating**
  - **—"Schmoozing"**
  - **—On-line communities**
- **Interacting**
  - **—Mentoring**
  - **—Peer tutoring**
  - **—Coaching**

Presenter's Notes

Informal learning comes in many forms, some more familiar than others. Use vivid examples from your setting to make it come alive for your audience. Do your engineers regularly lunch together? A community of practice! Do experienced employees help colleagues who are less so? A peer-tutoring program!

Slide 8.7

What Are the Outcomes?

■ Some are tangible
- —New skills and knowledge
- —Improved performance
- —Bottom-line results
- —Successful teamwork
- —Timely assistance

■ And some are not
- —Increased confidence and motivation
- —Greater job satisfaction
- —A sense of community
- —Rewarding new relationships

Presenter's Notes

The slide says it all.

Slide 8.8

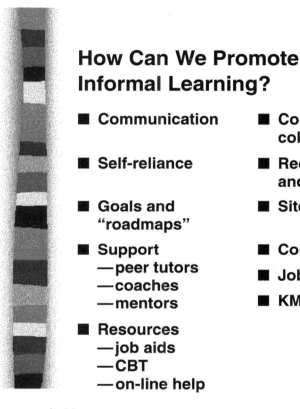

How Can We Promote Informal Learning?

- **Communication**

- **Self-reliance**

- **Goals and "roadmaps"**

- **Support**
  —peer tutors
  —coaches
  —mentors

- **Resources**
  —job aids
  —CBT
  —on-line help

- **Communication and collaboration**

- **Recognition, rewards, and heroes**

- **Site visits**

- **Community building**

- **Job documentation**

- **KM**

Presenter's Notes

Organizations cannot control or direct informal learning, but they can create an atmosphere to support and promote it. Think about your setting. Do you have a lounge where employees can meet and talk? Do you encourage employees to help each other and ask for help? Are there resources in the workplace that employees can refer to while on the job? How do you recognize informal efforts? What can you do to nurture the existing efforts and encourage the development of new forms of informal learning?

Resources

Armentrout, B. (1995). Making coaching your management metaphor. *Human Resources Focus, 72*(6).

Bell, C. (1997). *Managers as mentors: Building partnerships for learning.* San Francisco: Berrett-Koehler.

Bell, J., & Dale, M. (1999, August). *Informal learning in the workplace.* DEER report number 134. London: Department for Education and Employment.

Bischoff, R. (1998). Informal learning in the workplace announcement. (www.learning-org .com/98.01/0331)

Block, P. (1993, July). From paternalism to stewardship. *Training, 30*(7), 45.

Brown, J. S., & Duguid, P. (2000, May/June). Balancing act: How to capture knowledge without killing it. *Harvard Business Review, 78*(3), 73–80.

Center for Workforce Development. The teaching firm. Retrieved on-line February 16, 2001 at http://www.edc.org/CWD/Teaching.htm.

Doyle, M. E., & Smith, M. K. (1997). *Jean Jacques Rousseau: The informal education home page.* (www.infed.org/thinkers/et-rous.htm)

Foxon, M. (1999). *Closing the global leadership competency gap: The Motorola GOLD process.* Retrieved on-line March 22, 1999, at www.edweb.sdsu.edu/courses/EDTEC685/685_Spring99.

Jonassen, D. (Ed.). (1996). *Handbook of research for educational communications and technology.* New York: Simon & Schuster and MacMillan.

Jossi, F. (1997, August). Mentoring in changing times. *Training, 34*(8), 50.

Kearsley, G. (1999). *Social learning theory: The TIPS database.* www.coe.sdsu.edu/EDTEC544.

Khan, S. (2000, June 29). Ritz-Carlton opens with training tradition. *USA Today,* p. 3B.

Kiser, K. (1999). When those who do, teach. *Training, 36*(4), 42.

Marquardt, M. (1999). *Action learning in action.* Palo Alto, CA: American Society for Training and Development.

Marsick, V. J., & Volpe, M. (Eds.). (1999). Informal learning on the job. *Advances in Developing Human Resources, 3,* entire issue.

Micklethwait, J., & Wooldridge, A. (1996). *The witch doctors.* New York: Random House.

Morland, V. (undated). *Communities of practice.* www.geocities.com/CapeCanaveral/2414/ cop.htm.

Murray, M. (1991). *Beyond the myths and magic of mentoring: How to facilitate a mentoring program.* San Francisco: Jossey-Bass/Pfeiffer.

Petsca, K. (1999) *U.S. tops 100 million Internet users according to* Computer Industry Almanac. (Retrieved May 27, 2000, at www.c-i-a.com/index)

Rickett, D. (1993, February). Training today—Peer training: Not just a low-budget answer. *Training, 30*(2), 70.

Rossett, A., & Strayer, J. (1994). Coaching sales performance: A case study. *Performance Improvement Quarterly, 7*(4).

Russell, B. (1999, March/April). Experience-based learning theories. *The Informal Learning Review, 35,* 2.

Stamps, D. (1997). Communities of practice—Learning is social. Training is irrelevant? *Training, 34*(2), 34.

Stamps, D. (1998). *Learning ecologies.* (www.trainingsupersite.com/archive)

Thach, L. (1998). 14 ways to groom executives. *Training, 35*(8), 52.

Wenger, E. (1998). *Communities of practice: Learning, meaning, and identity.* New York: Cambridge University Press.

CHAPTER NINE

HOW CAN WE USE KNOWLEDGE MANAGEMENT?

Astrid: Just got an e-mail from a sales guy who told me he flat out wasn't going to contribute any of his sales proposals to the knowledge base.

Brock: You'd think he'd want to, with all the applause they're getting for putting customer materials, presentations, and proposals into the system. All you need is one good experience using the sales knowledge base and they turn around fast. I saw it with one of the senior reps from Sweden. He needed a presentation for a higher education group in Eastern Europe. He found one that had been done for Chile. He read the commentary from the sales leader and was able to edit it to work for his own needs. He said he saved five hours.

Astrid: Recently, I've been redesigning classes so that each includes introductions to our knowledge bases and related on-line communities.

Brock: I should do that too. I've been putting some of the training examples and tools into the bases, but I hadn't thought about pointing to the repositories in class.

Defining Knowledge Management

Knowledge management (KM) is about delivering the right knowledge to the right people at the right time. That, however, takes some doing. As Astrid complained above, not everybody is eager to pitch their ideas and work products into the collective knowledge

241

base. As Brock will soon see, there's still a strong preference for personal and unique inventions.

A famous quote attributed to the Hewlett-Packard founders goes something like this: "If HP only knew what HP knows. . . ." That sentiment rings bells in every kind of organization, from a school to a government agency to a corporation. Knowledge management (KM) is represented by large and small efforts to address that issue, to collect lessons learned in the organization in a way that facilitates continuous updates and wide distribution. Getting a grip on this knowledge, accumulating it, nurturing it, updating it, and making it vital are at the heart of KM. More than a decade ago, Prahalad and Hamel (1990) concluded that the core competencies—or the collective expertise—of an organization are the essence of competitive advantage. Knowledge management codifies that critical advantage, suggesting both content and interactions.

Schwen, Kalman, Hara, and Kisling (1998) and Horton (1999) noted two perspectives on knowledge management. The first views knowledge as content that can be captured and transferred. The second views knowledge as a social process that brings people into fruitful conversations across borders and boundaries. Of course, when suitably stirred, the content can serve as grist for the conversations, and the conversations can transform into archival aspects of the knowledge repository.

The "knowledge as content" perspective leads to the development of systems that encourage the efficient gathering, using, and disseminating of knowledge through, for example, knowledge repositories for business intelligence, anecdotes, presentations, and commentaries. A few years back, a global computer company asked its learning and education unit to establish an on-line place for sharing "smarts" across sales units, countries, and product groups. The envisioned purpose was to house sales presentations, product specifications, work sheets, proposals, and commentary about presentations and proposals. In addition, the hope was to provide a conduit to information about place-bound training and on-line classes related to generic sales skills and specific products. Imagine, for example, that a salesperson is scheduled to present to a utility company in Hanover, Germany. In preparation, she might access the database to see what others around the world have said and done in similar situations. She could look for information about this customer and this industry in the European Union and for others who have found themselves with a similar task, no matter the geography. She could rework prior presentations, duplicate FAQs and customer support materials, and even communicate with the originator of materials or approaches that interest her.

The "knowledge as an interactive and social process" provides her with other kinds of options. This perspective encourages the creation of "communities of practice," groups of individuals who communicate because they share opportunities, problems, customers, or other interests. The saleswoman might post a query to an on-line sales community, for example.

On-line communities exist outside organizations as well as within them. A favorite example is www.babycenter.com, an on-line community for pregnant women and related others. Babycenter transcends any one family, country, or organization, instead linking women and related others by the baby's due date. The government of the United States offers another instance. The United States Corporation for National Service supports listservs for agencies providing services to seniors volunteering in their communities. These listservs bring together the people who share that important mission.

There is obvious value in interactions within organizations too. The technology sales organization described above supports parallel conversations for people who sell products into higher education, telecommunications, insurance, energy, and government, for example. They also launch on-line connections to talk about new and extant product groups. Although the purposes of these particular interactions are conventional, internal connections happen for other reasons too, just as they would at the water cooler.

Friends within large corporations report participation in on-line communities that focus on such things as corporate child care centers or gay and lesbian issues. Another example is a Website called egroups (www.egroups.com), which concentrates on the challenges confronted by on-line community moderators (www.egroups.com/group/eModerators).

Why Knowledge Management Matters

Knowledge management is attracting attention everywhere. The World Bank has labeled knowledge management an "urgent necessity" for global development and is spearheading knowledge management initiatives in Third World countries. IBM's corporate strategy is replete with KM perspectives, emphasizing shared lessons, repurposed efforts, and collaboration across geographies.

Studies by KPMG and the Conference Board found that 80 percent of the world's biggest companies have KM initiatives in progress (Barth, 2000). The nonprofit Knowledge Management Consortium, founded in 1997, promotes practical, measurable applications of KM to business and other organizations. Their magazine, *Knowledge Management,* distributed in print and on the Web (www.kmmag.com), covers KM initiatives, pioneers, and software options.

A study done by Rossett and Marshall (1999) found that consulting companies were leading the way with knowledge management, both through support of their internal efforts and through services for clients. Marshall and Rossett found that people in consulting firms were four times more likely to have a formal KM system comprising dedicated staff and technology than were other kinds of organizations. The consulting firms distinguished themselves in many ways, including greater unrestricted access to information and reduction in command-and-control management policies.

Even school-based educators are intrigued with KM. They are establishing knowledge bases and communities of practice on-line, such as www.21ct.org, www .eduhound.com, www.parentsoup.com, www.par-inst.com, and www.kn.pacbell .com/wired/bluewebn. These useful, non-commercial sites model the possibilities for commercial organizations, whose KM efforts are often shrouded behind intranet firewalls.

Not surprisingly, the Web that has spurred the growth of KM also provides extensive coverage of it. A KM Website, www.brint.com, has grown like Topsy, evoking oohs and ahhs from a group of students impressed and overwhelmed by the profusion of resources. Joe Katzman, a KPMG senior consultant, links to many KM resources at www.pathcom.com/~kat/k-windows/knowledge/links.htm. A favorite on-line KM site of ours is www.knowledge-nurture.com. Sponsored by Buckman Laboratories, it is a free, rich source of information about knowledge management. Figure 9.1 shows some of what Buckman Labs is doing.

One company that started as a training and development consulting firm has altered its strategy to emphasize knowledge management. LeadingWay, headquartered in Irvine, California, developed a technology to integrate knowledge management and learning. Jill Funderburg-Donello, chief knowledge officer, put it this way: "While many of our clients still choose to deliver their knowledge in the form of training, especially in an on-line format, what differentiates us is that we don't limit them to delivering knowledge only in a learning environment. The content is held inside the knowledge system, so the format for delivery is flexible. The efforts that previously went into developing training, one delivery method, now can be leveraged to many formats, such as job aids and audio coaching. That same content that was used in sales training is also available as just-in-time performance support, sales presentations, product specification sheets, and other marketing materials. . . . Update the knowledge once, it's automatically updated everywhere. We treat knowledge as something that needs to be accessible in many different places—not just the training room."

Why so much attention to KM? What attracts LeadingWay, teachers, and consulting companies to the concept? Why does KM intrigue executives, when a conversation about training has traditionally produced MEGO (my eyes glaze over)? We think the answer hearkens back to that quote attributed to Hewlett-Packard at the beginning of this chapter. There is a widespread realization that value is being frittered away through carelessness and attrition. Research conducted by Szulanski (1996) for the American Productivity and Quality Center

FIGURE 9.1. SAMPLE KM SITE.

Buckman LABORATORIES

- LOBBY
- BUCKMAN ROOM
- LIBRARY
- EVENT BOARD
- WHAT'S NEW
- STARTER KIT
- Search

KNOWLEDGE *Nurture* **Articles About Knowledge Management at Buckman Laboratories**

As pioneers in the field of knowledge management, we have been featured in numerous articles in a number of publications. Most of the articles given below are on-line.

Knowledge Sharing at Buckman
These articles provide an overview of our efforts in knowledge management. They are either written by Buckman associates or featured interviews with our associates.

Information Technology
Information technology is a critical enabler for any knowledge management effort. Our IT infrastructure has been instrumental in establishing a framework for global knowledge sharing.

Culture
Although we have built on existing strengths in our culture, we also have devoted much thought an effort to changing our culture. Culture is the most important factor in any knowledge management effort.

Bulab Learning Center
Investing in the knowledge of our associates is a vital part of our knowledge management strategy. Our Bulab Learning Center enables us to deliver training not only in the classroom, but also across time and distance to wherever on the globe our associates are located.

Source: Copyright © 2000, Buckman Laboratories. Used by permission.

(APQC) revealed that successful practices typically linger in a company for years, often unrecognized and unshared. When they were recognized, he found that it took over two years before other entities within a company began to adopt best practices actively, if at all. Knowledge management is an attempt to do far better with the "smarts" within people and organizations.

Knowledge Management and Training

Training professionals have typically focused on *developing* brainpower more than *managing* it. Neuhaser, Bender, and Stromberg (2000), in a book that focuses on the culture of knowledge work, defined knowledge management as "managing people's brain power and the company's collective memory." That is exactly the point here. Training professionals must claim a leadership role in *managing the wealth of intellectual resources* extant in the organization. Although that endeavor includes training events, of course, it is also much more than any event or product.

Training professionals have typically focused on developing brainpower more than managing it.

As Rossett and Funderburg-Donello (in press) wrote, "KM distinguishes itself from traditional methods in its emphases and the ways it takes advantage of new technologies *to shift the wealth of individual knowledge into organizational resources.* KM boosts performance by shifting from structured, targeted learning events to the creation of dynamic databases that capture knowledge and connect people without the limits of time and space." They continued, "Where training builds capacity to help people respond IF a need emerges, KM creates resources that are there WHEN they are needed."

The San Diego Sandbox helped Rossett and Funderburg-Donello transfer their passion for the link between KM and training into a tangible resource; they developed a Website (www.defcon.sdsu.edu/3/objects/km/email) devoted to this fertile ground. Figure 9.2 is an example of how this site welcomes training professionals to the topic of KM. Figure 9.3, also from that site, highlights three ways that KM matters to the individual training professional.

FIGURE 9.2. SDSU'S KM AND TRAINING HOME PAGE.

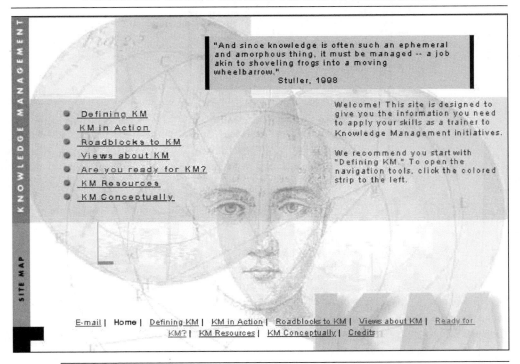

FIGURE 9.3. SOME REASONS TRAINERS SHOULD CONSIDER KM.

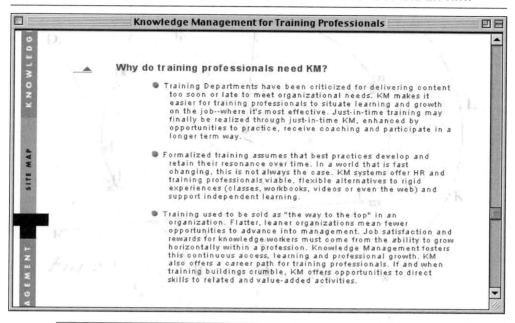

Source: Copyright © 1999, San Diego State University. Used by permission.

Table 9.1 highlights the distinctions between training and KM. The right-hand column, associated with KM, is generous. It doesn't preclude conventional training activities, but encourages new and broader ways for the professional to contribute to people and organizations.

As Rossett and Funderburg-Donello (in press) argued, there is much in KM that feels familiar:

- Devotion to human development and performance improvement
- Interest in capturing facts, information, knowledge, and expertise and in making all of it more readily available
- Connections among individuals for the purpose of deepening and distributing expertise, relationships, and work products
- Recognition that training alone cannot provide certain performance improvement
- Dedication to making certain that what is learned in class or on-line contributes to practice at work

TABLE 9.1. KM AND TRAINING.

Training Typically	*Knowledge-Management Perspectives*
The goal is development of individual capacity and memory.	The goal is creating, nurturing, and refreshing organizational resources and interactions.
The focus is on building up what's inside the individual.	The focus is on constructing a robust environment to surround people and enrich the organization.
A customer might say, "When can we schedule a class to introduce sales reps to the product?"	The customer will not typically come to us for KM. How can we change that?
Our responsibility is products and services that teach.	Responsibility expands to content development and social interactions.
We develop individual brainpower.	We collaborate to manage the organization's brainpower.
We communicate the right way to do it.	We attempt to show many ways to handle it, with commentary that illuminates standards and customization.
We work to build events, classes, and programs that will stand the test of time.	We contribute to materials and systems that enrich the organization and are updated readily, regularly.
Interventions must be of sufficient length and magnitude to justify travel costs.	The system is salient for problems and opportunities that are great and small, important and mundane.

The solution is cognitive distribution. Gery (1989), Rossett and Gautier-Downes (1991), and Pea (1993) encouraged others in the field to accept the concept of distributing performance-enhancing materials into learning experiences, such as training, *as well as into other means,* such as job aids, on-line help systems, and documentation. Trainers know that take-away materials extend the influence of the classroom. Knowledge management is a supercharged and systemic manifestation of that realization. Responsiveness to this concern is part of the strong case for KM, as wraparound knowledge bases and conversations accompany participants back to where the work gets done.

What Trainers with KM Perspectives Do

It is hard to argue about the potential for fruitful interplay between training and KM. Stamps (1997), however, reported that a review of seventy knowledge management projects by the American Productivity and Quality Center (APQC) found that only two projects involved training staff or human resource managers. Has time improved the situation? Are training and human resource professionals now capitalizing on the possibilities presented by KM?

Perhaps. Some signs of progress are provided as examples in this chapter. Look at LeadingWay. Consider Saba Systems. Visit Mindlever and Generation 21. We cannot yet point to a groundswell of change, but there are optimistic and tangible changes.

We're attempting here to encourage movement toward a definition of training that includes knowledge management perspectives, services, and products. Figure 9.4 presents an expanded view of the possibilities for the training and development professional. Note the parallel and linked work and the way that people, services, and materials move freely from one aspect of the work to the other.

A discussion of some of the new opportunities for you as a trainer presented by KM perspectives follows.

Create a Rich Environment

Where once trainers attended to the richness of rooms, lessons, and classroom interactions, KM prompts us to see, manage, and shape the learning and support possibilities within a larger environment. Consider two aspects of KM, the content and the social.

How can you contribute on both sides of the coin? What can you add to the knowledge bases? How can you salt on-line communities with cases, commentary, and examples? How might instructors and training professionals increase their influence by participating in on-line communities? Can you provide opportunities for individuals to self-assess in light of changes in services, products, and markets? Can you launch communities that target training and HR initiatives, such as safety or the rollout of a new operating system? Which aspects of classes create the most interest? For what materials do you receive requests? Those are the objects that should find their way into the organizational knowledge bases.

Bust the Boundaries of Classrooms

Knowledge management does not signal an end to classroom instruction. Instead, it means *sharing the best of the classroom with the rest of the organization*. The arms of the instructor are extended when training and KM come closer together. The instructor's "war stories" can be distributed across the organization. His examples can be posted on-line, along with commentary and caveats. His genius can now be coded in various kinds of support at the employee's fingertips. Other perspectives on the topic can accompany his and provide intriguing contrasts.

Knowledge management does not signal an end to classroom instruction. Instead, it means sharing the best of the classroom with the rest of the organization.

FIGURE 9.4. AN EXPANSIVE PROFESSIONAL ROLE FOR TRAINERS.

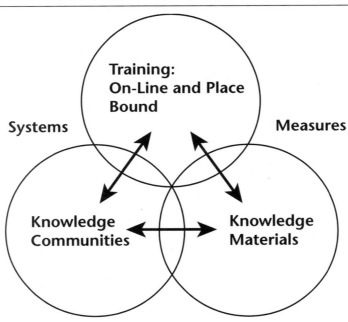

Visit on-line communities to solicit emergent problems so that classes are directed at pressing issues. Use the time in the classroom to test drive the rich KM resources to which participants may refer later after the class, when problems and opportunities are pressing.

Knowledge management transports relationships and ideas beyond four walls and into the organization (Barron, 2000). A pharmaceutical company provides an example. One of the key goals for their KM investment is to bring scientists from diverse fields and geographies together, on-line. Boundaries, especially disciplinary ones, are often viewed as stifling innovation. They believe that moderated KM communities tweak ingrained preferences.

Establish Broader Access to Information

Marshall and Rossett (2000) found that access to information did not occur with regularity in their respondents' organizations. Most managers were expected to justify *sharing* information, not *restricting* it. When the default is restricted access, it presents a barrier to KM. What can you do as a trainer? How can you draw attention to the problem? How can you serve as a voice for a freer flow of information?

Nurture Relationships

Most trainers are devoted to nurturing warm and supportive relationships in the classroom. Their careers often started because of those very talents, now extending to mentoring and coaching relationships. There is no need to abandon these inclinations. Instead, bring caring from the training center into the field. Help people with similar interests find one another. Provide a place where people can go to examine alternative approaches to selling X or repairing Y. Create a way for relationships commenced in classes to continue electronically. Tend to concerns about employment security and intellectual property. This topic is discussed in detail in Chapter Eight.

Ask Familiar and New Questions

Here we go from instructional designer to knowledge engineer, a leap that is not so great as many perceive it to be. One on-line resource from the Netherlands about concept mapping offers a list of software tools for representing content: www.to.utwente.nl/user/ism/lanzing/cm_home.htm

Resources associated with knowledge engineering and data mining are available at www.kdnuggets.com/companies. Tables 9.2 and 9.3 present questions that are at the heart of the KM effort. Notice that they are similar to those we've asked when trying to get at the essence of expertise.

Ask Different Things of Instructors

Two organizations, one associated with government and the other with manufacturing, bemoaned the many ways that their instructors have been dragging their heels regarding learning technologies and knowledge management. The instructors preferred the podium. They enjoyed engaging their students in classrooms. Many liked to travel to teach. Although some of that will continue, of course, the time has come for moving many critical lessons from the training center to the knowledge mainstream of the organization. As a trainer, you can help instructors to think of themselves as content sources. Assist them in transferring examples, commentary, and tools into knowledge repositories. Work to allay their concerns about doing so.

Instructors share our frustrations with failures associated with transfer. Through KM, instructors extend their influence, reaching beyond the classroom

TABLE 9.2. PLANNING FOR KM SUCCESS.

Anticipate Potential Obstacles

Has the organization attended to both sides of the equation, both the people and the technology?

How will the organization create a sharing and secure culture? How will it recognize and honor contributions?

How will you counter cultural resistance to putting favorite ideas where others might use, adapt, or even criticize them? Wim J. Nijhof, from the University of Twente in the Netherlands, described a European KM project that foundered because of inattention to culture and work preferences.

Do employees have the research and reference skills necessary for using the KM system?

Are they curious about their work, eager to find appropriate resources?

How will the system refresh itself?

How will it maintain quality and meaningfulness?

What kinds of approaches will be used to solicit feedback from users and potential users? How will this information inform the system? How will it help users assess contributions?

How can we slice and dice documentation and training materials to increase their use within the KM system? How can we infuse KM resources into classes and coaching sessions?

TABLE 9.3. WORTHY QUESTIONS.

KM Encourages Us to Ask Questions

What is keeping our people up at night? Where are they most proud?

What decisions are most difficult? To what might people refer for support and guidance?

What URLs are people pointing to? What strategic goals are related?

What examples and stories are repeated to new folks?

What know-how would have the most value if captured and archived?

What stories will provide critical lessons?

Where can other perspectives and approaches deepen knowledge? Save time?

How can we take the approaches of experts and bring several of their approaches together to look at core problems and opportunities?

What aspects of classes deserve wider distribution? Are there any checklists, cases, problems, tools, or war stories that deserve more eyeballs?

What elements from on-line conversations would enrich the system?

and into on-line communities and knowledge bases. In a KM world, instructors are valued most for what they know and the economic worth it brings to the organization, rather than for their ability to deliver in a classroom.

Not to be overlooked is concern about the employment security of experts and instructors. If what they know is captured and accessible, some are concerned about whether they continue to add value. Imagine that an instructor thinks, "If I give it to the knowledge base, how do I maintain importance in the organization?" It's a fair question.

The response involves a two-part role for instructors: (1) assuming new roles, including coaching, tailoring, participating on-line, and assessment, and (2) taking responsibility for continuing refreshment of the classes and resources so that they reflect emergent concepts, best practices, and line priorities.

Establish Alliances

As a trainer, you must seek new allies to educate about this expanded view of training. What is your relationship with information technology (IT)? Are you familiar with the databases used in the organization? Do you have access to them? When was the last time you contributed? When was the last time you worked with the line to update entries and add materials related to a growing concern or opportunity? Are you at the table when KM discussions are held? Do colleagues across the organization know of your interest? Can colleagues describe the fertile ground between training and KM? Find ways to *demonstrate* the rich possibilities inherent in this relationship. Mount pilot programs that illustrate those possibilities.

Repurpose Nearly Everything

Why is there a distinction between training materials and other materials? Why are the examples and work products housed within knowledge bases, rather than typically and generously sprinkled throughout classes? Why are the examples and war stories that enrich training not yet populating knowledge bases? The most valuable aspects of classes and knowledge bases should be starring on both stages. You must focus on building and encouraging materials that are actionable and on giving them featured roles via KM systems *and* learning opportunities.

Structure Materials and Conversations
to Enhance Meaningfulness and Quality

Marshall and Rossett (2000) found that *information overload* is an issue for training and performance professionals. Information overload is antithetical to KM. This has led some organizations to employ "cybrarians" or content managers to rationalize resources, refresh content, and then assure that it matches contemporary work and priorities. Jakob Nielsen's Website reiterates the importance of good information design with far-reaching commentary, ideas, and examples (www.useit.com).

Junk, and torrents of it, should worry us. In Barth's article, IBM's Scott Smith admitted just such a concern. According to Smith, in the past, the IBM Global Knowledge Management Consulting and Solutions organization encouraged contributions to the knowledge base with bonuses. What did they get? They got many, many contributions; most just beating the deadline set for the end of the year. Smith was quoted as saying, "Not only did they all come in at one time, they were incredibly long and unintelligible." Learning leaders must play a role in establishing systems to encourage, honor, and authenticate *useful* contributions.

Attend to the Social and Tacit Aspects

Knowledge management focuses on capturing that which is both critical *and* subtle. A 1997 Ernst and Young study of KM in 431 firms, reported by Pfeffer and Sutton (2000), found that firms were investing in knowledge repositories, such as intranets and data warehouses, building networks to identify internal resources, and implementing technologies to facilitate collaboration. Pfeffer and Sutton complained that this snapshot of KM reflected a limited view of the possibilities, one that showed a preference for codified information, such as statistics, canned presentations, and written reports, over stories, gossip, and insight into the way things *really work*.

Knowledge management focuses on capturing that which is both critical and subtle.

Many teachers, for example, have said that what they heard in the teacher's lounge encouraged success during their first years of teaching. Sales professionals often talk in similar fond ways about their informal social learning networks. Knowledge bases should be populated with anecdotal lessons just like those that once were shared in the lounge or local restaurant. It also points to the importance of communities of practice, where social networks are established and nurtured. An on-line paper by Hill and Raven (www.it.coe.uga.edu/itforum/paper46/paper46.htm) discussed factors contributing to on-line community successes.

Contribute to a Sharing, Positive Culture

It is almost trite to urge attention to establishing a sharing culture. Barth's article about KM horror stories reiterates that point (Barth, 2000). After an initial gush of enthusiasm for the topic, how is the organization telling its people that sharing, rather than hoarding, is expected and honored? If organizations fail to encourage sharing, knowledge bases and communities will languish, no matter the investment in technology.

What role can training and human resources play here? How can you as a trainer and performance professional help the organization anticipate stumbling blocks? How can you collaborate with colleagues to grapple with these issues? Pfeffer and Sutton (2000) cite a study by Teresa Amabile in which she showed that people who gave negative book reviews were perceived by others as more competent, leading to her conclusion that pessimism tends to be honored more than optimism. Would you toss your work products into a system where people are likely to criticize them? How can you protect willing participants in ways not so different than those employed in classrooms to nurture effort and bravery? There's a role for training professionals in fostering a culture that encourages people to risk and share, not hesitate, fear, and hoard.

Use Classes and Orientations to Create KM Habits

Examine classes. Look at on-line instruction. Are you showing off the knowledge bases in both venues? Are you talking up the communities of practice? Are you presenting real problems and then showing students how existing materials from the knowledge bases will help solve them? When you orient new people, do you talk about the organization's on-line communities and knowledge repositories? Do you provide information about those rich resources, just as you would connect new people to the on-line catalogues of classes? Establish habits that encourage seamless movement between classes and organizational knowledge resources.

Attend to Individuals Not Yet Ready to Be Self-Reliant

Are potential participants ready, willing, and able to engage with knowledge bases and communities of practice? Some are not. Many lack the meta-cognitive skills to search, find, adapt, and use the nuggets they do find. This creates a growing and critical role for training and development professionals.

Concentrate on Strategy, Management, and Integration

Conventional metrics typically incline training professionals toward staffing classes and boosting attendance. Knowledge management has the potential to change that, at least in part, as success depends on management and integration of a rich knowledge environment. Why move in this direction? There are many reasons, of course. One that appeals to executives is that brick-and-mortar classes have limits on enrollment. The resource can be used up; this happens when the seats are filled or the instructor is jet-lagged. Knowledge management bases cannot be exhausted.

How will you manage a steady and productive stream of knowledge assets? How will you distribute those resources through many delivery channels? How will you integrate them into mundane work? What communications systems will you wrap around them? How will you tailor the systems to meet the needs of diverse constituencies?

Dabbling in KM is futile. KM, much like training, must be an integrated aspect of the organization. Marshall and Rossett (2000) found that when resources are allocated to *both* KM technology *and* personnel, representing a significant commitment, those organizations reported strong evidence of KM.

Strengthen the Organization Afterward

A knowledge base offers rich resources to individuals. For example, it might help a salesman generate a sales proposal; it also might show him alternative ways to compare his company's product to competitors' goods. And after the salesman made his case to the customer, that same repository can welcome his labor. The system that coached and prompted his efforts now turns into a home for his contributions. When and if he chooses to leave the company, some ideas and artifacts will remain behind, enriching the organization. This seems fair and, not surprisingly, it appeals to organizational leaders.

Live the Expanded Role

Brook Manville, profiled by Stuart Silverstone (2000), has a career that reflects the possibilities inherent in bringing KM and learning together. Manville was a McKinsey and Company leader in global knowledge management. In early 2000 he joined Saba Software, a learning management systems company that has recently moved into end-to-end e-learning services. Now, Manville is Saba's chief learning officer and "customer evangelist." When asked by Silverstone about how KM is changing, he said (as we've been saying too), "First is the convergence of training—learning and learning programs—with knowledge management. Second, the Internet and markets on the Internet will play an increasing role in the distribution of knowledge and learning assets."

Why KM Falters

Our excitement about KM should be tempered with caution. The success rate is not yet what it ought to be. Knowledge management will not deliver unless we can anticipate the obstacles and make a concerted effort.

Johanna Ambrosio (2000) reported that at least half of all KM initiatives fail; some peg the failure rate as high as 70 percent. Why? Ambrosio offered several reasons, especially when HR and IT aren't involved together in the KM effort. She pointed to the failure of organizations to tailor compensation systems to support the unselfish values inherent in KM.

In the article, Viant's Chris Newell describes a better way: "We have eight different ways to earn stock, and five are directly related to growth and learning." Ambrosio also highlighted the importance of sponsorship for KM initiatives.

KPMG's Knowledge Management Report 2000 (Barth, 2000) found that the benefits of KM did not live up to expectations. They cited the following reasons for those frustrating results: lack of updates; failure to integrate KM into normal working practices; complicated systems; lack of training; and the fact that users did not perceive personal benefits.

Here are some key questions we should bring to the table when discussing KM initiatives in our organizations:

- What elements in the culture will encourage sharing rather than hoarding?
- In what substantive ways can the organization counter resistance to putting favorite ideas where others might use, adapt, or even criticize them?
- How will the organization deal with the issue of ownership, identity, and security?
- How will the organization recognize and honor contributions?
- How can we assure both quantity and quality of contributions? (See epinions [www.epinions.com] and fathom [www.fathom.com] for two different approaches to this issue.)
- How will we direct our system and top priority issues?
- What are people most concerned about? Where do they spend time?
- How do the systems address concerns and save time?
- Is the sponsor able to rivet attention across the organization? To maintain interest and commitment?
- Are the sponsor's interest and attention dependable or will they shift capriciously?
- Is the purpose of sufficient weight in the view of organizational leaders to attract and hold interest *and* resources?
- How will contributors be afforded the security and status that come from being the unique ones with knowledge about the topic at hand? (Marshall and Rossett found that only one-third of respondents' organizations offered incentives for contributions to a knowledge base and that not just any incentives would do.)
- How does the organization discourage restricting access to information?
- What makes the content in the repositories worthy? What is good stuff? What has meaning? (Because you can't guarantee perfection in a system that typically favors *rich options* over *one right answer,* you must seek customer and user reactions.)

TABLE 9.4. QUESTIONS AND ANSWERS.

Questions	Suggested Answers
You're in training. Why are you talking to me about knowledge management?	I am in training. Most important is that I am focused on learning and performance for the organization. That brings me to want to extend the reach of our classrooms and instructors and create a more learning-oriented environment throughout the organization.
What does training bring to KM?	We know the kinds of issues, questions, and problems that are plaguing people in the organization. We can help focus knowledge bases on what really matters. We also have many wonderful examples and tools in training that should be featured in the KM system. And the KM repositories and communities must be introduced in classes and encouraged. It's an opportunity to build good habits.
Any hesitations about KM for training?	Yes. In fact, an on-line interview with Dave Jonassen in Elearning Post (http://www.elearningpost.com/elthemes/jonassen.asp) raised important questions about KM and training. His main point: knowledge and learning cannot be managed—they depend on generative activities by learners. What do you think?
What about IT?	What about IT? They must be front and center in KM efforts, of course. No argument there. Our intention is to work with them to keep the efforts fresh and focused.
I love training. KM sounds like something that a database person or a librarian ought to be doing. How does a training person fit in?	Training events will endure, just be more carefully selected, and often supported by knowledge objects now available wherever and whenever needed. Rather than looking at KM as threatening training, see it as a way to extend the arms of the instructor. By the way, database and library reference skills are of great value too.
IT won't let us into the action.	Have you shown them reasons to invite you in? What knowledge objects are you contributing? In what ways are you adding value to the communities of practice? How are you creating knowledge and reference habits in the organization? What's the history of your relationship to their training efforts? This is a critical relationship, for many reasons. Why not use KM to forge closer ties?

- Do the knowledge bases reflect user priorities? (Although one salesperson might be compelled by product templates, fact sheets, and FAQs, others might crave commentary and war stories.)
- Where else might the systems founder?

Examine the questions listed above, in the literature, and in *Knowledge Management*. Even though the idea of separating knowledge from owners and sharing widely has immediate appeal to most executives, recognize that some individuals and constituents will be put off by the concept. How are you protecting intellectual property and answering employees' concerns that KM will capture their ideas in order to replace their labor? Although there are no easy answers here, these are issues that can bring the best of systems to a halt.

Questions and Answers

Table 9.4 presents typical questions that might be raised by sponsors and executives—and by you—as you examine the possibilities inherent in KM. We also offer some possible responses.

Knowledge Management in a Hurry

Table 9.5 lists resources keyed to the time you are able to devote to them.

TABLE 9.5. RESOURCES.

Time	Resources
"I have an hour"	Visit www.kmmag.com
	Visit www.buckmanlabs.com and http://home.att.net/~nickols/articles.htm
"I have a day"	Read Tom Stewart's *Intellectual Capital*
	Read Horton (see chapter resources)
	Visit http://www.brint.com
"I've got a week"	Visit http://defcon.sdsu.edu/3/objects/km/email
	Read Tiwana's book on KM tools (see chapter resources)
	Read Leonard (see chapter resources)
	Attend a conference. They are listed at www.kmmag.com

Spotlight on People

James Z. Li

Dr. James Z. Li's adult life has been dedicated to the "science" of knowledge. In 1991 Dr. Li had a vision, which he described thus: "If you could manufacture cars, you can manufacture knowledge." Li is the founder and chief executive officer of LeadingWay Corporation.

Training and Knowledge Management Discussing the importance of knowledge management for trainers, Li was direct: "It's time for training professionals to think about this question: 'What business are you in?'

"A lot of people in the training business are a bunch of dodos. They don't know it but they are about to become extinct. You may think it's a result of the Internet and e-learning, but it's not. It's because of the way they think and the mind-set they have. They are like the people aboard the Titanic who believed that the ship was unsinkable. They are like railroad companies who thought they were in the railroad business. They forgot about the passengers and did not realize they were in the business of trans-porting people. For organizations to survive in the 21st Century, they really have to take a global view of how to move people from beginners to experts and how to move knowledge from the ones who have it to the ones who need it faster and cheaper. Training professionals are in a good position to help their companies pro-duce, distribute, and manage knowledge for peak performance."

Organizations and Knowledge Management Li commented, when asked about the future of organizations and knowledge management: "Ten years ago, both IT and training organizations were facing the same question: 'How can we be strategic to our organization?' Ten years later, if a CEO does not have an IT or Internet strategy, he/she gets fired. Did you ever know a CEO who got fired because he/she did not have a training strategy?"

Li believes that, in the future, "The companies who will flourish are the ones who can create, distribute, and manage knowledge the fastest and cheapest. Training is the first step on the journey to expertise. Performance support lets you perform like an expert along the way, and knowledge management accelerates the pace of those who follow and learn from your experiences. The combining of all three into a single knowledge system offers a powerful tool for companies to compete in the knowledge economy."

Li concluded, "It's time for training organizations to become knowledge organi-zations and integrate KM into training and performance support practices to form a knowledge system that will change the way people learn, work, and share expertise."

Example of a KM Initiative Li gave us an example of a KM initiative at his own com-pany, LeadingWay. He said, "We help our customers manufacture, distribute, and manage knowledge. We believe in the principle of 'eat our own dog food' so we have implemented a knowledge system for our own employees that covers finance, sales, operations, and development in the form of LeadingWay University. KM is our competitive weapon in growing our organization and making LeadingWay a star in the emerging e-learning industry."

Li described the initiative thus: "Each group and individual has a set of core performance measures, and a knowledge system is built for each functional group. A knowledge system is an integration of training, performance support, and a knowledge management system. When new employees are hired, they go to LeadingWay University to take just enough training to get them started doing simple tasks on their jobs. They can access the knowledge systems 'just in time' on the job through the performance support system. If they still cannot do their job with the help of the reference materials, they have access to training on that task, either through e-learning or direct learning help."

He explained, "Any time a knowledge gap is identified or a best practice is found, we update the knowledge system immediately so that new knowledge is immediately available through both training and performance support systems. Because we use our 'Create Once, Knowledge Everywhere' [COKE] technology, we can update the knowledge once and distribute it in training, support, and knowledge management systems without the duplication of effort. Over time, the knowledge system gets smarter and smarter and will become a critical component of our business."

Contributions of the System Li shared that the initiative improved morale, boosted productivity, and reduced training costs. Revenue also doubled, and so did the number of employees. Li said that the company also "achieved the highest customer satisfaction in corporate history."

Advice for Training and HR Professionals Li offered the following advice: "KM is not about technology. It is about out-of-the-box thinking. Every training initiative can be transformed into an integrated learning and KM initiative, if you are willing to refocus your attention from training to knowledge."

Recommended Resources Li recommended APQC and their series on KM best practices, as well as LeadingWay's own white paper, "The Promise of E-Learning and the Practice of Knowledge System Design," at www.leadingway.com.

Jim McGee

McGee is one of the founding partners of DiamondCluster International. He described his background as follows: "We started DiamondCluster in 1994 with the idea of integrating technology, strategy, and implementation skills into a single, coherent organization. Before coming to DiamondCluster, I was one of the initial research fellows at Ernst and Young's Center for Business Innovation in Boston. At the Center, Tom Davenport, Larry Prusak, and I did some of the early research in the KM arena. Before that I was at the Harvard Business School, where I was doing research and getting a doctorate in electronic commerce.

"At DiamondCluster, I've been in charge of both our learning and KM efforts. I don't like the titles of 'chief learning officer' or 'chief knowledge officer.' I think they're seriously misleading. Periodically, I've described myself as DiamondCluster's 'chief knowledge architect.'"

Training Professionals and Knowledge Management McGee described why training professionals must cultivate an interest in knowledge management in this way: "I think these are fundamentally the same question. The only reason *not* to be interested [in knowledge management] is if you think you're in an organization where all the relevant knowledge is already well-understood and codified. Then you can ignore KM. You can probably also forget about your job or your organization in due course.

"In most of the organizations I see, the half-life of the knowledge base is getting shorter and shorter. If the knowledge base is turning over more rapidly, the learning organization (I prefer learning to training for a lot of reasons) has to get itself involved in how to help connect that knowledge to the mission of the learning organization. In other words, if you don't get yourself embedded in the knowledge that matters (that is, what's most relevant as tested in the marketplace), you're left doing compliance training or otherwise becoming marginalized in the organization."

McGee continued, "What I'd like to see more of from training organizations are efforts to improve the learning capacities of the organization and the individuals in it. That's more a disappointed commentary on how poor the learning skills are of even some of our brightest college graduates than anything else. Most of them know how to get A's, but few of them remember how to learn (if, in fact, they really ever knew much about how that happens)."

KM at DiamondCluster International We asked McGee to tell us about a KM initiative that contributed in his organization. He said, "We've tried a number of things. Some worked well. Others were largely failures, in retrospect. As a rapidly growing organization, we've been willing to try lots of things and kill the bad ideas pretty quickly.

"Overall, one of the things we have done in our early years is to focus on establishing elements of our cultural norms to foster knowledge sharing and use. Our cultural efforts have been more impactful in our early years than have our technology centered efforts. That's beginning to shift as we get bigger, although I'm willing to bet that the cultural norms we've established will continue to pay off.

"For example, we had the notion early on of designating a number of our people as 'knowledge leaders,' who we expect to develop younger staff's knowledge expertise and to contribute to client projects on the basis of their specific expertise, rather than their client relationship management skills or project management skills."

McGee continued, "We've been a high communications culture from the first days—voice mail and e-mail as part of the tech base. On a cultural note, knowledge leaders are always expected to get back to people quickly with answers to questions. Further, everyone is pretty comfortable sending queries out into the 'ether' and expecting to get help from somewhere. We've used mailing lists, intranets, and a variety of other technology tools to help that process and to help keep some more permanent resource of answers to questions handy. Recently, we've been having pretty good luck using instant messaging tools as another element in the mix."

McGee described what he believes is the most interesting effort/experiment that DiamondCluster has done, something they affectionately call the "Bizarre Bazaar." He explained, "The bazaar is something we tried first in the summer of 1997. One of our culture-building and sustaining practices are regular 'all-hands' meetings, where we bring everyone in the firm together for a face-to-face meeting.

"Early on, these meetings were monthly; then we shifted to bimonthly; and now we hold them quarterly but have expanded them to a two-and-a-half-day session. For the July '97 meeting, we decided to devote half the agenda to a mini-trade show/ bazaar. Any project team that wanted to could volunteer to set up a booth about their project. People could then move from booth to booth to see what was going on among their peers. We handed out awards for the best displays and teams got seriously into showing off their projects. We called it the 'Bizarre Bazaar' to encourage a bit of playfulness and have succeeded on that score."

McGee said, "The bazaar has now become an annual event. We hold it now in January at an all-hands meeting where the various MBAs and undergraduates with outstanding job offers also attend. Obviously, the bazaar provides a venue for projects to show off their stuff and for our people to interact with one another in a very high-energy, high-intensity setting. The trade-show setting also gives us an opportunity to showcase the breadth and diversity of our client work. One of the side effects is that it lets teams see how interesting their work is to others."

He continued, "It's not unusual for a team to get bored with its work and feel that other teams are doing more interesting work. The bazaar setting offsets that effect quite nicely. There are other things I think are important about the bazaar. One, it shows the power of culture in leveraging knowledge—far more powerful than technology if you can focus on making it work. Two, it shows the role and limits of central management/authority. We set up the circumstances and venue for the bazaar, but we let the teams choose how and what to do about it. In an organization like ours, with a very wide scope of practice, it's very important to allow for a great deal of latitude and judgment on the part of the field."

Advice for Training and HR Professionals McGee gave the following advice for training and HR professionals:

- "Don't look for or expect silver bullet solutions
- Focus on understanding organizational dynamics

- Don't restrict your perspective to inside the boundaries of your organization
- Don't let the IT group get hung up on technology nits
- Take advantage of early encounters/contact with new employees to set them along good paths of practice—help them connect to the 'hidden' aspects of the organization faster
- Focus KM efforts on the real problems of K-workers in the field—don't get distracted by KM systems designed to appeal to the egos/distorted perspectives of senior management"

Recommended Resources For people who want to learn more about knowledge management, McGee recommended Drucker (1999), Davenport and Prusak (1998), and Wenger's *Communities of Practice* (1998).

The Heart of the Matter

As training professionals, there is much that we can do to promote, encourage, and support knowledge management, but the first step is potentially the most difficult: selling your organization and its employees on knowledge management.

Slide 9.1

Defining Knowledge Management

Knowledge management (KM) is about getting the right knowledge to the right people at the right time.

Presenter's Notes

Core expertise, intellectual capital, wisdom—these are all words which describe the unique skills and knowledge that employees possess. Together, they are the collective wealth of the organization, its most valuable asset. Knowledge management is about accumulating this knowledge, growing it, updating it, making it vital, and spreading it throughout an organization. It is no simple task.

Slide 9.2

Knowledge Is Content

- Business intelligence
- Anecdotes
- Presentations
- Commentaries
- War stories

Presenter's Notes

When organizations view knowledge as content, they create systems to capture, organize, disseminate, and use it in meaningful ways.

Slide 9.3

Knowledge Is a Social Process

- ■ **Conversations**
- ■ **Communities of practice**
- ■ **On-line communities**
- ■ **Listservs**

Presenter's Notes

If you think about it, much of what we know we learned from other people—not from a class, a book, or a magazine. In this way, knowledge is a social process. People in a community of practice, in an on-line community, or on a listserv, for example, learn from one another *and* create new knowledge as they communicate, share opportunities, and solve problems together.

Slide 9.4

Why Does It Matter?

Incredibly, 80 percent of the world's biggest companies have KM initiatives in progress (Barth, 2000). The Knowledge Management Consortium was founded in 1997 to promote KM to business and other organizations. The World Bank calls KM an "urgent necessity" for global development, and a recent study found that consulting firms are leading the way with KM initiatives (Rossett and Marshall, 1999). KM is on the Web, in print, in schools, and in companies. Why? *KM Captures and disseminates knowledge that would otherwise be lost through carelessness and attrition.*

Slide 9.5

Training—and KM??

- Moving toward managing brain power
- Focusing on the organization and the individual
- Retaining the wealth of the organization through collection.
- Establishing artifacts and rich communities
- Repurposing everything

Presenter's Notes

When training professionals embrace knowledge management (KM), it expands the role they play in organizations and enables them to meet the unique needs of employees with customized, tailored information or training, exactly when they need it. For example, a sales rep in Zaire could tap into the company intranet or knowledge-management system and learn about customs in the United Kingdom or read "war stories" from colleagues. This enables employees to learn from their colleagues, rather than "reinvent the wheel" every time they are confronted with a new situation, challenge, or problem.

Slide 9.6

What Can a Training Professional Do?

- ■ **Repurpose nearly everything**
- ■ **Attend to the social and tacit aspects of knowledge**
- ■ **Contribute to a sharing, positive culture**
- ■ **Use classes and orientations to create KM habits**
- ■ **Concentrate on management and integration**
- ■ **Contribute to the "learningfulness" of the system**
- ■ **Live the expanded role**

Presenter's Notes

Knowledge management requires nothing less than a new organizational mind-set, one that recognizes knowledge and wisdom as the wealth of the organization; encourages interaction, collaboration, and cooperation; and understands that learning is a lifelong process that benefits employers and workers alike.

As training professionals, there is much that we can do to promote, encourage, and support knowledge management, but the first step is potentially the most difficult: selling your organization and its employees on knowledge management.

Resources

Ambrosio, J. (2000, July 3). Knowledge management mistakes. *Computer World*. www .computerworld.com/cwi/story/0,119, NAV47_ST046693,00.html.

Barron, T. (2000). A smarter Frankenstein: The merging of e-learning and knowledge management. *Learning Circuits*. Retrieved December 15, 2000 from the World Wide Web: www.learningcircuits.org/aug2000/barron.html.

Barth, S. (2000, October). KM horror stories. *KM Magazine, 3*(8), 37–40.

Davenport, T. H., & Prusak, L. (1998). *Working knowledge: How organizations manage what they know*. Boston: Harvard Business School Press.

Drucker, P. E. (1999, Winter). Knowledge worker productivity: The biggest challenge. *California Management Review, 41*(2).

Eisenhart, M. (2000, October). Around the virtual water cooler. *Knowledge Management, 3*(10),49–52.

Gery, G. (1989). The quest for electronic performance support. *CBT Directions, 2*(7), 21–23.

Hackos, J. T., & Stevens, D. M. (1997). *Standards for online communication*. New York: John Wiley & Sons.

Horton, W. (1999). *WBT and knowledge management, allies or arch-enemies*. Paper presented at the WBT Conference, San Diego, California, April 1999.

Hutchins, E., & Hollan, J. (1999). *COGSCI: Distributed cognition syllabus*. (www.hci.ucsd.edu/ 131/syllabus/index)

Lakewood Publications. (1998). Third world KM: The best place to start? *Online Learning News, 1*(39). www.ollo98.com/resource/newsletters/content.htm

Leonard, D. (1995). *Wellsprings of knowledge: Building and sustaining the sources of innovation*. Boston: Harvard Business School Press.

Marshall, J., & Rossett, A. (2000). An exploratory study of the relationship between knowledge management and performance professionals. *Performance Improvement Quarterly, 13*(3), 23–40.

Martinez, M. N. (1998, February). The collective power of employee knowledge. *HR Magazine, 43*, 88–92.

Neuhauser, P. C., Bender, R., & Stromberg, K. L. (2000). *Culture.com*. Toronto, Ontario: John Wiley & Sons.

Nickols, F. (2001). Knowledge management. On-line at http://home.att.net/~nickols/ articles.htm.

O'Dell, C., & Grayson, C.J., Jr. (1998). *If only we knew what we know*. New York: The Free Press.

Pea, R. (1993). Practices of distributed intelligence and designs for education. In G. Salomon (Ed.), *Distributed cognitions* (pp. 88–110). London: Cambridge University Press.

Pfeffer, J., & Sutton, R. I. (2000). *The knowing-doing gap*. Boston: Harvard Business School Press.

Prahalad, C. K., & Hamel, G. (1990, May/June). The core competence of the corporation. *Harvard Business Review, 68*, 79–87.

Prusak, L. (Ed.). (1997). *Knowledge in organizations*. Newton, MA: Butterworth—Heinemann.

Rossett, A. (1999). *First things fast: A handbook for performance analysis*. San Francisco: Jossey-Bass/ Pfeiffer.

Rossett, A., & Funderburg-Donello, J. (in press). Knowledge management and the performance professional. *Performance Improvement*.

Rossett, A., & Gautier-Downes, J. (1991). *A handbook of job aids*. San Francisco: Jossey-Bass/Pfeiffer.

Rossett, A., & Marshall, J. (1999). Signposts on the road to knowledge management. In K. P. Kuchinke (Ed.), *Proceedings of the 1999 AHRD Conference* (Vol. 1). (pp. 496–503). Baton Rouge, LA: Academy of Human Resource Development.

Rossett, A., & Tobias, C. (1999). A study of the journey from training to performance. *Performance Improvement Quarterly, 12*(3), 30–42.

Schwen, T. M., Kalman, H. K., Hara, N., & Kisling, E. L. (1998). Potential knowledge management contributors to human performance technology research and practice. *Educational Technology Research and Development, 46*(4), 73–89.

Silverstone, S. (2000, August). A conversation with knowledge management pioneer Brook Manville. *Knowledge Management, 3*(8), 45–48.

Stamps, D. (1997, August). Managing corporate smarts. *Training, 34*, 40–44.

Stewart, T. A. (1997). *Intellectual capital: The new wealth of organizations*. New York: Doubleday.

Szulanski, G. (1996, Winter). Exploring internal stickiness: Impediments to the transfer of best practices within the firm. *Strategic Management Journal, 17*, 27–43.

Tiwana, A. (2000). *The Knowledge Management Toolkit*. Englewood Cliffs, NJ: Prentice Hall.

Ulrich, D. (1997). *Human resource champions: The next agenda for adding value and delivering results*. Boston: Harvard Business School Press.

Wenger, E. (1998). *Communities of practice: Learning, meaning, and identity*. New York: Cambridge University Press.

CHAPTER TEN

WHERE TO FROM HERE?

Omar: I majored in engineering in college and got a job doing that right out of school. It's OK, but I think I want to build what they call "e-learning" programs.

Herta: I don't have any technical background at all. I was a psych major, and I've been out of college for fourteen years raising my kids. I've always had good public speaking skills; people tell me that training might be right for me.

Glenda: I bet I might have the job you're hoping for, Herta. I've been in corporate training for nine years now, but today all anybody is talking about is e-learning portals. Once they make a decision about which portal to go with, *if* they make a decision, I don't know what my role is going to be. Things are up in the air.

Allison: I think this field we call training will acquire a new and larger definition than you are considering. It won't be about on-line or instructor-led classes as much as it will be about relationships with customers, knowledge distribution, tailoring solutions that include these options, and integration of learning throughout the organization. Oh sure, we'll continue to deliver some of what we do in classrooms, but even more important will be anticipation of needs, speedy response, and follow-up with managers and participants.

All: That's training???

Into the Future

That is indeed the training we think we're moving toward. Although some manifestations of training and development are familiar, the outcomes, relationships, and services are shifting.

The future can be glimpsed in Chapter One. Look at Tables 1.1 through 1.3. Note the expanded view of the field. Those tables present emerging purposes, roles, relationships, products, and services. Training professionals are encouraged to anticipate, attend to individual *and* organizational growth, nurture knowledge bases, and systematically sprinkle development opportunities everywhere, from the intranet to the cafeteria, from the individual learner to on-line communities and knowledge repositories.

It's also clear that we are not yet there. We have taken baby steps on the road to that future. Look around you. Where are the surprising alliances? What has the training and development unit ceased doing? Commenced doing? Where are the continuous, expanded measurements? The rich knowledge bases? The link between training and knowledge management?

[R]ecording hits on Websites is not more consequential than was counting butts in training seats.

Of course, many training and development groups are currently moving classes on-line, but we are concerned that this movement is with the same perspectives and metrics that were brought to classes and workshops in the past century. For example, recording hits on Websites is not more consequential than was counting butts in training seats. Where are the hard questions about value added to the organization? Where is the check against the issues that precipitated training in the first place?

The 1999 ASTD State of the Industry study found large increases in the amount of training provided to individuals, with approximately 82 percent receiving training in 1999, compared to 69 percent in 1996. The Billcom *Training* magazine Census 2000 also presented a picture of a robust training enterprise, with $54 billion allocated and $19 billion spent externally for materials, vendors, and services. What remains to be done is to turn so much activity and so many transactions to strategic advantage.

The times thus present opportunities for Herta, Omar, Glenda, and the rest of us. Executives are more interested in training and development than they have ever been. But it will not be the career we once envisioned. Thus, in this chapter we go beyond the podium and into the future by highlighting eight key opportunities in the training and development field.

Opportunity 1: E-Business and Training and Development

Business Week (September 25, 2000) predicted that 50 percent of Koreans would be on-line by the end of 2000. The United States has already passed that mark. The Web will grow in importance for individuals and for organizations, especially as what *Business Week* (October 9, 2000, p. 145) calls "pokey copper wires" are replaced by speedy, broadband optical networks.

We're moving much of work and play to the World Wide Web. One of our friends gambles on-line. Another searches out patterns for quilts. Yet a third ponders his ancestral roots; a fourth researches her husband's chronic illness; and a fifth studies potential investments. This semester, seventy students are taking on-line graduate classes with San Diego State University's Department of Educational Technology. They hail from all over the world.

There are Websites that plan funerals, and even one that provides excuses if you are cheating on a loved one. All this, and e-learning too, is fueled by the promise of e-business.

What is e-business, and why is it interesting to us? E-business links the geographically separated through a transparent, speedy, and information-rich environment, the Internet, which provides a place for businesses and customers to do what they need and want to do. E-business provides many opportunities to fuel transactions, large and small. For example, Wal-Mart now expects its diaper suppliers to electronically track Wal-Mart's diaper sales and then to deliver the necessary stock in the required sizes. Wal-Mart relies on its diaper suppliers to use their expertise, bolstered by access to immediate internal Wal-Mart sales information. The benefit to Wal-Mart is that they avoid inventory costs and focus instead on what they do best.

What does the diaper story say to us about e-business? First, it *redefines* who does what. Second, note that Wal-Mart is *providing information* about its sales to organizations that are not Wal-Mart. Even before Wal-Mart knows, their supplier knows that a particular store in Paris or Portland is about to run out of jumbo diapers. Next, ponder these *new and trusting relationships* in the supply chain. Also, note how *speed and responsiveness* are honored. And finally, consider the *customer focus* that Wal-Mart and its suppliers are demonstrating.

How will e-business influence training and development in the future? The truth is, we don't know for sure. Let's speculate, however, on the possibilities, focusing on three different perspectives: the learner, the leader of an internal training and development organization, and the developer or designer of learning experiences and products.

The Individual Learner

The learner turns into a customer in an e-business world. That's a good place to be if caring and service accompany the jargon. Power and options shift to individuals. A senior citizen in Poland can choose to take an on-line class originating in Canada, and a college student at a state university in Idaho can enrich her academic program by taking business classes on-line with internationally renowned faculty through UNEXT (www.unext.com) or Quisic (www.quisic.com). Simultaneously, a telecommunications salesman in Mexico City can avail himself of references about data warehousing.

Size matters. E-business now provides the possibility to purchase one chapter of a book instead of the entire book. It also opens the door to acquiring one or two music cuts instead of the whole CD. Such benefits are significant for training and development. The salesman in Mexico City can purchase a short overview, a self-assessment, and some customer support materials. As his interest in data warehousing grows, he can bite off more learning and support materials, as needed.

More choices are great, but even better is that effective Web learning businesses will use *prior* choices and profiles to tailor *subsequent* services for customers. What they learn will help the companies suggest, otherwise known as "push," on-line classes, knowledge objects, products, and even brick-and-mortar conferences to people who might be presumed to need and want them. In the not-too-distant future, they'll infer preferences for learning and assessment strategies and nudge people to study in ways that congeal into desirable certificates, credentials, and career opportunities.

[E]ffective Web learning businesses will use prior choices and profiles to tailor subsequent services for customers.

The windows into individual preferences, needs, and proclivities do raise questions about privacy and security. E-businesses, including those devoted to learning, must develop approaches that earn and retain customer trust. If that special relationship is honored, the learner/customer will perceive that his or her personal information has been collected for reasons with merit.

Leaders of the Organization

If you are the leader of an organization charged with training and development, you already feel the hot breath of e-business and e-learning on your neck. It might sound like this: "I want 75 percent of our classes on-line by the end of next year" or "Which learning management system (LMS) is it going to be?" or "We've got to keep track of what they know, the classes they've been in, their career paths. Put it on-line where we can see it, and they and their managers can, too."

Competing vendors cannot help but confuse leaders. ASTD's Donna Abernathy reviewed the landscape in ASTD's free on-line magazine, www .learningcircuits.org/oct2000. She wrote, "You'll soon realize the hefty challenge of determining what businesses some of them are in. And you can chalk up part of the haziness to the shear speed of e-learning. The blur. There's increasing overlap among vendor offerings as companies expand and enhance their services. For instance, IBM Mindspan Solutions—presented here as a service provider—is also a key technology player. VCampus and RWD Technologies straddle those two segments, as well. Learn2.com and eMind.com fall into the services and content groups. And Pensare, Ninth House, SmartForce, Mentergy, Knowledge-Planet, and DigitalThink are considered to be key players in all three areas: content, technology, and services."

How might e-business perspectives and technologies change your performance and learning strategy?

- Many organizations, such as Smartforce, Click2Learn, DigitalThink, and Playback Media, want to partner with internal human resources. We are no longer alone, smack dab in the middle of an organization, waving our arms to attract attention to education and training. Others are eager to aggregate and provide on-line people development opportunities, no matter where employees are or what they need.
- The distinctions between the inside and the outside will blur, especially in the ways they appear to employees within organizations. When employees visit their corporate learning portal, it will be branded in a way that suggests that it is a resource that is theirs and theirs alone, tailored to their organization. It will be up to internal professionals to tailor the participants' experience so that relevance is more than the corporate logo.
- Potential partners will want to help you track people by providing insight into their participation, performance, and progress. Learning management systems (LMS), such as Saba, Docent, Ingenium, and Arista, have the potential to serve individual employees and line leaders. The challenge is to put into place indicators that transcend hits on Websites.
- External vendors are beginning to offer a compelling array of end-to-end services that reflect standing priorities in the training business. They are promising options tailored to individuals, assessments, and progress tracking. Note that Arista and DigitalThink are now one. Ingenium and Click2Learn have long been joined at the hip. Saba, with an early strategy focused on learning management, is now offering learning content.

How will you discern quality? In the midst of so many options, discerning which is best must become a growing aspect of the job. Brand will help, of course. For example, fathom.com promises authenticated content from prestigious and ancient institutions. Unext uses a similar model. How could you doubt business classes offered by faculty from the London School of Economics and the University of Chicago? But brand isn't the whole story. Lguide (www.lguide.com) and trainseek (www.trainseek.com) provide independent reviews of on-line classes on topics as diverse as software, sexual harassment, and leadership. Lguide offers head-to-head comparison on popular topics and recently even presented a vivid review of a class about Islamic investing.

Although historically line executives tossed employees and responsibility to centralized training units, the Web enables us to provide continuous windows into employee needs, performance, and persistence to the people who *should* most want it, their managers. The crux is to concentrate manager attention on this new data and to help them use it.

Designers and Developers

The Web provides designers and developers with better ways to build programs. Of most obvious benefit is access to fresh information about learners and their preferences and priorities. That knowledge will extend to insight into the attractiveness and effectiveness of training materials, using reactions, choices, pauses, leaps, glitches, disappearances, and performance outcomes.

The Point. E-business is all about speed, an attribute rarely associated with the work of instructional designers and developers. More templates, tools, wizards, and resources will characterize the future. With access to archived learning objects, templates, tools that nudge development, and shared on-line workspaces for feedback, we will grow faster at the work.

Relationships with on-line providers and other vendors will enable internal professionals to attend to preparing employees for learning and to working with managers and sibling colleagues to follow up. Just as Proctor and Gamble is aware of Wal-Mart's diaper needs, so too will on-line providers signal us about employees who have neglected compliance obligations, such as safety or sexual harassment training. On-line partners will be there with options that promise both compliance and proof of compliance with a keystroke.

But does that guarantee meaning? Internal training organizations must help everyone in the organization play roles in converting on-line experiences into individual and organizational expertise and habit. Creating value from all this training will come from within the organization, from contracts that have been established with the line, and from supervisors who engage their employees in conversations after brick-and-mortar or e-learning experiences.

Not too long ago, altering a class was a great big deal. It involved cracking into an existing course, editing numerous sections to reflect changes, reworking time frames and expectations, and tweaking endlessly. Most believed that it was best if the person who built the class did the revisions, as only he held the keys to what was there and where it was located. In truth, often the developer preferred to leave well enough alone.

That is no longer the case with object-oriented design and development. Very much in keeping with the e-business discussion above and knowledge management in the prior chapter, "objects" present a responsive, flexible, economical, and speedy way to do what we do.

Opportunity 2: Building Objects

"Objects" Defined. Instead of producing long, unbroken learning sequences, an object-oriented developer slices and dices so that content morsels are accessible, updatable, and available for ready redeployment. Objects are housed in databases with tags that make it possible to find what

[A]n object-oriented developer slices and dices so that content morsels are accessible, updatable, and available for ready redeployment.

you need, when you need it. Hunting for an example of a contracting procedure? Seeking a case that illustrates a concept, such as shared decision making, or looking for a short sequence that teaches a particular kind of negotiating or the way the electoral college works? All that is in the database, and because it is tagged and its context is independent, it can be found and repurposed by someone not the original author.

Warren Longmire's article in ASTD's *Online Learning Circuits* offers an excellent primer on the topic (www.learningcircuits.org/mar2000/primer).

Bob Hoffman (see Chapter Six) is making the object concept come alive for advanced graduate students at San Diego State University. What SDSU classmates are piloting has been influenced by the CISCO Re-Usable Learning Objects Strategy (www.cisco.com/warp/public/10/wwtraining/elearning/learn/whitepaper_docs/rlo_strategy_v3–1.pdf). Also see www.leadingway.com and www.gen21.com for efforts inspired by object-oriented perspectives.

The objects movement is likely to mean:

- *More sharing and less repeat work.* For example, at a very decentralized financial services company, they tried an objects approach for a priority need. Instead of having each distinct unit build separate classes and fact sheets and customer materials about the new Roth IRA accounts, they created a database of reusable objects that could be called on across the organization. Available for adaptation were worked examples, job aids on how to fill out the forms, sample questions to qualify customers, and a basic introduction to the concept.

- *Smaller morsels to be accessed and updated.* One of the problems in our business is legacy materials that linger and burden. An object orientation makes it easier to appreciate legacy elements, toss the aged, update the salvageable, flexibly re-configure, and tailor for the circumstances. Professionals will be more willing to entertain change and updates if past efforts can be swiftly accessed and altered.
- *Shorter courses and materials.* Why are courses as long as they are? Is it that people learn better in longer gulps over days and weeks? No, it's because most orga-nizations see little value in transporting people for thirty minutes, one hour, or even two hours of training. That reluctance has encouraged the development of engagements that are flabbier than they need to be.
- *Context to give meaning and life to objects.* An issue that accompanies context-independent objects is that they can be dull, dull, dull, because they are distant from an authentic context or a dynamic professor. They are not much fun to read, but they are very useful to employ. Training professionals and in-structors will assume the job of investing them with meaning and context—of tailoring them so that they become interesting. Training and performance professionals must activate the assets. The challenge will be to fold objects into experiences and environments that grab and retain attention.
- *Speed and customization.* When the organization has a rich array of small objects on topics that matter, such as customer service, safety, spreadsheets, or team-ing, good things happen. Tasked with constructing an on-line or instructor-led class on any of those topics, rich resources are just keystrokes away. The orga-nization knows what it has. Links between the sales knowledge base and sales training become tighter and more obvious as examples, cases, and customer materials can be extracted from the database and used for both purposes.

Opportunity 3: New Roles and Permeable Boundaries

Publishing houses have seen themselves as content developers for a long time. Some professors are coming around to that definition of themselves as well. Even newspaper publishers have begun to see themselves in that view. And so do many of the up-and-coming e-learning developers, such as Quisic, UNEXT, Ninth House, ElementK, Pensare, and DigitalThink.

What do these sources intend to do with all this content? They hope to sell it to organizations and individuals. They're going into the conventional training and development business as your personal portals or as your corporate university. Most surprising of all, they don't intend to stop at the doors of government and industry. They also want to be your alma mater, without hassling with the campus, ivy, and tenure.

If UNEXT and Quisic can take on academia, then academia can ponder using its content and brand wealth to provide learning to even the unmatriculated. Yes, universities are busting the boundaries of the ways they think about themselves and their treasured resources. Visit www.ucla.edu. The drop-down menu on the opening screen provides a glimpse of the future for higher education. Define your relationship with UCLA, and the screen and offerings are tailored to you. It's similar to Yahoo, except that it's stocked with on-line and campus courses, expert professors, public funding, and brand.

As you can see, conventional boundaries will erode in the future, as publishers, universities, and start-ups redefine themselves, seeking ways to be your education, training, and information providers. Content will be the nose under the camel's tent, but it will not stop there. Access to organizations will commence with materials that teach time management, ancient history, or spreadsheets, but will grow to organizational services.

They will jump from e-learning content to *linking their content to organizational competencies*. For example, a recent start-up is focused on moving away from the course model to matching smaller learning and information support objects to career competencies and performance management systems.

Others will concentrate on delivery, wherever you are, whenever you want it, *even if you can't plug in*. Names like Palm, Blackberry, PageWriter, and OmniSky will attempt to deliver on this promise, already of interest to the hospitality and medical industries. These wireless options are the next frontier for providing what employees need, when they need it.

Opportunity 4: Taming Choices

Consider the choices. There are brick-and-mortar options, such as coaching, classes, and mentoring. Then there are electronic options, ranging from e-learning classes, to on-line help systems, to templates, decision support tools, and knowledge bases. E-learning gurus Elliott Maisie and Brandon Hall recognize the many options and encourage combined systems, which they call "brick and click," or "blended."

But what would the combinations look like? How much brick and how much click? How do performance and need data transfer into those decisions? Will the issue be brick-ness versus click-ness or the strategies used within the particular delivery systems, a point of view that hearkens back to Clark's (1983) work on strategies and media. His strong case focused attention on learning strategies over any particular medium.

A presentation by Parrish and Wang (2000) at the Association for Educational Communications and Technology raised intriguing questions about strategies and choices. Parrish and Wang's work at the University Corporation for Atmospheric Research (UCAR) serves the meteorology community. Meteorologists have been fortunate to be treated to programs that model the best of cognitive theory delivered on-line, including opportunities to work on cases and simulations and to reflect and interact with authentic situations.

Recently, the UCAR team turned to webcasts (www.meted.ucar.edu), a more directive and instructor-dominant strategy. Wang and Parrish reported a reaction that was surprisingly positive. Quotes from participating meteorologists suggested that UCAR had now gotten it right.

The point, of course, is not that directed, streamed, and archived strategies are "right," with independent learner-led approaches the "wrong" way to go. Rather, the point is that our approaches remain debatable. Brick *or* click? Brick *and* click? Instructor-led? Learner choices? Instructor *and* learner-led? The devil lurks in the details and the answers remain to be seen.

Opportunity 5: International Vistas

Fruitful and difficult challenges are presented by global organizations, employees, and customers. When you cast your eyes beyond traditional borders and into new alliances close and far, opportunities and dangers expand exponentially. Simple solutions are seductive; we know a global company that tried to reduce its "American-ness" by creating word-processed documents in British English.

As good as boundary busting is, there are substantial indirect costs associated with interactions outside the core unit. It takes resources to interoperate. The ability to do that well, to take advantage of partners' core capabilities, to give up habitual aspects of the work and seize on others, and to not squander resources in interaction costs will demand our attention in the future. Languages, cultures, oceans, and mountains enlarge the challenges.

People in the training and development business are finding themselves with much broader vistas. A training and development consultant might live in London, but focus on change management in Eastern Europe and Asia. Another colleague, also in this field we loosely call "training," may work in a cubicle in India to build an authoring tool that will make it possible for subject-matter experts all over the world to move their ideas and expertise on-line. A third internal consultant may head up a team attempting to establish international project management standards. Her team could span the globe. Her task might be to transcend the differences in time zones, languages, and cultures to produce approaches that will generate classes and performance support tools of use to her organization's employees, no matter where they live.

People in the training and development business are finding themselves with much broader vistas.

Yesterday, one of the authors received a call from a telecommunications company. Successful in the United States, they are now buying and partnering around the world in order to facilitate wireless communications. They must crystallize and communicate processes that have made them what they are so that distant acquisitions can mimic, adapt, and eventually enjoy similar results. How will they capture and promulgate the content and standards at the heart of their current efforts, while simultaneously incorporating the strengths of other cultures?

Executives, not surprisingly, would prefer to believe that there are eternal verities, that what we know to be successful in Des Moines and Dublin will transfer neatly to Lisbon and Pretoria. Sanchez and Curtis (2000) raised questions about such sweeping generalizations, providing explanations for why cross-cultural efforts sometimes try our patience. Although it would be great to hold hands across the oceans and build programs for shipment worldwide, Sanchez and Curtis's recent discussion of Hofstede's landmark work (1980) made a convincing case otherwise.

Ever noticed how different the Germans are? Or how the Malaysians seem to be very much one way rather than another? Sanchez and Curtis (2000) note that people from outside cultures are often more conscious of country characteristics than those who are inside. They say that training and development professionals must walk a tightrope when noting and honoring country and cultural differences and laboring to avoid limiting stereotypes.

Hofstede's research pointed at four dimensions: (1) avoidance of uncertainty; (2) masculinity; (3) power distance; and (4) individualism. Hofstede added a fifth dimension, time orientation.

These authors' work provides some explanation for why people in different cultures love or hate rules, hang on to or eschew security, crave or avoid collaboration, are timely or tardy, or share or hoard their best ideas. Who hasn't noticed differences? Who doesn't worry about success and appropriateness when outside one's own comfort zone? It becomes even more daunting when one is developing print or electronic materials for dissemination *everywhere*. This topic will claim much more of our attention in the future.

Sanchez and Curtis highlight the concept of individualism versus collectivism, noting implications for supervision, performance management, and rewards and recognition.

What is the training professional to do? First, recognize that the differences feel greater when you are outside the culture. There are many similarities. People are people, but they are also formed by their history, religious backgrounds, and organizational experiences. Start by appreciating the similarities; then be prepared for differences. Examine some of the dimensions noted in Hofstede's work. Form committees with representatives from across the globe so that diverse views and examples can be discussed.

Finally, build every program so that there is standard content that establishes the core message. Provide reasons why the material is the central focus. Then seek out opportunities to localize and incorporate the intriguing differences in cultures and countries. For example, the wireless telecommunications equipment company mentioned earlier will proclaim a common set of processes. At the same time, they will build materials that ask country leaders to check for congruence and adapt processes to respect local regulations and mores. Anticipate abrasiveness between the core, repeated messages and local realities. Establish processes to resolve the inevitable issues when they emerge.

A final suggestion is longer term. Many who are successful at working in global contexts have had experiences outside their countries of origin. Although American finance and technology consultants often spend months and years abroad as part of their career trajectories, training and development professionals rarely do. We and the organizations we serve will profit from those experiences and networks.

Opportunity 6: The Knowledge Cocoon

Training professionals will continue to lament their problems with transfer of training. One way around that concern, according to Jill Funderburg-Donello, chief learning officer at Leading Way in Irvine, California, is knowledge management. Knowledge management circumvents the transfer issue by *embedding information and guidance in the job, where people can reach for it when they need it.* This approach to enriching the environment contrasts with treating learning as a separate event with the *potential* to matter to the student, perhaps some time in the future.

Consider knowledge as a cocoon that can wrap around workers. It is there when a doctor is weighing the benefits and detriments of a particular drug for a particular patient; there when the accountant is auditing a project; and there when a teacher is explaining a standardized test to parents. The impetus behind KM systems is that they can be used to distribute and archive ideas, subtle know-how, and standard messages across far-flung organizations. It's there to guide and boost performance when the need emerges. Visit a wonderful, free resource about electronic performance support by Bill Miller at www.epssinfosite.com/index.htm.

Our knowledge management future will present the following opportunities:

- Knowledge management will help us to extend expertise, wisdom, and thoughtfulness beyond the classroom and into the places where the real work is done.
- Our job will involve capturing individual and organizational "smarts" (What's in? What's out? How is it distributed? Who maintains it?).
- We must focus on the culture of the organization and answer questions such as: Why will employees share rather than hoard? What will encourage generosity? How will the organization earn the trust of individuals so that they will donate their individual efforts, ideas, and products to the system for the collective good?
- Knowledge management will expand the training professional's role in the organization from a focus on events and individual capability to include responsibility for a rich organizational repository, useful tools, and wizards, and ongoing dialogue.

Senge (1990) captured the attention of business leaders and training professionals when he wrote about the learning organization. This is where his ideas will come true.

Opportunity 7: Career Self-Reliance

The future will bring more choices to individuals. Not only will most individuals perceive that as appropriate, but their organizations have come to share this view. For example, a pharmaceutical company shifted from bureaucratic arrays of classes to career self-reliance for global employees. Leading human resource thinkers, such as David Ulrich (1998), acknowledge the shift to a greater role for the individual employee in her own growth and development.

With career self-reliance the individual takes over more of the planning, execution, and self-management associated with career planning and development. Silicon Valley has many knowledge workers who look at themselves, their careers, and their opportunities in just this way.

As Suzanne Valery, a San Diego-based consultant, said, "Career self-reliance in the new world of work will mean focusing on the skills needed to maintain one's 'employability.' It is less about career pathing *within a particular organization* and more about *identifying with one's profession as a whole.* Self-reliant workers prepare for continued employment in a rapidly changing environment by applying concepts of strategic management in planning their career. They must remain informed of the changes in their industry and take responsibility for learning the skills that will be required three to five years in the future" (personal communication to author).

An example is Canadian Imperial Bank of Commerce, which devised an approach to developing human capital that essentially snubbed formal curricula and classroom-based training methods (Stewart, 1997). Rather than offering classes to the staff, managers were instructed to let employees learn by shadowing colleagues. Learners retained independent access to traditional training materials, books, and software—even formal classes when necessary. More initiative and scheduling falls to employees.

Does this take the organization out of the loop? May executives wash their hands of support for ongoing professional development. No! Most likely, the organization will retain three critical roles:

1. Providing *leadership* in defining the future, including offering guidance on the directions the organization and key specializations will take and providing strategies for self-assessment and supervisory assessment
2. Supporting and tailoring *resources* to encourage and enable development and support, such as classes, on-line modules, on-line job aids, knowledge bases, and coaching programs
3. Tracking *progress* so that employees and their managers know their current status and readiness for the future

At the same time, while organizations set goals, provide resources, and track progress, individuals will be encouraged to power their own growth and development. The tractable employee who meekly toddled off to training class is a dying breed, to be replaced by another who says what he needs, asks for targeted development and support, and finds them for himself, perhaps on-line, if necessary. We can envision that this employee might even depart the organization if critical needs are not being met.

Some years back, one of the authors was asked to look at engineering retention in a global petrochemical company. Engineers were leaving the company to work for competitors, and the company wanted to know why. Exit interviews and internal focus groups told the story. Prized engineers were willing to leave in part because they perceived that their careers and skills were not being sufficiently valued and attended to by the company. Without a sense of being valued, they chose to move to competitors who paid more. This shows what happens when the organization removes itself from development. Organizational loyalty can be threatened.

How can a company take advantage of the strengths of motivated and self-reliant individuals, and yet boost loyalty? The organization must manifest interest in individual employees, provide tailored opportunities, and enable concerted, effective, and supportive experiences at work. Career self-reliance should not be code for spending less money on employee development.

Irrelevant, burdensome training will be less tolerated by employees when they have many other choices for professional development. . . .

The career self-reliance that grants more agency to employees also forces internal training professionals to increase the quality of what they offer or broker. Irrelevant, burdensome training will be less tolerated by employees when they have many other choices for professional development and of places to work.

Retention of talent is a growing part of the work of training and human resource professionals. It includes providing the highest quality learning and support for employees.

Opportunity 8: Sorting a Pile of This from a Pile of That

More individuality, portability, and job shifting will increase demand for recognizable quality and credentials. Organizations need ways to know what a candidate knows and to determine the value of a degree or certificate. Did an employee who studied on-line with an e-learning dot-com acquire more than a piece of paper? Which e-learning providers offer the most quality? These are vital questions about *any* learning experience or vendor, but the current flood of new providers and new formats make decisions even more difficult.

Complicating the situation is the trend toward distant managers who specialize in project management rather than a technical area. They must be effective at assessing candidates, credentials, and performance.

Even the U.S. Senate is taking notice of the flood of new options and recognitions. For example, Nebraska Senator Bob Kerrey chaired a careful look at Web-based education (www.hpcnet.org/webcommission). Although evaluation companies such as Lguide (www.lguide.com) and Trainseek (www.trainseek.com) make on-line products more transparent to the marketplace, many buyers continue to perceive their options as overwhelming and impenetrable.

Busy individuals continue to be surrounded by regulations constructed *before* the Internet created so many e-learning options. A true story from one author's e-mail illustrates the point. It was written by the husband of a harried nurse and mother:

"By now we were in the last week of September. My wife's nursing license re-
newal, complete with a CEU provider number, needs to be postmarked by
September 30. Janet became a distance learning student. The course layout
was a simple read and click. Read sixteen articles and answer a 100-question
true/false test on-line. Knowing that it would be impossible to sit at a computer
reading sixteen articles on-line, she decided to download the articles and test
to print them. Given our 28.8 Internet connection, this task took about thirty
minutes.

"If you ever had small kids, it is amazing how fast time gets sucked into the
past. On Saturday morning, September 30th, Janet wakes up early to start her
'distance learning course.' But instead of printing all the articles, Janet printed
the 100-question test and then opened each article on her desktop in Microsoft
Word. That way, she simply read the test question and used the SEARCH and
FIND feature in Word to look up the answers for each of the true/false questions
(okay, I'll admit, I gave her the suggestion about the search-and-find shortcut).
By lunch, the mission was accomplished.

"The last step was to go back on-line to actually take the test. By now, I am
sitting alongside as a cheerleader, observer, and coach. As Janet worked her way
through the screens, she read, 'Seventy percent is passing and you are entitled
to one retake of the exam before paying for the course.' She looked at me and
said, 'If I knew that, I could have taken the test cold turkey. I bet I could have
passed and saved myself the morning!' An hour later, after two computer crashes
and a very poor logic flow for completing the test and paying for it on-line,
Janet received: (a) a score of 92 percent (eight questions were obviously poorly
worded); (b) a $47 charge to her credit card; and (c) the CEU certificate and
provider number. She was officially an e-graduate and, more importantly, certified as competent to be a nurse for yet one more year."

Another friend, Sharon, was caught sneaking through the end of a green
light. One week later, she found a picture of her misdeed in the mail, with a ticket
for $301 and information about driving schools. Sharon jumped at the on-line
option. She signed up and took her class exactly as Janet did. (Interesting, each
independently found her success strategy of not bothering with the learning materials, but instead relying on the test questions and the search function.) What
did Sharon learn? Not a thing. Will it influence her driving? Not at all. Was she
a satisfied on-line student. Yes indeed. Her experience fulfilled her requirements,
with little fuss or bother.

The easy way is attractive to humans. And so is the promise of a stunning
value proposition. In their June 2000 white paper about return on investment,

Docent, Inc., wrote, "A docent e-learning solution is expected to deliver a minimum of 400 percent return on investment in the first twelve months versus traditional education and training approaches."

Such promises can't help but attract the attention of executives. They should rivet us as well, because we must provide the discernment and organizational support necessary to convert hope into some version of reality. Verification of promises and quality assurance will become a growing focus of our work.

More Than Pieces of Paper

In the past decade, we have witnessed the popularity of Novell and Microsoft technical certificates. These were a harbinger of things to come. The "goodness" of a single class or coached experience appears to be greatly increased by its proximity to others on a certificate or by its association with a recognized entity through accreditation or branding. This bundling of experiences, classes, coaching, and knowledge objects into something with more substantial identity will grow in importance to individuals and to organizations.

Certification. *Certification* is granted to individuals in recognition for learning a collection of useful skills in, for example, maintaining Novell networks, life saving, technical writing, or taking x-rays. Would you rather entrust your child at a pool with certified life guards or to some teens from the neighborhood?

Accreditation. *Accreditation,* on the other hand, is granted to institutions or agencies. In light of some set standards, institutions make a case that they have the wherewithal (faculty, libraries, standards, concern about equity, access, and so forth) to be recognized as an accredited college, dental graduate program, or barber school. An independent accrediting agency examines the institution. With accreditation comes the ability to grant degrees, typically recognized as the manifestation of the institution's worth and the individual graduate's worth as well.

Brand. Bigger even than a single certificate or degree is *brand*. Harvard has it. The London School of Economics does too. So do the Culinary Institute of America and the Sorbonne. Their very names connote excellence. Of course, just like Coca-Cola and Mercedes Benz, they must protect that brand by monitoring quality. Learning professionals must also determine if they have lived up to that responsibility. Some questions about certificates, credentials, and brands are presented in Table 10.1.

TABLE 10.1. QUESTIONS ABOUT CERTIFICATES, CREDENTIALS, AND BRANDS.

Ask these questions before you "buy" the program or the credentials of the person

Can you see why they bundled these skills together? Can you see the value that is added by this combination of programs or classes?

When did they last update their offerings?

How is effectiveness measured?

Will they ask your organization to participate in measurement?

What data does the program have from graduates? From organizations that have employed their graduates? Can they point to return on investment data?

Are they accredited? What did the accrediting body ask of them? When were they last accredited? Has anybody *not* been accredited?

If they are making their case through their brand, are these programs associated with the university or entity that has earned the brand? Is this coming from Harvard, for example, or from their extension arm?

How much has the branded entity actually been involved in the programs you are contemplating? What has the famous expert or professor contributed? When was the last time the expert touched the program? Have they been exercising continuous involvement and quality control?

If a candidate for a position is pointing to a credential, ask: What did you learn? What can you do now that you couldn't do before? What problems did you solve as a result of your studies? How would you improve that program? What additional development is appropriate for you now?

Keep in mind that the our new world gives more power to individuals and markets and quite a bit less to cultural elites. Press entities to earn their brand, your respect, and your institution's business over and over again.

Questions and Answers

Table 10.2 presents possible questions from HR and training professionals about the future and their place within it.

TABLE 10.2. QUESTIONS AND ANSWERS.

Question	Answer
What am I going to do? I liked my old job.	Many aspects of your old job will endure. You'll continue to develop people. You'll continue to develop programs. You'll continue to worry about quality. You should remain concerned about the strength of individuals, but expand your attention to the *health of the organization* and its ability to support its people. The difference is in the accountability and the forms your efforts will take. Most likely, there will be less happening in the classroom, and more occuring through alliances with siblings in your organization and partners outside. Manage and integrate.
But I really, really liked delivering classes.	Well, opportunities for making presentations remain, but probably not in as many conventional classroom settings. Work with sponsors and customers. Brief them. Help them help their employees use independent learning opportunities.
I see myself as a program developer.	Good. The need for integrated programs tailored to situations and reaching across oceans will grow. However, try to begin to think of yourself less as a person writing programs and more as a *manager and integrator.* Oh, you'll still write, and plenty. But the success of the writing depends on the systems into which the writing is placed.
Do I have to be involved with technology? I'm a people person.	You must be involved with technology, but your focus need not be on Java scripting or XML. Focus instead on how technology delivers to people, on their readiness for the programs, on follow-up, and on selecting programs and management systems that deliver real meaning for the people and the organization. Put pressure on the technology to serve people.
You're painting a much more strategic role for training people. Will it happen?	We think so. But you must play a part in it. The needs are there. Executives are howling for more e-learning and cost savings. External vendors are at the walls with enticing options and big promises. Line leaders want what they want when they want it, with few loyalties to internal organizations or prior favored vendors. The opportunity is through responsiveness, busting boundaries, alliances, and quality assurance.
I'm sold. What do I do next?	You've just begun. You've read a book about the possibilities and now have electronic and print resources at your fingertips. Take advantage of contemporary interest in lifelong learning and knowledge management. Finally, our themes are at the vortex of most organizations' agenda. Go for it.

Spotlight on People

Janice Sibley

Janice Sibley is a consultant and the owner of Corporate Resources in Gaithersburg, Maryland. Her company offers strategic market planning and team facilitation services, as well as leadership in training development projects for organizations. Prior to starting Corporate Resources, Sibley directed training development and marketing processes for corporations within the computer software and optical publishing industries. She has eighteen years of experience directing development and marketing projects for various companies and associations, particularly within the scientific, medical, and technology producer industries.

The Future Sibley sees a strong role for knowledge management in the future. She said, "Training and development will increasingly evolve toward total knowledge management, with professionals being called on to create learning value for individuals as well as the organizations for which they work. I think we will see successful organizations wanting an integrated, multidimensional approach to learning—one that moves beyond organizing knowledge around individuals to address the needs of the group or organization."

Sibley also sees a continuing trend toward training being offered through multimedia and Web-based formats. She predicted, "Web-based training can reign king for providing customized, self-paced bits of information at the exact moment of learner need. But, you can't just throw Web-based training onto the Internet, walk away, and expect it to succeed. I think we'll see that the ultimate success of on-line training requires some sort of coaching and mentoring system that guides learners via their own unique performance plans."

Future Promise When we asked Sibley what impending changes stand out for her, she predicted that there would be a major shift in the field of training and development—one that will also become an important organizational trend. She said that there seems to be a greater focus on creating electronic performance support systems (EPSS) that deal with the interface between people and software. She explained, "I'm seeing more and more clients want to develop training systems that reach further than merely providing individualized solutions for skills and knowledge needs.

For example, I work with an international association of physician specialists whose members need highly focused training that is available to them at any time—five in the morning before they begin rounds or nine at night as they review patient cases. These doctors don't have time to attend classes or even sit at a computer taking courses for long periods of time. Yet, they work in hospitals and report to physician certifying organizations that require them to *demonstrate* an ongoing participation in

CME [continuing medical education] activities relevant to their individual knowledge gaps. We've created a five-year plan for converting the association's multimillion-dollar static CME curriculum into a dynamic 'just-in-time' knowledge database and EPSS. The system will assist physicians with identifying their knowledge gaps, offer customized Web-based training solutions (including peer coaching and mentoring accessible via handheld computers used at the patient bedside), and compile individual CME records for demonstrating ongoing learning activity. It's a massive and incredibly exciting project."

Sibley believes that training and performance improvement professionals will need to support learning efforts from all angles: "This means creating systems that provide dynamic access to training at the moment of need. It also means supporting the training transfer process through access to other knowledge management resources such as databases of effective practices, benchmarking studies, models, and forums for knowledge exchange, as well as plenty of coaching and training in successful learning practices."

Potential Potholes We asked Sibley what concerns her about the future that she has described. She replied, "Technology has made it so easy to amass information that it can get in the way of acquiring knowledge that has real strategic value for an organization. We all struggle with our ability to deal with vast amounts of knowledge—how many times have you thought to yourself 'Gosh, I wish someone would just help me figure out what stuff I really need to retain out of all this information.'"

This is where Sibley thinks that technology can play an important role in assisting us with knowledge management. She continued, "I have a client in the financial service industry who is struggling with cross-training employees. The use of technology has allowed this organization to streamline lots of repetitive activities and free up many employees to perform other tasks. But now the organization is faced with a massive retraining effort, and the relevant training and performance information mostly resides in the minds of the employees. Also, the organization wants to maintain exemplary customer service by making sure that each employee is trained to perform at least two different jobs. To solve this huge knowledge management problem without spending lots of time and money on training development, we've come up with a technology based system that relies on an appointed team of employee mentors to capture, sort, and transfer knowledge around the organization."

The Next Five Years Sibley confided, "Beyond technology, I think the next five years will bring a major cultural shift in the way that knowledge is acquired and shared. I think we've already seen that trend occurring with people's use of the Internet. Most of us conduct knowledge searches that are very non-linear—we move in and out of different search engines and Websites in paths that would resemble big bowls of spaghetti if we were to track them. What I really think we're experiencing through the Internet is a new way of learning where we are constantly renewing, replenishing, expanding, and creating more knowledge for ourselves and others. Here, technology may be the *means* . . . but the *end* is a distinctly human and cultural shift in learning strategy."

She added, "In the future, I think we'll see a lot of desire for self-management of training and performance improvement, but accompanied by a great need to be coached or mentored in various learning practices. I've got a client in the newspaper publishing industry who is producing Websites targeted to specific reader populations. We recently conducted a focus group with technology savvy senior citizens to assess their needs for a senior-targeted Website. I found it fascinating to learn that these individuals primarily use the Internet as a tool for acquiring new information. But they feel overwhelmed and frustrated by finding too much information. We learned that they want to be coached by other seniors on how to self-manage their learning efforts and improve their performance using the Internet. They also want mentoring systems set up for recommending reputable sites and suggesting efficient ways to obtain information. However, they distinctly *do not* want anybody deciding for them what particular topics seniors should explore."

Advice for the Future We asked Sibley what advice she would give to an organization that now calls itself "training" about how to assure a strong and productive future. She said, "I think that most organizations will seek guides, maps, and pathways for building knowledge across multiple performance levels. Besides training development, they will need consulting in performance coaching, performance management, and the efficient use of technology for self-managed learning. When technology is used for learning, training development professionals need to become mentors who assist individuals in acquiring knowledge that has strategic value. They'll also need to make sure that incentive systems are in place to encourage trainees to actually finish the training they start. Today's training departments should move rapidly towards fulfilling each of these needs."

Success into the Future Sibley discussed success in the future thus: "If there's one thing that the last decade has shown us, it's that we shouldn't assume knowledge is stationary. Instead, it is moving and perishable—so the power that usually comes with knowledge is fleeting. This has great implications for our careers. I've been through half a dozen directional turns in my own career, each one demanding a revised and updated set of knowledge and skills, but each one also being tremendously rewarding. I think that successful individuals will weave agility, self-management, goal setting, and lifelong learning into their futures."

Sivasailam "Thiagi" Thiagarajan

Sivasailam "Thiagi" Thiagarajan, based in Bloomington, Indiana, has been a member of NSPI/ISPI (International Society for Performance Improvement) since 1965. He has also served as the editor of ISPI periodicals for more than ten years, until he was, as he put it, "fired from the job." He currently makes a living by playing games and help-ing others improve their performance in an effective and enjoyable fashion. We inter-viewed Thiagi because he is, in our view, smart, funny, wise, and irreverent.

The Future We asked Thiagi to look into the future of the field of training and de-velopment and tell us what he saw and the changes that stand out for him. Thiagi said that he believes that, in the future, training will be provided on 24/7/365 basis, that there will be an increase in free-agent learners, and that the majority of training will be provided by on-line vendors around the world. Thiagi predicted that the demand for interactive training will increase significantly, that computers will permit mass in-dividualization of training, and that "face-to-face training will be provided in a variety of locales."

When we asked what concerns him about the future, Thiagi said, "Nothing."

The Next Five Years Thiagi said that in addition to the changes he described earlier, he foresees the following changes over the next five years:

- Softer technologies (based on psychology and sociology) will prescribe training approaches
- Participants will represent a heterogeneous mass of different ages, genders, cul-tures, and learning styles
- Most training will take place in teams that encourage people-to-people interactions
- ISD models will disappear and useful elements will be incorporated into main-stream training design
- Newer training design models will be based on complexity, chaos, and self-adapting systems
- Training will undergo disintermediation

Thiagi also believes that instructional designers and trainers will become obsolete and that learners will directly link themselves with subject-matter experts (SMEs) of their choice. He said, "As a part of 'formal education,' all SMEs will be taught how to teach, tutor, and coach others; everyone will be taught how to learn effectively, inde-pendently, and continuously using SMEs as one source of information."

Advice for Organizations Thiagi's advice for a "training" organization was: "Put yourself out of business. Explore fringe areas, such as complexity, chaos, and self-adaptive systems. Focus on techniques for individualizing instruction to suit cultural and individual differences. Learn how to help people achieve the same performance goals through at least a dozen different approaches. Be a continuous learner, using a variety of nontraditional (and nontechnological) approaches. Use an 'open-platform' approach to providing training, and get ready to appeal to the 'twitch-speed' gener-ation of learners who learn differently."

Advice for Individuals Thiagi advised individuals: "Accept what is inevitable. Let go of your assumptions. Trust people."

Resources

Abernathy, D. (2000, October). A guide to on-line learning service providers. *ASTD Learning Circuits.* (www.learningcircuits.org/oct2000)

Charchian, R., & Cohen, S. L. (2000, August). Playing a new game as a training professional: It's your move. *Performance Improvement, 39*(7), 12–17.

Clark, R. E. (1983). Reconsidering research on learning from media. *Review of Educational Research, 53*, 445–459.

Docent, Inc. (2000, June). *Calculating the return on your e-learning investment.* (www.docent.com/shared/wp/calculating_roi.pdf)

Greenberg, J. D., & Dickelman, D. J. (2000, July). Distributed cognition: A foundation for performance support. *Performance Improvement, 39*(6), 18–24.

Hofstede, G. (1980). *Culture's consequences: International differences in work-related values.* Beverly Hills, CA: Sage.

Hofstede, G. (1991). *Cultures and organizations: Software of the mind.* London: McGraw-Hill International.

McMurrer, D. P., Van Buren, M. E., & Woodwell, W. H. (2000). *The 2000 ASTD State of the Industry Report.* Alexandria, VA: ASTD.

Packer, A. (2000, August). Getting to know the employee of the future. *Training & Development, 54*(8), 39–43.

Parrish, P., & Wang, W. (2000). Presentation given at the Association for Educational Communications and Technology Conference, Denver, Colorado.

Paul, L. G. (2000, February). Internetification. *Inside Technology Training, 4*(2), 30–32.

Sanchez, C. M., & Curtis, D. M. (2000). Different minds and common problems: Geert Hofstede's research on national cultures. *Performance Improvement Quarterly, 13*(2), 9–19.

Senge, P. M. (1990). *The fifth discipline: The art and practice of the learning organization.* New York: Doubleday.

Stamps, D. (1997, August). Managing corporate smarts. *Training, 34*, 40–44.

Stewart, T. A. (1997). *Intellectual capital: The new wealth of organizations.* New York: Doubleday.

Ulrich, D. (1997). *Human resource champions: The next agenda for adding value and delivering results.* Boston: Harvard Business School Press.

Ulrich, D. (1998). A new mandate for human resources. *Harvard Business Review, 76*(1), 124–134.

Urdan, T. A., & Weggen, C. C. (2000). *Corporate e-learning: Exploring a new frontier.* (www.wrhambrecht.com/research.coverage/elearning/ir/ir_explore.pdf)

Werbach, K. (2000, May/June). Syndication: The emerging model for business in the Internet era. *Harvard Business Review*, pp. 86–93.

Wheatley, M. J., & Kellner-Rogers, M. (1998). *A simpler way.* San Francisco: Berrett-Koehler.

Wiley, D. A. (Ed.) (In press). *The instructional use of learning objects.* Bloomington, IN: Association for Educational Communications and Technology.

ABOUT THE AUTHORS

Allison Rossett is recognized for translating theory into practice in vivid ways. A long-time professor of educational technology at San Diego State University, Allison was the Year 2000 inductee into the *Training* magazine HRD Hall of Fame. A consultant in the design, development, and evaluation of performance and training systems, she was featured in the October 2000 *Fast Company*. Prior award-winning books are *First Things Fast: A Handbook for Performance Analysis* (with its supportive Website, www.jbp.com/rossett.html), *Training Needs Assessment,* and *A Handbook of Job Aids.* Her client list includes Taco Bell, Century 21 International, PriceWaterhouseCoopers, IBM, HP, the Getty Conservation Institute, AT&T, Fidelity Investments, Deloitte Consulting, Vanguard Investments, SBC, and several new media and learning start-ups. Rossett can be contacted at arossett@mail.sdsu.edu. Her Website is edweb.sdsu.edu/people/ARossett/ARossett.html

Kendra Sheldon is a writer and performance consultant living in San Diego, California. With a background in media, technology, and education, Kendra has had work appear in local television, radio, and news publications, including KGTV-Channel 10, KCNN-AM and FM, *CalPirg Reports,* the *La Jolla Light, Chiropractic Natural Health, Dental News and Views, Financial Strategies,* and more. Kendra's most recent work can be seen on the Web at the following sites, as well as many more:

www.jbp.com/rossett.html (The award-winning *First Things Fast* site)

defcon.sdsu.edu/1/objects/km/welcome/ (knowledge management)

www.sexualharass.com/) (sexual harassment in the workplace)

defcon.sdsu.edu/1/objects/online/ (on-line learning)

www.kn.pacbell.com/wired/webtime/ (Webtime Stories)

clipt.sdsu.edu/posit/tx/db.htm (POSIT)

Sheldon can be reached at kjsheldon@projects.sdsu.edu.

INDEX